English Literature for Schools

NORTH

PLUTARCH'S LIVES

SIR THOMAS NORTH

PLUTARCH'S LIVES

A SELECTION

EDITED BY

P. GILES, LITT.D.,

MASTER OF EMMANUEL COLLEGE, CAMBRIDGE

CAMBRIDGE
AT THE UNIVERSITY PRESS
1921

CAMBRIDGE
UNIVERSITY PRESS

University Printing House, Cambridge CB2 8BS, United Kingdom

Cambridge University Press is part of the University of Cambridge.

It furthers the University's mission by disseminating knowledge in the pursuit of
education, learning and research at the highest international levels of excellence.

www.cambridge.org
Information on this title: www.cambridge.org/9781107693067

© Cambridge University Press 1921

First published 1921
First paperback edition 2014

A catalogue record for this publication is available from the British Library

ISBN 978-1-107-69306-7 Paperback

CONTENTS

INTRODUCTION

I. THE AUTHOR AND THE BOOK

AMONG the authors of ancient Greek literature three have especially moved the world—Plato, Aristotle, Plutarch. Till the revival of learning in the fifteenth and sixteenth centuries Aristotle's philosophy adopted by the mediaeval church had for many centuries held fast the minds of men; from Plato all later philosophies, not excluding Aristotle's, draw their inspiration and to the renewed study of his works was due above all things the overthrow of mediaevalism. To Plutarch is owing not only much in literature but also much in the political changes of Europe. No small part of our knowledge of ancient history depends on Plutarch. To his *Lives* as translated by Thomas North we owe Shakespeare's *Coriolanus*, *Julius Caesar*, and *Antony and Cleopatra*, many passages of which are but North turned into verse. To the *Lives* also we owe a political movement the ideas of which profoundly influenced the whole world; the French version by Amyot from which North's translation was made was the chief text-book which inspired the French Revolution.

Yet Plutarch was neither historian nor revolutionary. Born about 45 A.D. in the reign of the Emperor Claudius at the little town of Chaeronea in Boeotia, he spent the greater part of his life in his native place discharging the humble duties at one time of a police commissioner, at another of

mayor.   Descended from a family long established
at Chaeronea he obtained the ordinary education
of a son of well-to-do parents in those days, spent
some years in Athens in attending the lectures of
the philosophers and on occasion visited Rome,
though he never understood Latin well.   Many
of his works are lost, but much still survives.
Plutarch's chief literary interest was in Ethics ;
the greater part of his extant works are essays,
some on literature, some on moral philosophy,
others on questions of religion or antiquities.   But
the work of Plutarch which has most influenced
later ages is his *Parallel Lives of Eminent Men*.
Plutarch's book has been the source of history, of
literature and of revolution, but when Plutarch
wrote it, he had none of those ends in view.   The
work seems to have been primarily intended as
studies in character, object lessons to elucidate
the author's theory of Ethics.   It is not a work of
original research.   Plutarch simply collected the
best sources he could obtain for the lives that he
intended to write.   The historical facts are therefore derived from other authors whom he quotes
by name.   For heroes of remote antiquity like
Theseus, Romulus, Lycurgus, Numa, there was
not much to be obtained beyond vague tradition.
For Solon he depended largely on a treatise on the
Athenian Constitution which is attributed to Aristotle.   This work, after being lost for many centuries,
was discovered in Egypt and published to the
modern world in 1891.   Even for Themistocles
it is clear that Plutarch had little to rely upon
but gossiping memoirs of a later generation.   For
others, such as Pericles, Nicias, Cicero, Julius Caesar,
information was abundant and trustworthy.   As
Plutarch's object was the study of character and
not history, anecdotes were useful for his purpose ;

an anecdote even if invented will not be out of
keeping with the character of the person of whom
it is told.

The *Lives* seem to have been the work of
Plutarch's later years. The arrangement is peculiar. Of the fifty biographies which are now extant
all except four are arranged in pairs, one member
being always Greek and the other Roman. The
four which are not included in this arrangement
are the lives of Aratus the general of the Achaean
league (of whom much is said also in the life of
Cleomenes), of Artaxerxes king of Persia, and of
Galba and Otho the Roman emperors who reigned
successively in the year of revolution which followed
the downfall of Nero in 68 A.D. The lives of Galba
and Otho are less studies of character than a history
of the time, and it has been conjectured that these
were Plutarch's first attempts and that he afterwards changed his method for another, which from
most points of view is decidedly worse.

Plutarch's reasons for adopting the parallel
method are not clear. M. Maurice Croiset, the
distinguished French historian of Greek literature,
conjectures that the moving cause was patriotism
combined with admiration for Roman character;
that Plutarch was filled with reverence for the lofty
love of country, the self-sacrifice and the prowess
of the heroes of the Roman Republic, and at the
same time was anxious to show that no less noble
exemplars of these qualities might be drawn from
the history of his own country. The resemblances
between the personalities thus coupled together are
sometimes striking and sometimes not. This is
obvious enough from the biographies contained in
this volume. The parallelism between Agis and
Cleomenes, who endeavoured to undermine the
power of the Ephors and return to the pristine con-

stitution of Lycurgus, and the brothers Tiberius and
Gaius Gracchus who, no less discontented with the
narrow self-seeking of the Roman Senate in their
day, wished to restore the farmer statesmen of the
age of Cincinnatus, is sufficiently obvious.   On the
other hand the resemblance between the career of
Timoleon and that of Aemilius Paulus is less striking.
They were both successful soldiers, both in their
careers passed through great sorrows and both lived
to enjoy a calm and honoured old age.   But these
are such common incidents of human life that it
would not be difficult to find other Romans no less
similar to Timoleon than Aemilius Paulus.   Both
it is true overthrew great empires, for the power of
the younger Dionysius in Sicily is fairly comparable
to that of Philip V in Macedon.   But the troubles
which beset their middle life were widely different.
Timoleon withdrew himself from the world because
his mother would not forgive him for the murder
of his brother in the cause of Corinthian liberty ;
Aemilius Paulus was the trusted general and statesman of Rome throughout, and the great sorrow
which befel him was the sudden death of his two
younger sons when he was about to celebrate his
triumph over Philip,—a disaster much magnified in
Roman eyes because he had allowed his two elder
sons to be adopted respectively by the son of the
first Scipio Africanus and the son of the great
Fabius Maximus, and had thus left his own house
without heirs.

Of Plutarch's life we know little except what
we gather from his own writings, but it is clear
that his literary achievement brought him much
honour and esteem in his old age.   He seems to
have died about 125 A.D.

2. THE FRENCH TRANSLATOR

Jacques Amyot whose translation of Plutarch's *Lives* is one of the most important landmarks in the history of French prose literature was born at Melun on October 30, 1513. His parents were poor working people and Jacques had to overcome many obstacles and undergo many hardships, before he was able to attain his ambition and become a scholar. His parents were unable to give him much help, but, when he was a student at Paris, his mother used to send him a loaf every week; whatever else he wanted he had to earn for himself. Though he translated various other Greek works, a large part of his life was devoted to the study and the translation of Plutarch. Before he was thirty he had translated a few lives which he dedicated to Francis I. Francis was a lover of learning and interested himself in the young student. He made him Abbot of the monastery of Bellozane and, admiring his Latin style, appointed him to draw up a letter which the king wished to send to the Great Council of the Church then being held at Trent. A still greater honour was conferred upon Amyot; he was sent to deliver this letter in person. It was not an easy task, for the members of the Council were inclined to regard it as an insult that so unimportant a person had been sent as envoy, and in their wrath were moved to pick holes in the envoy's Latinity. They were especially annoyed, because the Council was described in the letter, not as *Concilium*, but as *Conventus*, which they regarded as a veiled aspersion upon them. Amyot however was able to convince them not only that no insult was meant, but that *conventus* was a very good Latin word for the purpose, and returned home having carried out his mission very successfully. The successor of Francis, Henry II, made him tutor to his sons, who were later Charles IX and Henry III. Surely never had a tutor less credit by his pupils. It may be presumed that the translation of the *Lives* was intended for their benefit, for it was in 1559 while Amyot was still their tutor that the first edition of the completed work was published. If Charles and Henry had not many virtues they were at least always well-disposed towards Amyot. He was soon made Bishop of Auxerre and though on one occasion at least his life was threatened by Catherine the Queen-mother and he had to go into hiding for a little, Charles for once resisted his mother and brought Amyot back to court. When the Guises were murdered at the instigation of Henry III, Amyot it was said, probably without foundation, was accessory to the plot. When Henry III died in 1589, Amyot was already an old man. His last days were embittered by the wars of the League which he joined under compulsion, while the Huguenots sacked his palace. He died early in 1593 in his eightieth year.

Amyot was not merely a translator. In his youth he spent much time in collating Greek manuscripts of the text of Plutarch and it has been found that many supposed mistranslations really represent better readings which he had collected in his researches in French and Italian libraries, but which remained unpublished till the nineteenth century.

3. THE ENGLISH TRANSLATOR

Of Sir Thomas North who translated Amyot's French translation of the *Lives* into English in 1579 not very much is known. He was the younger son of Edward the first Lord North, and was born probably about 1535 A.D. The family estate is at Kirtling near Newmarket, and Thomas, like his father, is said to have been educated at Peterhouse, Cambridge. He seems to have lived in Cambridgeshire as he had the freedom of the town of Cambridge conferred upon him in 1568, commanded three hundred men of Ely when preparations were being made to receive the Spanish Armada, and after 1592 appears upon the list of justices for the county of Cambridge. The date of his death is unknown but it must have been soon after 1601. (See the article in the *Dictionary of National Biography*.)

North early devoted himself to literature. Like Amyot he translated other works but his most important achievement by far is his translation of Plutarch's *Lives*, which first appeared in 1579. Unlike Philemon Holland, who translated soon afterwards the rest of Plutarch's works, he was not a Greek scholar, and made no attempt to compare Amyot's version with the original. Consequently whenever Amyot adopts a French form for a Greek name North gives the French form, and whenever Amyot by inadvertence leaves out a phrase, it is wanting also in North's version. Though North makes occasional mistakes of his own, the translation is not a slavish copy of Amyot's, but is presented in strong, racy, and idiomatic English. As the first secular work on a large scale (the first edition contains over eleven hundred large folio pages closely printed) in modern English prose, it is no less important for the history of English literature than Amyot's translation is for French. It has received attention in recent times chiefly as a source for Shakespeare's plays, and the Lives most frequently reprinted are those which were so used. The other parts of North's work however deserve to be more widely known. In themselves the Lives from which Shakespeare borrowed are not more valuable either for matter or for style than many others. Probably no English prose book on the same scale except the English versions of the Bible has gone through so many editions in the first century of its existence. It was replaced in popular use by the version 'by various hands' which was edited by Dryden (1683), and later by the translation made by the brothers Langhorne in 1770. The most scholarly version in use is the revision of Dryden's translation made by the poet Arthur Hugh Clough. A new and accurate translation by Mr B. Perrin is now being published along with the Greek text in the Loeb series.

The English of North's *Plutarch* is often compared with that of the authorised version of the English Bible. The language of the two books is, however, by no means identical. It is easy to see that North represents a somewhat earlier stage in the formation of English style. The language is looser and more irregular in many respects. One characteristic feature may be mentioned. In the English Bible, sentences of the type 'The Lord, he is God' are rare and clearly used for emphasis. In North on the other hand it is very common to find both substantive and pronoun as subject to the same verb; if the sentence begins with a participial phrase containing the substantive, it is

North's regular practice to insert the pronoun before the verb. Such sentences occur on almost every page.

In this reprint the spelling has been modernised and the punctuation altered in a few cases, where it was likely to be ambiguous. Proper names also have been respelt according to modern practice with one exception. In North's own time, and for many generations after, Englishmen, learned and unlearned alike, spelt the Roman name Gaius as Caius, and this spelling has accordingly been left unaltered.

P. G.

August 20, 1920.

THE LIFE OF TIMOLEON

WHEN I first began to write these lives, my intent was to profit others; but since, continuing and going on, I have much profited my self by looking into these histories, as if I looked into a glass, to frame and fashion my life, to the mould and pattern of these virtuous noblemen. For running over their manners in this sort, and seeking also to describe their lives: methinks I am still conversant and familiar with them, and do as it were lodge them with me, one after another. And when I come to peruse their histories, and to weigh the virtues and qualities they have had, and what singularity each of them possessed: and to choose and cull out the chiefest things of note in them, and their best speeches and doings most worthy of memory: then I cry out,

O gods, can there be more passing pleasure in the world?

Or is there anything of more force, to teach man civil manners and a ruled life, or to reform the vice in man? Democritus the philosopher writeth, that we should pray we might ever see happy images and sights in the air, and that the good which is meet and proper to our nature, may rather come to us, than that is evil and unfortunate: presupposing a false opinion and doctrine in philosophy, which allureth men to infinite superstitions: that there are good and bad images flying in the air, which give a good or ill impression unto men, and incline men to vice, or to virtue. But as for me, by continual reading of ancient histories, and gathering these lives together which now I leave before you, and by keeping always in mind the acts of the most noble, virtuous, and best given men of former age, and worthy memory: I do teach and prepare my self to shake off and banish from me all lewd and dishonest conditions, if by chance the company and conversation of them whose company I keep, and must of necessity haunt, do acquaint me with some unhappy or ungracious touch. This is easy unto me, that do dispose my mind, being quiet and not troubled with any passion, unto the deep consideration of so many noble examples. As I do present unto you now in this volume, the lives of Timoleon the Corinthian, and of Paulus Aemilius the Roman, who had not only a good and upright mind with them, but were also fortunate and happy, in all the matters they both did take in hand. So as you shall hardly judge, when you have read over their lives, whether wisdom or good fortune brought them to achieve to such honourable acts and exploits as they did.

Before Timoleon was sent into Sicily, thus stood the state of the Syracusans. After that Dion had driven out the tyrant Dionysius, he himself after was slain immediately by treason, and those that aided him to restore the Syracusans to their liberty, fell out, and were at dissension among themselves. By reason whereof, the city of Syracuse changing continually new tyrants, was so troubled and turmoiled with all sorts of evils that it was left in manner desolate, and without inhabitants. The rest of Sicily in like case was utterly destroyed, and no cities in manner left standing, by reason of the long wars: and those few that remained, were most inhabited of foreign soldiers and strangers (a company of loose men gathered together that took pay of no prince nor city) all the dominions of the same being easily usurped, and as easy to change their lord. Insomuch Dionysius the tyrant, ten years after Dion had driven him out of Sicily, having gathered a certain number of soldiers together again, and through their help driven out Nysaeus, that reigned at that time in Syracuse: he recovered the realm again, and made himself king. So, if he was strangely expulsed by a small power out of the greatest kingdom that ever was in the world: likewise he more strangely recovered it again, being banished and very poor, making himself king over them, who before had driven him out. Thus were the inhabitants of the city compelled to serve this tyrant: who besides that of his own nature he was never courteous nor civil, he was now grown to be far more dogged and cruel, by reason of the extreme misery and misfortune he had endured. But the noblest citizens repaired unto Hicetes, who at that time as lord ruled the city of the Leontines, and they chose him for their general in these wars: not for that he was anything better than the open tyrants, but because they had no other to repair unto at that time, and they trusted him best, for that he was born (as themselves) within the city of Syracuse, and because also he had men of war about him, to make head against the tyrant.

But in the meantime, the Carthaginians came down into Sicily with a great army, and invaded the country. The Syracusans being afraid of them, determined to send ambassadors into Greece unto the Corinthians, to pray aid of them against the barbarous people, having better hope of them, than of any other of the Grecians. And that not altogether because they were lineally descended from them, and that they had received in times past many pleasures at their hands: but also for that they knew that Corinth was a city, that in all ages and times, did ever love liberty and hate tyrants, and that had always made their greatest wars, not for ambition of kingdoms, nor of covetous desire to conquer and rule, but only to defend and maintain the liberty of the Grecians. But Hicetes in another contrary sort, took upon him to be general, with a mind to make himself King of Syracuse. For he had secretly practised with the Carthaginians, and

openly notwithstanding in words he commended
the counsel and determination of the Syracusans,
and sent ambassadors from himself also with theirs
unto Peloponnesus: not that he was desirous any
aid should come from them to Syracuse, but because
he hoped, if the Corinthians refused to send them
aid (as it was very likely they would for the wars
and troubles that were in Greece), that he might
more easily turn all over to the Carthaginians
and use them as his friends, to aid him against the
Syracusans, or the tyrant Dionysius. And that this
was his full purpose and intent, it appeared plainly
soon after.

Now when their ambassadors arrived at Corinth,
and had delivered their message, the Corinthians,
who had ever been careful to defend such cities as
had sought unto them, and specially Syracuse, very
willingly determined in council to send them aid, and
the rather for that they were in good peace at that
time, having wars with none of the Grecians. So
their only stay rested upon choosing of a general to
lead their army. Now as the magistrates and
governors of the city were naming such citizens as
willingly offered their service, desirous to advance
themselves, there stept up a mean commoner who
named Timoleon, Timodemus' son, a man that until
that time was never called on for service, neither
looked for any such preferment. And truly it is to
be thought it was the secret working of the gods,
that directed the thought of this mean commoner to
name Timoleon; whose election fortune favoured
very much, and joined to his valiantness and virtues
marvellous good success in all his doings afterwards.
This Timoleon was born of noble parents, both by
father and mother: his father was called Timodemus,
and his mother Demareta. He was naturally inclined
to love his country and commonweal: and was always
gentle and courteous to all men, saving that he
mortally hated tyrants and wicked men. Furthermore nature had framed his body apt for wars and

for pains: he was wise in his greenest youth in all
things he took in hand, and in his age he shewed
himself very valiant.

He had an elder brother called Timophanes, who
was nothing like to him in condition: for he was a
rash harebrained man, and had a greedy desire to
reign, being put into his head by a company of mean
men, that bare him in hand they were his friends,
and by certain soldiers gathered together which he
had always about him. And because he was very
hot and forward in wars, his citizens took him for
a notable captain, and a man of good service, and
therefore oftentimes they gave him charge of men.
And therein Timoleon did help him much to hide the
faults he committed, or at the least, made them seem
less, and lighter than they were, still increasing that
small good gift that nature brought forth in him. As
in a battle the Corinthians had against the Argives
and the Cleoneians, Timoleon served as a private
soldier amongst the footmen: and Timophanes his
brother, having charge of horsemen, was in great
danger to be cast away, if present help had not been.
For his horse being hurt, threw him on the ground in
the midst of his enemies. Whereupon part of those
that were about him, were afraid and dispersed themselves here and there: and those that remained with
him, being few in number, and having many enemies
to fight withal, did hardly withstand their force and
charge. But his brother Timoleon seeing him in such
instant danger afar off, ran with all speed possible to
help him, and clapping his target before his brother
Timophanes, that lay on the ground, receiving many
wounds on his body with sword and arrows, with great
difficulty he repulsed the enemies, and saved his own
and his brother's life. Now the Corinthians fearing
the like matter to come that before had happened
unto them, which was to lose their city through
default of their friends' help, they resolved in council,
to entertain in pay continually four hundred soldiers
that were strangers, whom they assigned over to

Timophanes' charge. Who, abandoning all honesty and regard of the trust reposed in him, did presently practise all the ways he could to make himself lord of the city: and having put divers of the chiefest citizens to death without order of law, in the end he openly proclaimed himself king. Timoleon being very sorry for this, and thinking his brother's wickedness would be the very highway to his fall and destruction, sought first to win him, with all the good words and persuasions he could, to leave his ambitious desire to reign, and to seek to salve (as near as might be) his hard dealing with the citizens. Timophanes set light by his brother's persuasions, and would give no ear unto them. Thereupon Timoleon then went unto one Aeschylus his friend, and brother unto Timophanes' wife, and to one Satyrus a soothsayer (as Theopompus the historiographer calleth him, and Ephorus calleth him Orthagoras) with whom he came again another time unto his brother: and they three coming to him instantly besought him to believe good counsel, and to leave the kingdom. Timophanes at the first did but laugh them to scorn, and sported at their persuasions: but afterwards he waxed hot, and grew into great choler with them. Timoleon seeing that, went a little aside, and covering his face fell a-weeping: and in the mean season, the other two drawing out their swords, slew Timophanes in the place.

This murder was straight blown abroad through the city, and the better sort did greatly commend the noble mind and hate Timoleon bare against the tyrant: considering that he being of a gentle nature, and loving to his kin, did notwithstanding regard the benefit of his country, before the natural affection of his brother, and preferred duty and justice before nature and kindred. For before he had saved his brother's life, fighting for the defence of his country: and now in seeking to make himself king and to rule the same, he made him to be slain. Such then as misliked popular government and liberty, and always

followed the nobility, they set a good face on the
matter, as though they had been glad of the tyrant's
death.   Yet still reproving Timoleon for the horrible
murder he had committed against his brother, declaring how detestable it was both to the gods and men,
they so handled him, that it grieved him to the heart
he had done it.   But when it was told him that his
mother took it marvellous evil, and that she pronounced horrible curses against him, and gave out
terrible words of him, he went unto her in hope to
comfort her : howbeit she could never abide to see
him, but always shut her door against him.   Then he
being wounded to the heart with sorrow, took a
conceit suddenly, to kill himself by abstaining from
meat: but his friends would never forsake him in
this despair, and urged him so far by entreaty and
persuasion that they compelled him to eat.   Thereupon he resolved thenceforth to give himself over to
a solitary life in the country, secluding himself from
all company and dealings : so as at the beginning, he
did not only refuse to repair unto the city, and all
access of company, but wandering up and down in
most solitary places, consumed himself and his time
with melancholy.

And thus we see, that counsels and judgment are
lightly carried away (by praise or dispraise) if they
be not shored up with rule of reason and philosophy,
and rest confounded in themselves.   And therefore
it is very requisite and necessary, that not only the
act be good and honest of itself, but that the resolution thereof be also constant, and not subject unto
change : to the end we may do all things considerately :
lest we be like unto lickerous-mouthed men, who as
they desire meats with a greedy appetite, and after
are soon weary, disliking the same : even so do we
suddenly repent our actions grounded upon a weak
imagination of the honesty that moved us thereunto.   For repentance maketh the act naught, which
before was good.   But determination, grounded upon
certain knowledge and truth of reason, doth never

change, although the matter enterprised have not
always happy success. And therefore Phocion the
Athenian having resisted (as much as in him lay)
certain things which the general Leosthenes did,
and which contrary to his mind took good effect:
and perceiving the Athenians did open sacrifice unto
the gods, to give them thanks for the same, and much
rejoice at the victory they had obtained: I would
have rejoiced too (said he) if I had done this: but sc
would I not for anything, but I had given the counsel.
And after that sort, but more sharply did Aristides
Locrian (a very friend and companion of Plato's)
answer Dionysius the elder, tyrant of Syracuse: who
asked his goodwill to marry one of his daughters.
I had rather see my daughter dead (said he) than
married unto a tyrant. And within a certain time after,
the tyrant put all his sons to death: and then he
asked him in derision, to grieve him the more, if he
were still of his former opinion for the marrying of
his daughter. I am very sorry (said he), with all my
heart for that which thou hast done: but yet I do
not repent me of that I have said. That peradventure
proceeded of a more perfect virtue.

But to return again unto Timoleon. Whether
that inward sorrow struck him to the heart for the
death of his brother Timophanes, or that shame did
so abash him, as he durst not abide his mother,
twenty years after he did never any notable or
famous act. And therefore, when he was named to
be general of the aid that should be sent into Sicily,
the people having willing chosen and accepted of
him: Teleclides, who was chief governor at that time
in the city of Corinth, standing upon his feet before
the people, spake unto Timoleon, and did exhort him
to behave himself like an honest man, and valiant
captain in his charge. For, said he, if that you
handle your self well, we will think you have killed
a tyrant; but if you do order your self otherwise
than well, we will judge you have killed your brother.
Now Timoleon being busy in levying of men, and

preparing himself, letters came to the Corinthians from Hicetes, whereby plainly appeared, that Hicetes had carried two faces in one hood, and that he was become a traitor. For he had no sooner despatched his ambassadors unto them, but he straight took the Carthaginians' part, and dealt openly for them, intending to drive out Dionysius, and to make himself King of Syracuse. But fearing lest the Corinthians would send aid before he had wrought his feat, he wrote again unto the Corinthians, sending them word that they should not need now to put themselves to any charge or danger for coming into Sicily, and specially, because the Carthaginians were very angry, and did also lie in wait in the way as they should come, with a great fleet of ships to meet with their army : and that for himself, because he saw they tarried long, he had made league and amity with them, against the tyrant Dionysius. When they had read his letters, if any of the Corinthians were before but coldly affected to this journey, choler did then so warm them against Hicetes, that they frankly granted Timoleon what he would ask, and did help to furnish him to set him out.

When the ships were ready rigged, and that the soldiers were furnished of all things necessary for their departure, the nuns of the goddess Proserpina, said they saw a vision in their dream, and that the goddesses Ceres and Proserpina did appear unto them, apparelled like travellers to take a journey : and told them that they would go with Timoleon into Sicily. Upon this speech only, the Corinthians rigged a galley they called the galley of Ceres and Proserpina : and Timoleon himself before he would take the seas, went into the city of Delphi, where he made sacrifice unto Apollo. And as he entered into the sanctuary where the answers of the Oracle are made, there happened a wonderful sign unto him. For amongst the vows and offerings that are hung up upon the walls of the sanctuary, there fell a band directly upon Timoleon's head, em-

broidered all about with crowns of victory: so that
it seemed Apollo sent him already crowned, before
he had set out one foot towards the journey.   He
took ship, and sailed with seven galleys of Corinth,
two of Corfu, and ten the Leucadians did set out.
When he was launched out into the main sea, having a
frank gale of wind and large, he thought in the night
that the element did open, and that out of the same
there came a marvellous great bright light over his
ship, and it was much like to a torch burning, when
they shew the ceremonies of the holy mysteries.
This torch did accompany and guide them all their
voyage, and in the end it vanished away and seemed
to fall down upon the coast of Italy, where the
shipmasters had determined to arrive.   The wise
men's opinions being asked what this might signify,
they answered that this wonderful sight did betoken
the dream the nuns of the goddess Ceres dreamed,
and that the goddesses favouring his journey, had
shewed them the way, by sending of this light from
heaven: because that the isle of Sicily is consecrated
unto the goddess Proserpina, and specially for that
they report her ravishment was in that isle, and
that the whole realm was assigned unto her for her
jointure, at the day of her marriage.

Thus did this celestial sign of the gods both encourage
those that went this journey and deliver them also
assured hope, who sailed with all possible speed they
could: until such time as, having crossed the seas,
they arrived upon the coast of Italy.   But when they
came thither, the news they understood from Sicily
put Timoleon in great perplexity, and did marvellously
discourage the soldiers he brought with him.   For
Hicetes having overthrown the battle of the tyrant
Dionysius, and possessed the greatest part of the city
of Syracuse, he did besiege him within the castle,
and within that part of the city which is called the
Isle, where he had pent him up, and enclosed him in
with walls round about.   And in the meantime he had
prayed the Carthaginians, that they would be careful

to keep Timoleon from landing in Sicily, to the end
that by preventing that aid, they might easily divide
Sicily between them, and no man to let them. The
Carthaginians following his request, sent twenty of
their galleys unto Rhegium, amongst which Hicetes'
ambassadors were sent unto Timoleon, with testimony
of his doings: for they were fair flattering words to
cloak his wicked intent he purposed. For they willed
Timoleon that he should go himself alone (if he
thought good) unto Hicetes, to counsel him, and to
accompany him in all his doings, which were now so
far onwards in good towardness, as he had almost
ended them all. Furthermore, they did also persuade
him, that he should send back his ships and soldiers
to Corinth again, considering that the war was now
brought to good pass, and that the Carthaginians
would in no case that his men should pass into Sicily,
and that they were determined to fight with them, if
they made any force to enter. So the Corinthians at
their arrival into the city of Rhegium, finding there these
ambassadors, and seeing the fleet of the Carthaginians'
ships, which did ride at anchor not far off from them:
it spited them on the one side to see they were thus
mocked and abused by Hicetes. For every one of
them were marvellous angry with him, and were
greatly afeard also for the poor Sicilians, whom too
plainly they saw left a prey unto Hicetes for reward
of his treason, and to the Carthaginians for recompense of the tyranny, which they suffered him to
establish. So, on the other side they thought it impossible to conquer the ships of the Carthaginians,
which did lie in wait for them and so near unto them:
considering they were twice as many in number as
they, and hard for them to subdue the army also that
was in the hands of Hicetes in Sicily, considering
that they were not come to him, but only for the
maintenance of the wars.

Notwithstanding, Timoleon spake very courteously
unto those ambassadors, and captains of the
Carthaginians' ships, letting them understand that

he would do as much as they would have him: and
to say truly, if he would have done otherwise, he could
have won nothing by it.   Nevertheless he desired for
his discharge, they would say that openly, in the
presence of the people of Rhegium (being a city of
Greece, friend and common to both parties), which
they had spoken to him in secret: and that done, he
would depart incontinently, alleging that it stood him
very much upon for the safety of his discharge, and
that they themselves also should more faithfully keep
that they had promised unto him touching the
Syracusans, when they had agreed upon it and
promised it before all the people of Rhegium, who
should be witness of it.   Now all this was but a fetch
and policy delivered by him, to shadow his departure,
which the captains and governors of Rhegium did
favour, and seem to help him in : because they wished
Sicily should fall into the hands of the Corinthians,
and feared much to have the barbarous people for
their neighbours.   For this cause they commanded a
general assembly of all the people, during which time,
they caused the gates of the city to be shut: giving
it out, that it was because the citizens should not go
about any other matters in the meantime.   Then
when all the people were assembled, they began to
make long orations without concluding any matter:
the one leaving always to the other a like matter to
talk of, to the end they might win time, until the
galleys of the Corinthians were departed.   And staying
the Carthaginians also in this assembly, they mistrusted nothing, because they saw Timoleon present:
who made a countenance, as though he would rise to
say something.   But in the meantime, some one did
secretly advertise Timoleon, that the other galleys
were under sail and gone away, and that there was
but one galley left, which tarried for him in the haven.
Thereupon he suddenly stole away through the press,
with the help of the Rhegians, being about the chair
where the orations were made : and trudging quickly
to the haven, he embarked incontinently, and hoised

sail also.   And when he had overtaken his fleet, they
went all safe together to land at the city of Tauromenion, which is in Sicily : there they were very well
received by Andromachus, who long time before had
sent for them, for he governed this city as if he had
been lord thereof.   He was the father of Timaeus the
historiographer, and honestest man of all those that
did bear rule at that time in all Sicily.   For he did
rule his citizens in all justice and equity, and did
always show himself an open enemy to tyrants.   And
following his affection therein, he lent his city at that
time unto Timoleon, to gather people together, and
persuaded his citizens to enter into league with the
Corinthians, and to aid them, to deliver Sicily from
bondage, and to restore it again to liberty.

But the captains of the Carthaginians, that were in
Rhegium, when they knew that Timoleon was under
sail and gone, after that the assembly of the Council
was broken up, they were ready to eat their fingers
for spite to see themselves thus finely mocked and
deceived.   The Rhegians on the other side, were
merry at the matter, to see how the Phoenicians
stormed at it, that they had such a fine part played
them.   Howbeit in the end, they determined to send
an ambassador unto Tauromenion, in one of their
galleys.   This ambassador spake very boldly and
barbarously unto Andromachus, and in a choler : and
last of all, he showed him first the palm of his hand,
then the back of his hand, and did threaten him that
his city should be so turned over hand, if he did
not quickly send away the Corinthians.   Andromachus
fell a-laughing at him, and did turn his hand up and
down as the ambassador had done, and commanded
him that he should get him going and that with all
speed out of his city, if he would not see the keel of his
galley turned upward.   Hicetes now understanding of
Timoleon's coming, and being afraid, sent for a great
number of galleys unto the Carthaginians.   Then the
Syracusans began to despair utterly when they saw
their haven full of the Carthaginians' galleys, the best

part of their city kept by Hicetes, and the castle by the tyrant Dionysius. And on the other side, that Timoleon was not yet come but to a little corner of Sicily, having no more but the little city of Tauromenion, with a small power, and less hope: because there was not above a thousand footmen in all, to furnish these wars, neither provision of victuals, nor so much money as would serve to entertain and pay them: besides also, that the other cities of Sicily did nothing trust him. But by reason of the violent extortions which they had of late suffered, they hated all captains and leaders of men of war to the death, and specially for the treachery of Callippus and Pharax, whereof the one was an Athenian, and the other a Lacedaemonian. Both of them said they came to set Sicily at liberty, and to drive out the tyrants: and yet nevertheless, they had done so much hurt unto the poor Sicilians, that the misery and calamity which they had suffered under the tyrants, seemed all to be gold unto them, in respect of that which these captains had made them to abide. And they did think them more happy, that had willingly submitted themselves unto the yoke of servitude, than those which they saw restored and set at liberty.

Therefore persuading themselves, that this Corinthian would be no better unto them, than the other had been before, but supposing they were the self same former crafts and alluring baits of good hope and fair words, which they had tasted of before, to draw them to accept new tyrants: they did sore suspect it and rejected all the Corinthians' persuasions, saving the Adranitans only, whose little city being consecrated to the god Adranus (and greatly honoured and reverenced through all Sicily) was then in dissension one against another: in so much as one part of them took part with Hicetes and the Carthaginians, and the other sent unto Timoleon. So it fortuned that both the one and the other, making all the possible speed they could, who should come first, arrived both in manner at one self time.

Hicetes had about five thousand soldiers. Timoleon had not in all, above twelve hundred men, with which he departed to go towards the city of Adranum distant from Tauromenion about three hundred and forty furlongs. For the first day's journey he went no great way, but lodged betimes: but the next morning he marched very hastily, and had marvellous ill way. When night was come, and daylight shut in, he had news that Hicetes did but newly arrive before Adranum, where he encamped. When the private captains understood this, they caused the vaward to stay, to eat, and repose a little, that they might be the lustier, and the stronger to fight. But Timoleon did set still forwards, and prayed them not to stay, but to go on with all the speed they could possible, that they might take their enemies out of order (as it was likely they should) being but newly arrived, and troubled with making their cabins, and preparing for supper. Therewith as he spake these words, he took his target on his arm, and marched himself the foremost man, as bravely and courageously as if he had gone to a most assured victory. The soldiers seeing him march with that life, they followed at his heels with like courage. So they had not passing thirty furlongs to go, which when they had overcome, they straight set upon their enemies, whom they found all out of order, and began to fly, so soon as they saw they were upon their backs before they were aware. By this means there were not above three hundred men slain, and twice as many more taken prisoners, and so their whole camp was possessed. Then the Adranitans opening their gates, yielded unto Timoleon, declaring unto him with great fear and no less wonder, how at the very time when he gave charge upon the enemies, the doors of the temple of their god opened of themselves, and that the javelin which the image of their god did hold in his hand, did shake at the very end where the iron head was, and how all his face was seen to sweat.

This (in my opinion) did not only signify the victory he had gotten at that time, but all the notable exploits he did afterwards, unto the which, this first encounter gave a happy beginning. For immediately after, many cities sent unto Timoleon, to join in league with him. And Mamercus, the tyrant of Catana, a soldier and very full of money, did also seek his friendship. Furthermore, Dionysius the tyrant of Syracuse, being weary to follow hope any longer, and finding himself in manner forced unto it by long continuance of siege : made no more reckoning of Hicetes, when he knew that he was so shamefully overthrown. And contrariwise, much esteeming Timoleon's valiantness, he sent to advertise him, that he was contented to yield himself and the castle into the hands of the Corinthians. Timoleon being glad of this good hap unlooked for, sent Euclides and Telemachus, two captains of the Corinthians, to take possession of the castle with four hundred men, not all at a time, nor openly (for it was impossible, the enemies lying in wait in the haven), but by small companies and by stealth he conveyed them all into the castle. So the soldiers possessed the castle, and the tyrant's palace, with all the movables and munition of war within the same. There were a great number of horse of service, great store of staves and weapons offensive of all sorts, and engines of battery to shoot far off, and sundry other weapons of defence, that had been gathered together of long time, to arm threescore and ten thousand men. Moreover, besides all this, there were two thousand soldiers, whom with all the other things rehearsed, Dionysius delivered up into the hands of Timoleon : and he himself, with his money and a few of his friends, went his way by sea, Hicetes not knowing it, and so came to Timoleon's camp. This was the first time that ever they saw Dionysius a private man, in base and mean estate. And yet within few days after, Timoleon sent him from thence unto Corinth in a ship, with little store of money. Who was born and brought up in the greatest and most famous tyranny and kingdom conquered by force, that ever was in the world : and which himself had kept by the space of ten years after the death of his father. Since Dion drave him out, he had been marvellously turmoiled in wars, by the space of twelve years: in which time, although he had done much mischief, yet he had suffered a great deal more. For he saw the death of his sons when they were men grown and able to serve and carry armour. He saw his daughters ravished by force and deflowered of their virginity. He saw his own sister (who was also his wife) first of all shamed and cruelly handled in her person, with the greatest villainies and most vile parts done unto her, that his enemies could devise : and afterwards horribly murdered with her children, and their bodies in the end thrown into the sea, as we have more amply declared in the life of Dion.

Now when Dionysius was arrived in the city of Corinth, every Grecian was wonderful desirous to go see him, and to talk with him. And some went thither very glad of his overthrow, as if they had trodden him down with their feet, whom fortune had overthrown, so bitterly did they hate him. Other pitying him in their hearts, to see so great a change, did behold him as it were with a certain compassion, considering what great power secret and divine causes have over men's weakness and frailty, and those things that daily pass over our heads. For the world then, did never bring forth any work of nature, or of man's hand, so wonderful as was this of fortune : who made the world see a man, that before was in manner lord and king of all Sicily, sit then commonly in the city of Corinth, talking with a victualler, or sitting a whole day in a perfumer's shop, or commonly drinking in some cellar or tavern, or to brawl and scold in the midst of the streets, with common women in the face of the world, or else to teach common minstrels in every lane and alley, and to

dispute with them with the best reason he had, about
the harmony and music of the songs they sang in
the theatres.   Now some say he did this, because he
knew not else how he should drive the time away, for
that indeed he was of a base mind, and an effeminate
person, given over to all dishonest lusts and desires.
Other are of opinion, he did it to be the less regarded,
for fear lest the Corinthians should have him in
jealousy and suspicion, imagining that he did take the
change and state of his life in grievous part, and that
he should yet look back, hoping for a time to recover
his state again : and that for this cause he did it, and
of purpose feigned many things against his nature,
seeming to be a stark idiot, to see him do those
things he did.

Some notwithstanding have gathered together
certain of his answers, which do testify that he did
not all these things of a base brutish mind, but to fit
himself only to his present misery and misfortune.
For when he came to Leucas, an ancient city built by
the Corinthians, as was also the city of Syracuse, he
told the inhabitants of the same, that he was like to
young boys, that had done a fault.   For as they fly
from their fathers, being ashamed to come to their
sight, and are gladder to be with their brethren ; even
so is it with me, said he, for it would please me
better to dwell here with you, than to go to Corinth
our head city.   Another time, being at Corinth, a
stranger was very busy with him (knowing how
familiar Dionysius was with learned men and
philosophers, while he reigned in Syracuse) and asked
him in the end in derision : what benefit he got by
Plato's wisdom and knowledge ? he answered him
again : How thinkest thou, hath it done me no good,
when thou seest me bear so patiently this change of
fortune ?   Aristoxenus a musician, and others, asking
him what offence Plato had done unto him : he
answered, that tyrants' state is ever unfortunate,
and subject to many evils ; but yet no evil in their
state was comparable to this : that none of all those

they take to be their most familiars, dare once tell them truly anything; and that through their fault, he left Plato's company. Another time there cometh a pleasant fellow to him, and thinking to mock him finely, as he entered into his chamber, he shook his gown, as the manner is when they come to tyrants, to shew that they have no weapons under their gowns. But Dionysius encountered him as pleasantly, saying to him: Do that when thou goest hence, to see if thou hast stolen nothing. And again, Philip King of Macedon, at his table one day descending into talk of songs, verse, and tragedies, which Dionysius his father had made, making as though he wondered at them, how possibly he could have leisure to do them: he answered him very trimly, and to good purpose. He did them even at such times (quoth he) as you and I, and other great lords whom they reckon happy, are disposed to be drunk, and play the fools. Now for Plato, he never saw Dionysius at Corinth. But Diogenes Sinopian, the first time that ever he met with Dionysius, said unto him: Oh, how unworthy art thou of this state! Dionysius stayed suddenly, and replied: Truly I thank thee, Diogenes, that thou hast compassion of my misery. Why, said Diogenes again: Dost thou think I pity thee? Nay it spiteth me rather, to see such a slave as thou (worthy to die in the wicked state of a tyrant like thy father) to live in such security and idle life, as thou leadest amongst us. When I came to compare these words of Diogenes with Philistus' words the historiographer, bewailing the hard fortune of the daughters of Leptines, saying that they were brought from the top of all worldly felicity, honour and goods (whereof tyrannical state aboundeth) unto a base, private, and humble life: methinks they are the proper lamentations of a woman, that sorroweth for the loss of her boxes of painting colours, or for her purple gowns, or for other such pretty fine trims of gold, as women use to wear. So, methinks these things I have intermingled concerning Dionysius, are not impertinent to

the description of our lives, neither are they trouble-
some nor unprofitable to the hearers, unless they
have other hasty business to let or trouble them.

But now if the tyrant Dionysius' wretched state
seem strange, Timoleon's prosperity then was no less
wonderful. For within fifty days after he had set
foot in Sicily, he had the castle of Syracuse in his
possession, and sent Dionysius as an exile to Corinth.
This did set the Corinthians in such a jollity, that
they sent him a supply of two thousand footmen, and
two hundred horsemen, which were appointed to land
in Italy, in the country of the Thurians. And perceiving that they could not possibly go from thence
into Sicily, because the Carthaginians kept the seas
with a great navy of ships, and that thereby they were
compelled to stay for better opportunity : in the mean
time they bestowed their leisure in doing a notable
good act. For the Thurians, being in wars at that
time with the Bruttians, they did put their city into
their hands, which they kept very faithfully and
friendly, as it had been their own native country.
Hicetes all this while did besiege the castle of Syracuse,
preventing all he could possible, that there should
come no corn by sea unto the Corinthians that kept
within the castle : and he had hired two strange
soldiers, which he sent unto the city of Adranum, to
kill Timoleon by treason, who kept no guard about
his person, and continued amongst the Adranitans,
mistrusting nothing in the world, for the trust and
confidence he had in the safeguard of the god of the
Adranitans. These soldiers being sent to do this
murder, were by chance informed that Timoleon
should one day do sacrifice unto this god. So upon
this, they came into the temple, having daggers under
their gowns, and by little and little thrust in through
the press, that they got at the length hard to the
altar. But at the present time as one encouraged
another to despatah the matter, a third person they
thought not of, gave one of the two a great cut in the
head with his sword, that he fell to the ground. The

man that had hurt him thus, fled straight upon it, with his sword drawn in his hand, and recovered the top of a high rock. The other soldier that came with him, and that was not hurt, got hold of a corner of the altar, and besought pardon of Timoleon, and told him he would discover the treason practised against him. Timoleon thereupon pardoned him. Then he told him how his companion that was slain, and himself, were both hired, and sent to kill him. In the meantime, they brought him also that had taken the rock, who cried out aloud, he had done no more than he should do : for he had killed him that had slain his own father before, in the city of the Leontines. And to justify this to be true, certain that stood by did affirm it was so indeed. Whereat they wondered greatly to consider the marvellous working of fortune, how she doth bring one thing to pass by means of another, and gathereth all things together, how far asunder soever they be, and linketh them together, though they seem to be clean contrary one to another, with no manner of likeness or conjunction between them, making the end of the one, to be the beginning of another. The Corinthians examining this matter throughly, gave him that slew the soldier with his sword, a crown of the value of ten minas, because that by means of his just anger, he had done good service to the God that had preserved Timoleon. And furthermore, this good hap did not only serve the present turn, but was to good purpose ever after. For those that saw it, were put in better hope, and had thenceforth more care and regard unto Timoleon's person, because he was a holy man, one that loved the gods, and that was purposely sent to deliver Sicily from captivity.

But Hicetes having missed his first purpose, and seeing numbers daily drawn to Timoleon's devotion, he was mad with himself, that having so great an army of the Carthaginians at hand at his commandment, he took but a few of them to serve his turn, as if he had been ashamed of his fact, and had used their friendship by stealth. So he sent thereupon for Mago their general, with all his fleet. Mago at his request brought an huge army to see too, of a hundred and fifty sail, which occupied and covered all the haven : and afterwards landed threescore thousand men, whom he lodged every man within the city of Syracuse. Then every man imagined the time was now come, which old men had threatened Sicily with many years before, and that continually : that one day it should be conquered, and inhabited by the barbarous people. For in all the wars the Carthaginians ever had before in the country of Sicily, they could never come to take the city of Syracuse ; and then through Hicetes' treason, who had received them, they were seen encamped there. On the other side, the Corinthians that were within the castle, found themselves in great distress, because their victuals waxed scant, and the haven was so straitly kept. Moreover, they were driven to be armed continually to defend the walls, which the enemies battered, and assaulted in sundry places, with all kinds of engines of battery, and sundry sorts of devised instruments and inventions to take cities : by reason whereof, they were compelled also to divide themselves into many companies.

Nevertheless, Timoleon without gave them all the aid he could possible : sending them corn from Catana, in little fisher-boats and small crayers, which got into the castle many times, but specially in stormy and foul weather, passing by the galleys of the barbarous people, that lay scatteringly one from another, dispersed abroad by tempest, and great billows of the sea. But Mago and Hicetes finding this, determined to go take the city of Catana, from whence those of the castle of Syracuse were victualled : and taking with them the best soldiers of all their army, they departed from Syracuse, and sailed towards Catana. Now in the mean space, Leon Corinthian, captain of all those that were within the castle, perceiving the enemies within the city kept but slender

ward, made a sudden sally out upon them, and taking
them unawares, slew a great number at the first
charge, and drave away the other.   So by this occasion
he won a quarter of the city, which they call Achradina,
and was the best part of the city, that had received
least hurt.   For the city of Syracuse seemeth to be
built of many towns joined together.   So having
found there great plenty of corn, gold, and silver, he
would not forsake that quarter no more, nor return
again into the castle : but fortifying with all diligence
the compass and precinct of the same, and joining it
unto the castle with certain fortifications he built up
in haste, he determined to keep both the one and the
other.   Now were Mago and Hicetes very near unto
Catana, when a post overtook them, purposely sent
from Syracuse unto them : who brought them news,
that the Achradina was taken.   Whereat they both
wondered, and returned back again with all speed
possible (having failed of their purpose they pretended)
to keep that they had yet left in their hands.

Now for that matter, it is yet a question, whether
we should impute it unto wisdom and valiancy, or
unto good fortune : but the thing I will tell you now,
in my opinion, is altogether to be ascribed unto
fortune.   And this it is.   The two thousand footmen
and two hundred horsemen of the Corinthians, that
remained in the city of the Thurians, partly for fear
of the galleys of the Carthaginians that lay in wait
for them as they should pass, Hanno being their
admiral : and partly also for that the sea was very
rough and high many days together, and was always
in storm and tempest : in the end, they ventured to
go through the country of the Bruttians.   And partly
with their good-will (but rather by force) they got
through, and recovered the city of Rhegium, the sea
being yet marvellous high and rough.   Hanno the
admiral of the Carthaginians, looking no more than
for their passage, thought with himself that he had
devised a marvellous fine policy, to deceive the
enemies.   Thereupon he willed all his men to put

garlands of flowers of triumph upon their heads, and therewithal also made them dress up, and set forth his galleys, with targets, corslets, and brigantines after the Grecians' fashion. So in this bravery he returned back again, sailing towards Syracuse, and came in with force of oars, rowing under the castle's side of Syracuse, with great laughing and clapping of hands: crying out aloud to them that were in the castle, that he had overthrown their aid which came from Corinth, as they thought to pass by the coast of Italy into Sicily, flattering themselves that this did much discourage those that were besieged. But whilst he sported thus with this fond device, the two thousand Corinthians being arrived through the country of the Bruttians in the city of Rhegium, perceiving the coast clear, and that the passage by sea was not kept, and that the raging seas were by miracle (as it were) made of purpose calm for them: they took sea forthwith in such fisher boats and passengers as they found ready, in the which they went into Sicily, in such good safety as they drew their horse (holding them by the reins) alongst their boats with them.

When they were all passed over, Timoleon having received them, went immediately to take Messina, and marching thence in battle array, took his way towards Syracuse, trusting better to his good fortune, than to his force he had: for his whole number in all, were not above four thousand fighting men. Notwithstanding, Mago hearing of his coming, quaked for fear, and doubted the more upon this occasion. About Syracuse are certain marshes, that receive great quantity of sweet fresh water, as well of fountains and springs, as also of little running brooks, lakes, and rivers, which run that way towards the sea: and therefore there are great store of eels in that place, and the fishing is great there at all times, but specially for such as delight to take eels. Whereupon the Grecians that took pay on both sides, when they had leisure, and that all was quiet between them,

they intended fishing. Now, they being all countrymen, and of one language, had no private quarrel one
with another: but when time was to fight, they did
their duties, and in time of peace also frequented
familiarly together, and one spake with another, and
specially when they were busy fishing for eels: saying,
that they marvelled at the situation of the goodly
places thereabouts, and that they stood so pleasantly
and commodious upon the sea-side. So one of the
soldiers, that served under the Corinthians, chanced
to say unto them: Is it possible that you that be
Grecians born, and have so goodly a city of your
own, and full of so many goodly commodities: that
ye will give it up unto these barbarous people, the
Carthaginians, and most cruel murderers of the
world? where you should rather wish that there
were many Sicilies betwixt them and Greece. Have
ye so little consideration or judgment to think, that
they have assembled an army out of all Africk, unto
Hercules' pillars, and to the sea Atlantic, to come
hither to fight to establish Hicetes' tyranny? who, if
he had been a wise and skilful captain, would not
have cast out his ancestors and founders, to bring
into his country the ancient enemies of the same:
but might have received such honour and authority
of the Corinthians and Timoleon, as he could reasonably have desired, and that with all their favour and
good-will. The soldiers that heard this tale reported
it again in their camp: insomuch they made Mago
suspect there was treason in hand, and so sought
some colour to be gone. But hereupon, notwithstanding that Hicetes prayed him all he could to
tarry, declaring unto him how much they were
stronger than their enemies, and that Timoleon did
rather prevail by his hardiness and good fortune,
than exceed him in number of men: yet he hoised
sail, and returned with shame enough into Africk,
letting slip the conquest of all Sicily out of his hands,
without any sight of reason or cause at all.

The next day after he was gone, Timoleon presented

battle before the city, when the Grecians and he
understood that the Carthaginians were fled, and that
they saw the haven rid of all the ships: and then
began to jest at Mago's cowardliness, and in derision
proclaimed in the city, that they would give him a
good reward, that could bring them news, whither the
army of the Carthaginians were fled. But for all this,
Hicetes was bent to fight, and would not leave the
spoil he had gotten, but defend the quarters of the
city he had possessed, at the sword's point, trusting
to the strength and situation of the places, which were
hardly to be approached. Timoleon perceiving that,
divided his army, and he with one part thereof did set
upon that side which was the hardest to approach,
and did stand upon the river of Anapus: then he
appointed another part of his army to assault all
at one time, the side of Achradina, whereof Isias
Corinthian had the leading. The third part of his
army that came last from Corinth, which Dinarchus
and Demaretus led, he appointed to assault the
quarter called Epipolae. Thus, assault being given
on all sides at one time, Hicetes' bands of men were
broken, and ran their way. Now that the city was
thus won by assault, and come so suddenly to the
hands of Timoleon, and the enemies being fled, it
is good reason we ascribe it to the valiantness of the
soldiers, and the captain's great wisdom. But where
there was not one Corinthian slain, nor hurt in this
assault, sure methinks herein, it was only the work
and deed of fortune, that did favour and protect
Timoleon, to contend against his valiantness. To
the end that those which should hereafter hear of his
doings, should have more occasion to wonder at his
good hap, than to praise and commend his valiantness.
For the fame of this great exploit, did in few days
not only run through all Italy, but also through all
Greece. Insomuch as the Corinthians (who could
scant believe their men were passed with safety into
Sicily) understood withal that they were safely arrived
there, and had gotten the victory of their enemies: so

prosperous was their journey, and fortune so speedily did favour his noble acts.

Timoleon having now the castle of Syracuse in his hands, did not follow Dion. For he spared not the castle for the beauty and stately building thereof, but avoiding the suspicion that caused Dion first to be accused, and lastly to be slain, he caused it to be proclaimed by trumpet, that any Syracusan whatsoever, should come with crows of iron and mattocks, to help to dig down and overthrow the fort of the tyrants. There was not a man in all the city of Syracuse but went thither straight, and thought that proclamation and day to be a most happy beginning of the recovery of their liberty. So they did not only overthrow the castle, but the palace also, and the tombs: and generally all that served in any respect for the memory of any of the tyrants. And having cleared the place in few days, and made all plain, Timoleon at the suit of the citizens, made councilhalls, and places of justice to be built there : and did by this means stablish a free state and popular government, and did suppress all tyrannical power. Now, when he saw he had won a city that had no inhabitants, which wars before had consumed, and fear of tyranny had emptied, so as grass grew so high and rank in the great market-place of Syracuse, as they grazed their horses there, and the horsekeepers lay down by them on the grass as they fed : and that all the cities, a few excepted, were full of red deer and wild boars, so that men given to delight in hunting, having leisure, might find game many times within the suburbs and town ditches, hard by the walls: and that such as dwelt in castles and strongholds in the country, would not leave them to come and dwell in cities, by reason they were all grown so stout, and did so hate and detest assemblies of council, orations, and order of government, where so many tyrants had reigned: Timoleon thereupon seeing this desolation, and also so few Syracusans born that had escaped, thought good, and all his captains,

to write to the Corinthians, to send people out of
Greece to inhabit the city of Syracuse again. For
otherwise the country would grow barren and unprofitable, if the ground were not ploughed. Besides, that
they looked also for great wars out of Africk: being
advertised that the Carthaginians had hung up the
body of Mago their general upon a cross (who had
slain himself for that he could not answer the dishonour laid to his charge) and that they did levy
another great mighty army, to return again the next
year following, to make wars in Sicily.

These letters of Timoleon being brought unto
Corinth, and the ambassadors of Syracuse being
arrived with them also, who besought the people to
take care and protection over their poor city, and that
they would once again be founders of the same: the
Corinthians did not greedily desire to be lords of so
goodly and great a city, but first proclaimed by the
trumpet in all the assemblies, solemn feasts, and
common plays of Greece, that the Corinthians having
destroyed the tyranny that was in the city of Syracuse,
and driven out the tyrants, did call the Syracusans that
were fugitives out of their country, home again, and
all other Sicilians that like to come and dwell there,
to enjoy all freedom and liberty, with promise to
make just and equal division of the lands among them,
the one to have as much as the other. Moreover,
they sent out posts and messengers into Asia, and
into all the islands where they understood the
banished Syracusans remained, to persuade and
entreat them to come to Corinth, and that the
Corinthians would give them ships, captains, and
means to conduct them safely unto Syracuse, at their
own proper costs and charges. In recompense
whereof, the city of Corinth received every man's
most noble praise and blessing, as well for delivering
Sicily in that sort from the bondage of tyrants, as
also for keeping it out of the hands of the barbarous
people, and restoring the natural Syracusans and
Sicilians to their home and country again. Never-

theless, such Sicilians as repaired to Corinth upon
this proclamation (themselves being but a small
number to inhabit the country) besought the Corinthians to join to them some other inhabitants, as
well of Corinth itself, as out of the rest of Greece : the
which was performed. For they gathered together
about ten thousand persons, whom they shipped and
sent to Syracuse. Where there were already a
great number of others come unto Timoleon, as well
out of Sicily itself, as out of all Italy besides : so that
the whole number (as Athanis writeth) came to threescore thousand persons. Amongst them he divided
the whole country, and sold them houses of the city
unto the value of a thousand talents. And because
he would leave the old Syracusans able to recover
their own, and make the poor people by this means
to have money in common to defray the common
charge of the city, as also their expenses in time of
wars : the statues or images were sold, and the
people by most voices did condemn them. For they
were solemnly indited, accused, and arraigned, as if
they had been men alive to be condemned. And it
is reported that the Syracusans did reserve the statue
of Gelo, an ancient tyrant of their city, honouring his
memory because of a great victory he had won of the
Carthaginians, near the city of Himera : and condemned all the rest to be taken away out of every
corner of the city, and to be sold.

Thus began the city of Syracuse to replenish again,
and by little and little to recover itself, many people
coming thither from all parts to dwell there. Thereupon Timoleon thought to set all the other cities at
liberty also, and utterly to root out all the tyrants of
Sicily : and to obtain his purpose, he went to make
wars with them at their own doors. The first he
went against was Hicetes, whom he compelled to
forsake the league of the Carthaginians, and to
promise also that he would raze all the fortresses he
kept, and to live like a private man within the city of
the Leontines. Leptines in like manner, that was

tyrant of the city of Apollonia, and of many other little
villages thereabouts, when he saw himself in danger
to be taken by force, did yield himself.   Whereupon
Timoleon saved his life, and sent him unto Corinth:
thinking it honourable for his country, that the other
Grecians should see the tyrants of Sicily in their
chief city of fame, living meanly and poorly like
banished people.   When he had brought this to pass,
he returned forthwith to Syracuse about the
establishment of the common-weal, assisting Cephalus
and Dionysius, two notable men sent from Corinth
to reform the laws, and to help them to stablish the
goodliest ordinances for their common-weal.   And
now in the meantime, because the soldiers had a
mind to get something of their enemies, and to avoid
idleness, he sent them out abroad to a country
subject to the Carthaginians, under the charge of
Dinarchus and Demaretus: where they made many
little towns rebel against the barbarous people, and
did not only live in all abundance of wealth, but they
gathered money together also to maintain the wars.

The Carthaginians on the other side, while they
were busy about these matters, came down into
Lilybaeum, with an army of threescore and ten
thousand men, two hundred galleys, and a thousand
other ships and vessels that carried engines of battery,
carts, victuals, munition, and other necessary provision for a camp, intending to make sporting wars
no more, but at once to drive all the Grecians again
quite out of Sicily.   For indeed it was an able army
to overcome all the Sicilians, if they had been whole
of themselves, and not divided.   Now they being
advertised that the Sicilians had invaded their
country, they went towards them in great fury led by
Hasdrubal and Hamilcar, generals of the army.   This
news was straight brought to Syracuse, and the
inhabitants were so stricken with fear of the report
of their army: that being a marvellous great number
of them within the city, scant three thousand of them
had the hearts to arm themselves, and to go to the

field with Timoleon. Now the strangers that took
pay, were not above four thousand in all: and of
them, a thousand of their hearts failed, and left him
in midway, and returned home again: saying, that
Timoleon was out of his wits, and more rash than his
years required, to undertake with five thousand footmen, and a thousand horse, to go against threescore
and ten thousand men: and besides, to carry that
small force he had to defend himself withal, eight
great days' journey from Syracuse. So that if it
chanced they were compelled to fly, they had no place
whither they might retire themselves unto with safety,
nor man that would take care to bury them, when
they were slain. Nevertheless, Timoleon was glad he
had that proof of them before he came to battle.
Moreover, having encouraged those that remained
with him, he made them march with speed towards
the river of Crimesus, where he understood he should
meet with the Carthaginians.

. So getting up upon a little hill, from whence he
might see the camp of the enemies on the other side:
by chance certain mules fell upon his army, laden
with smallage. The soldiers took a conceit at the
first upon sight of it, and thought it was a token of
ill-luck: because it is a manner we use, to hang
garlands of this herb about the tombs of the dead.
Hereof came the common proverb they use to speak,
when one lieth a-passing in his bed: He lacketh but
smallage: as much to say, he is but a dead man.
But Timoleon to draw them from this foolish super-
stition and discourage they took, stayed the army.
And when he had used certain persuasions unto them,
according to the time, his leisure, and occasion: he
told them that the garland of itself came to offer
them victory beforehand. For, said he, the Corinthians do crown them that win the Isthmian games
(which are celebrated in their country) with garlands
of smallage. And at that time also even in the
solemn Isthmian games, they used the garland of
smallage for reward and token of victory: and at this

present it is also used in the games of Nemea. And
it is but lately taken up, that they have used branches
of pine-apple trees in the Isthmian games. When
Timoleon had thus encouraged his men, as you have
heard before: he first of all took of this smallage,
and made himself a garland, and put it on his head.
And after him the captains and all the soldiers
also took of the same, and made themselves the like.
The soothsayers in like manner at the very same
time, perceived two eagles flying towards them: the
one of them holding a snake in her talons, which she
pierced through and through, and the other as she
flew, gave a terrible cry. So they shewed them both
unto the soldiers, who did then all together with one
voice call upon the gods for help.

Now this fortuned about the beginning of summer,
and towards the latter end of May, the sun drawing
towards the solstice of summer : when there rose
a great mist out of the river, that covered all the
fields over, so as they could not see the enemy's
camp, but only heard a marvellous confused noise of
men's voices, as it had come from a great army : and
rising up to the top of the hill, they laid their targets
down on the ground to take a little breath: and the
sun having drawn and sucked up all the moist vapours
of the mist unto the top of the hills, the air began to
be so thick, that the tops of the mountains were all
covered over with clouds, and contrarily, the valley
underneath was all clear and fair, that they might
easily see the river of Crimesus, and the enemies also,
how they passed it over in this sort. First they had
put their carts of war foremost, which were very
hotly armed and well appointed. Next unto them
there followed ten thousand footmen, armed with
white targets upon their arms: whom they seeing
afar off so well appointed, they conjectured by their
stately march and goodly order, that they were the
Carthaginians themselves. After them, divers other
nations followed confusedly one with another, and
so they thronged over with great disorder. There

Timoleon considering the river gave him opportunity
to take them before they were half passed over, and
to set upon what number he would: after he had
shewed his men with his finger, how the battle of
their enemies was divided in two parts by means of
the river, some of them being already passed over,
and the other to pass: he commanded Demaretus
with his horsemen to give a charge on the vaward, to
keep them from putting themselves in order of battle.
And himself coming down the hill also with all his
footmen into the valley, he gave to the Sicilians the
two wings of his battle, mingling with them some
strangers that served under 'him: and placed with
himself in the midst, the Syracusans with all the
choice and best liked strangers. So he tarried not
long to join, when he saw the small good his horsemen did. For he perceived they could not come to
give a lusty charge upon the battle of the Carthaginians, because they were paled in with these armed
carts, that ran here and there before them: whereupon they were compelled to wheel about continually
(unless they would have put themselves in danger to
have been utterly overthrown), and in their returns to
give venture of charge, by turns on their enemies.
Wherefore Timoleon taking his target on his arm,
cried out aloud to his footmen, to follow him
courageously, and to fear nothing. Those that heard
his voice, thought it more than the voice of a man,
whether the fury of his desire to fight did so strain it
beyond ordinary course, or that some god (as many
thought it then) did stretch his voice to cry out so
loud and sensibly. His soldiers answered him again
with the like voice: and prayed him to lead them
without longer delay. Then he made his horsemen
understand, that they should draw on the one side
from the carts, and that they should charge the
Carthaginians on the flanks: and after he did set the
foremost rank of his battle, target to target against the
enemies, commanding the trumpets withal to sound.

Thus with great fury he went to give a charge

upon them, who valiantly received the first charge,
their bodies being armed with good iron corslets,
and their heads with fair murrions of copper, besides
the great targets they had also, which did easily
receive the force of their darts, and the thrust of the
pike.   But when they came to handle their swords,
where agility was more requisite than force, a fearful
tempest of thunder, and flashing lightning withal,
came from the mountains. After that came dark
thick clouds also (gathered together from the top of
the hills) and fell upon the valley, where the battle
was fought, with a marvellous extreme shower of rain,
fierce violent winds, and hail withal.   All this tempest
was upon the Grecians' backs, and full before the
barbarous people, beating on their faces, and did
blindfold their eyes, and continually tormented them
with the rain that came full upon them with the
wind, and the lightnings so oft flashing amongst
them, that one understood not another of them.
Which did marvellously trouble them, and specially
those that were but fresh-water soldiers, by reason of
the terrible thunderclaps, and the noise the boisterous
wind and hail made upon their harness: for that made
them they could not hear the order of their captains.
Moreover, the dirt did as much annoy the Carthaginians, because they were not nimble in their
armour, but heavily armed, as we have told you : and
besides that also, when the plates of their coats were
through wet with water, they did load and hinder
them so much the more, that they could not fight
with any ease.   This stood the Grecians to great
purpose, to throw them down the easier.   Thus when
they were tumbling in the dirt with their heavy armour,
up they could rise no more.   Furthermore, the river
of Crimesus being risen high through the great rage
of waters, and also for the multitude of people that
passed over it, did overflow the valley all about:
which being full of ditches, many caves, and hollow
places, it was straight all drowned over, and filled
with many running streams, that ran overthwart the

field, without any certain channel. The Carthaginians being compassed all about with these waters, they could hardly get the way out of it ; so as in the end they being overcome with the storm that still did beat upon them, and the Grecians having slain of their men at the first onset, to the number of four hundred of their choicest men, who made the first front of their battle : all the rest of the army turned their backs immediately and fled for life. Insomuch as some of them, being followed very near, were put to the sword in the midst of the valley : others, holding one another hard by the arms together, in the midst of the river as they passed over, were carried down the stream and drowned, with the swiftness and violence of the river. But the greatest number, thinking by footmanship to recover the hills thereabouts, were overtaken by them that were light armed, and put to the sword every man. They say that of ten thousand which were slain in this battle, three thousand of them were natural citizens of Carthage, which was a very sorrowful and grievous loss to the city. For they were of the noblest, the richest, the lustiest, and valiantest men of all Carthage. For there is no chronicle that mentioneth any former wars at any time before, where there died so many of Carthage at one field and battle, as were slain at that present time. For before that time, they did always entertain the Libyans, the Spaniards, and the Nomads, in all their wars : so as when they lost any battle, the loss lighted not on them, but the strangers paid for it.

The men of account also that were slain, were easily known by their spoils. For they that spoiled them, stood not trifling about getting of copper and iron together, because they found gold and silver enough. For the battle being won, the Grecians passed over the river, and took the camp of the barbarous people, with all their carriages and baggage. And as for the prisoners, the soldiers stole many of them away, and sent them going : but of them that came to light in the common division of the spoil,

3—2

they were about five thousand men, and two hundred
carts of war that were taken besides. Oh, it was a
noble sight to behold the tent of Timoleon their
general, how they environed it all about with heaps
of spoils of every sort: among which there were
a thousand brave corslets gilt and graven with
marvellous curious works, and they brought thither
with them also ten thousand targets. So the conquerors being but a small number to take the spoil
of a multitude that were slain, they filled their purses
even to the top. Yet were they three days about
it, and in the end, the third day after the battle,
they set up a mark or token of their victory. Then
Timoleon sent unto Corinth, with the news of this
overthrow, the fairest armours that were gotten in
the spoil: because he would make his country and
native city spoken of and commended through the
world, above all the other cities of Greece. For
that at Corinth only, their chief temples were set
forth and adorned, not with spoils of the Grecians,
nor offerings got by spilling the blood of their
own nation and country (which to say truly, are
unpleasant memories), but with the spoils taken
from the barbarous people their enemies, with in-
scriptions witnessing the valiancy and justice of
those also, who by victory had obtained them.
That is to wit, that the Corinthians and their captain
Timoleon (having delivered the Grecians dwelling
in Sicily, from the bondage of the Carthaginians) had
given those offerings unto the gods, to give thanks for
their victory.

That done, Timoleon leaving the strangers he had
in pay, in the country subject to the Carthaginians,
to spoil and destroy it: he returned with the rest of
his army unto Syracuse. Where at his first coming
home, he banished the thousand soldiers that had
forsaken him in his journey, with express charge that
they should depart the city before sunset. So these
thousand cowardly and mutinous soldiers passed over
into Italy, where, under promise of the contrary,

they were all unfortunately slain by the Bruttians: such was the justice of the gods to pay the just reward of their treason. Afterwards, Mamercus the tyrant of Catana, and Hicetes (whether it was for the envy they did bear to Timoleon's famous deeds, or for that they were afraid of him) perceiving tyrants could look for no peace at his hands: they made league with the Carthaginians, and wrote unto them that they should send another army and captain suddenly, if they would not utterly be driven out of Sicily. The Carthaginians sent Gisco thither with threescore and ten sail, who at his first coming took a certain number of Grecian soldiers into pay, which were the first the Carthaginians ever retained in their service: for they never gave them pay until that present time, when they thought them to be men invincible, and the best soldiers of the world. Moreover, the inhabitants of the territory of Messina, having made a secret conspiracy amongst themselves, did slay four hundred men that Timoleon had sent unto them: and in the territories subject unto the Carthaginians, near unto a place they call Hierae, there was another ambush laid for Euthymus Leucadian, so as himself and all his soldiers were cut in pieces. Howbeit the loss of them made Timoleon's doings notwithstanding more fortunate: for they were even those that had forcibly entered the temple of Apollo in the city of Delphi, with Philomelus the Phocian, and with Onomarchus, who were partakers of their sacrilege. Moreover, they were loose people and abjects, that were abhorred of everybody, who vagabond-like wandered up and down the country of Peloponnesus, when Timoleon for lack of other was glad to take them up. And when they came into Sicily, they always overcame in all battles they fought, whilst they were in his company. But in the end, when the fury of wars was pacified, Timoleon sending them about some special service to the aid of some of his, they were cast away every man of them: and not all together,

but at divers times. So as it seemed that God's
justice, in favour of Timoleon, did separate them from
the rest, when he was determined to plague them for
their wicked deserts, fearing lest good men should
suffer hurt by punishing of the evil. And so was the
grace and good-will of the gods wonderful towards
Timoleon, not only in matters against him, but in
those things that prospered well with him.

Notwithstanding, the common people of Syracuse
took the jesting words and writings of the tyrants
against them, in marvellous evil part. For Mamercus
amongst other, thinking well of himself, because he
could make verses and tragedies, having in certain
battles gotten the better hand of the strangers which
the Syracusans gave pay unto, he gloried very much.
And when he offered up the targets he had gotten of
them, in the temples of the gods, he set up also
these cutting verses, in derision of them that were
vanquished:

> With bucklers pot-lid like, which of no value were,
> We have these goodly targets won, so richly trimmèd here,
> All gorgeously with gold, and eke with ivory,
> With purple colours finely wrought, and deckt with ebony.

These things done, Timoleon led his army before
the city of Calauria, and Hicetes therewhile entered
the confines of the Syracusans with a main army,
and carried away a marvellous great spoil. And after
he had done great hurt, and spoiled the country,
he returned back again, and came by Calauria, to
despite Timoleon, knowing well enough he had at
that time but few men about him. Timoleon suffered
him to pass by, but followed him afterwards with his
horsemen and lightest armed footmen. Hicetes understanding that, passed over the river called Damyrias,
and so stayed on the other side as though he would
fight, trusting to the swift running of the river, and
the height of the banks on either side of the same.
Now the captains of Timoleon's bands fell out marvellously amongst themselves, striving for honour of
this service, which was cause of delaying the battle.

For none would willingly come behind, but every
man desired to lead the vaward, for honour to begin
the charge: so as they could not agree for their
going over, one thrusting another to get before his
companion. Wherefore Timoleon fell to drawing of
lots, which of them should pass over first, and took
a ring of every one of them, and cast them all within
the lap of his cloak: so rolling them together, by
chance he plucked one at the first, whereon was
graven the marks and tokens of a triumph. The young
captains seeing that, gave a shout of joy, and without
tarrying drawing of other lots, they began every man
to pass the river as quickly as they could, and to set
upon the enemies as suddenly. But they being not
able to abide their force, ran their ways, and were
fain to cast their armour away to make more haste:
howbeit there were a thousand of them lay dead in
the field.

And within few days after, Timoleon leading his
army to the city of the Leontines, took Hicetes alive
there, with his son Eupolemus, and the general of
his horsemen, who were delivered into his hands by
his own soldiers. So Hicetes and his son were put
to death, like traitors and tyrants: and so was
Euthydemus also, who though he was a valiant
soldier, had no better mercy shewed him, than the
father and the son, because they did burthen him
with certain injurious words he spake against the
Corinthians. For they say, that when the Corinthians
came first out of their country into Sicily, to make
wars against the tyrants: that he making an oration
before the Leontines, said amongst other things, that
they should not need to be afraid, if

> The women of Corinth were come out of their country.

Thus we see, that men do rather suffer hurt, than
put up injurious words: and do pardon their enemies,
though they revenge by deeds, because they can do
no less. But as for injurious words, they seem to
proceed of a deadly hate, and of a cankered malice.

Furthermore, when Timoleon was returned again to Syracuse, the Syracusans arraigned the wives of Hicetes, and his son, and their daughters: who being arraigned, were also condemned to die by the judgment of the people. Of all the acts Timoleon did, this of all other (in my opinion) was the foulest deed: for if he had listed, he might have saved the poor women from death. But he passed not for them, and so left them to the wrath of the citizens, who would be revenged of them, for the injuries that were done to Dion, after he had driven out the tyrant Dionysius. For it was Hicetes that caused Arete, the wife of Dion, to be cast into the sea, his sister Aristomache, and his son that was yet a sucking child, as we have written in another place in the life of Dion.

That done, he went to Catana against Mamercus, who tarried for him by the river Abolus, where Mamercus was overthrown in battle, and above two thousand men slain, the greatest part whereof were the Carthaginians, whom Gisco had sent for his relief. Afterwards he granted peace to the Carthaginians, upon earnest suit made to him, with condition, that they should keep on the other side of the river of Lycus, and that it should be lawful for any of the inhabitants there that would, to come and dwell in the territory of the Syracusans, and to bring away with them their gods, their wives and children: and furthermore, that from thenceforth the Carthaginians should renounce all league, confederacy, and alliance with the tyrants. Whereupon Mamercus having no hope of good success in his doings, he would go into Italy, to stir up the Lucanians against Timoleon and the Syracusans. But they that were in his company, returned back again with their galleys in the midway: and when they were returned into Sicily, they delivered up the city of Catana into the hands of Timoleon, so as Mamercus was constrained to save himself, and to fly unto Messina, to Hippo the tyrant thereof. But Timoleon followed him, and besieged the city both by sea and by land. Whereat

Hippo quaked for fear, and thought to fly by taking of
ship, but he was taken starting. And the Messinians
having him in their hands, made all the children come
from the school to the theatre, to see one of the
goodliest sights that they could devise: to wit, to see
the tyrant punished, who was openly whipped, and
afterwards put to death. Now for Mamercus, he did
yield himself unto Timoleon, to be judged by the
Syracusans, so that Timoleon might not be his
accuser. So he was brought unto Syracuse, where
he attempted to make an oration to the people,
which he had premeditated long before. But seeing
that the people cried out, and made a great noise,
because they would not hear him, and that there was
no likelihood they would pardon him: he ran overthwart the theatre, and knocked his head as hard as
he could drive, upon one of the degrees whereon they
sat there to see their sports, thinking to have dashed
out his brains, and have rid himself suddenly out of
his pain. But he was not happy to die so, for he was
taken straight being yet alive, and put to death as
thieves and murderers are.

Thus did Timoleon root all tyrants out of Sicily,
and made an end of all wars there. And whereas he
found the whole isle, wild, savage, and hated of the
natural countrymen and inhabitants of the same, for
the extreme calamities and miseries they suffered, he
brought it to be so civil, and so much desired of
strangers, that they came far and near to dwell there,
where the natural inhabitants of the country self
before, were glad to fly and forsake it. For Agrigentum and Gela, two great cities, did witness this,
which after the wars of the Athenians, had been
utterly forsaken and destroyed by the Carthaginians,
and were then inhabited again: the one, by
Megellus and Pheristus, two captains that came from
Elea; and the other by Gorgos, who came from the
isle of Ceos. And as near as they could, they gathered
again together the first ancient citizens and inhabitants of the same: whom Timoleon did not only

assure of peace and safety to live there, to settle
them quietly together: but willingly did help them
besides, with all other things necessary, to his utter-
most mean and ability, for which they loved and
honoured him as their father and founder. And this
his good love and favour was common also to all
other people of Sicily whatsoever. So that in all
Sicily there was no truce taken in wars, nor laws
established, nor lands divided, nor institution of any
policy or government thought good or available, if
Timoleon's device had not been in it, as chief director
of such matters: which gave him a singular grace to
be acceptable to the gods, and generally to be beloved
of all men.

For in those days, there were other famous men in
Greece, that did marvellous great things: amongst
whom were these, Timotheus, Agesilaus, Pelopidas
and Epaminondas, which Epaminondas Timoleon
sought to follow in all things, as near as he could,
above any of them all. But in all the actions of
these other great captains, their glory was always
mingled with violence, pain, and labour: so as some
of them have been touched with reproach, and other
with repentance. Whereas contrariwise, in all
Timoleon's doings (that only excepted which he was
forced to do to his brother) there was nothing but
they might with truth (as Timaeus said) proclaim the
saying of Sophocles:

O mighty gods of heaven, what Venus stately dame,
Or Cupid (god) have thus yput their hands unto this same?

And like as Antimachus' verses, and Dionysius'
painting, both Colophonians, are full of sinews and
strength, and yet at this present we see they are
things greatly laboured, and travelled with much
pain: and that contrariwise in Nicomachus' tables,
and Homer's verses, besides the passing workman-
ship and singular grace in them, a man findeth at the
first sight, that they were easily made, and without
great pain. Even so in like manner, whosoever will

compare the painful bloody wars and battles of
Epaminondas and Agesilaus, with the wars of
Timoleon, in the which, besides equity and justice,
there is also great ease and quietness : he shall find,
weighing things indifferently, that they have not
been fortune's doings simply, but that they came of
a most noble and fortunate courage.   Yet he himself
doth wisely impute it unto his good hap, and favourable fortune.   For in his letters he wrote unto his
familiar friends at Corinth, and in some other
orations he made to the people of Syracuse, he
spake it many times, that he thanked the almighty
gods, that it had pleased them to save and deliver
Sicily from bondage by his means and service, and
to give him the honour and dignity of the name.
And having built a temple in his house, he dedicated
it unto Fortune, and furthermore did consecrate his
whole house unto her.   For he dwelt in a house the
Syracusans kept for him, and gave him in recompense
of the good service he had done them in the wars,
with a marvellous fair pleasant house in the country
also, where he kept most when he was at leisure.
For he never after returned unto Corinth again, but
sent for his wife and children to come thither, and
never dealt afterwards with those troubles that fell
out amongst the Grecians, neither did make himself
to be envied of the citizens (a mischief that most
governors and captains do fall into, through their
unsatiable desire of honour and authority), but lived
all the rest of his life after in Sicily, rejoicing for the
great good he had done, and specially to see so many
cities and thousands of people happy by his means.

But because it is an ordinary matter, and of
necessity (as Simonides saith), that not only all larks
have a tuft upon their heads, but also that in all
cities there be accusers, where the people rule : there
were two of those at Syracuse, that continually
made orations to the people, who did accuse Timoleon,
the one called Laphystius, and the other Demaenetus.
So this Laphystius appointing Timoleon a certain

day to come and answer to his accusation before the
people, thinking to convince him : the citizens began
to mutiny, and would not in any case suffer the
day of adjournment to take place. But Timoleon
did pacify them, declaring unto them that he had
taken all the extreme pains and labour he had done,
and had passed so many dangers, because every
citizen and inhabitant of Syracuse, might frankly
use the liberty of their laws.   And another time
Demaenetus, in open assembly of the people, reproving many things Timoleon did when he was general:
Timoleon answered never a word, but only said unto
the people, that he thanked the gods they had
granted him the thing he had so oft requested of
them in his prayers, which was, that he might once
see the Syracusans have full power and liberty to
say what they would.   Now Timoleon in all men's
opinion, had done the noblest acts that ever Grecian
captain did in his time, and had alone deserved the
fame and glory of all the noble exploits, which the
rhetoricians with all their eloquent orations persuaded
the Grecians unto, in the open assemblies, and
common feasts and plays of Greece, out of the which
fortune delivered him safe and sound before the
trouble of the civil wars that followed soon after:
and moreover he made a great proof of his valiancy
and knowledge in wars, against the barbarous people
and tyrants, and had shewed himself also a just and
merciful man unto all his friends, and generally to
all the Grecians.   And furthermore, seeing he won
the most part of all his victories and triumphs,
without the shedding of any one tear of his men, or
that any of them mourned by his means, and also
rid all Sicily of all the miseries and calamities reigning at that time, in less than eight years' space: he
being now grown old, his sight first beginning a little
to fail him, shortly after he lost it altogether.   This
happened, not through any cause or occasion of
sickness that came unto him, nor that fortune had
casually done him this injury: but it was in my

opinion, a disease inheritable to him by his parents, which by time came to lay hold on him also. For the voice went, that many of his kin in like case had also lost their sight, which by little and little with age, was clean taken from them. Howbeit Athanis the historiographer writeth, that during the wars he had against Mamercus and Hippo, as he was in his camp at Mylae, there came a white spot in his eyes, that dimmed his sight somewhat : so that every man perceived that he should lose his sight altogether. Notwithstanding that, he did not raise his siege, but continued his enterprise, until he took both the tyrants at last : and so soon as he returned to Syracuse again, he did put himself out of his office of general, praying the citizens to accept that he had already done, the rather because things were brought to so good pass, as they themselves could desire.

Now, that he patiently took this misfortune to be blind altogether, peradventure men may somewhat marvel at it : but this much more is to be wondered at, that the Syracusans after he was blind, did so much honour him, and acknowledge the good he had done them, that they went themselves to visit him oft, and brought strangers (that were travellers) to his house in the city, and also in the country, to make them see their benefactor, rejoicing and thinking themselves happy, that he had chosen to end his life with them, and that for this cause he had despised the glorious return that was prepared for him in Greece, for the great and happy victories he had won in Sicily. But amongst many other things the Syracusans did, and ordained to honour him with, this of all other methinketh was the chiefest : that they made a perpetual law, so oft as they should have wars against foreign people, and not against their own countrymen, that they should ever choose a Corinthian for their general. It was a goodly thing also to see how they did honour him in the assemblies of their Council. For if any trifling matter fell in question among them, they despatched it of them-

selves: but if it were a thing that required great
counsel and advice, they caused Timoleon to be sent
for. So he was brought through the market-place in
his litter, into the theatre, where all the assembly of
the people was, and carried in even so in his litter as
he sat: and then the people did all salute him with
one voice, and he them in like case. And after he
had paused awhile to hear the praises and blessings
the whole assembly gave him, they did propound
the matter doubtful to him, and he delivered his
opinion upon the same: which being passed by the
voices of the people, his servants carried him back
again in his litter through the theatre, and the
citizens did wait on him a little way with cries of
joy and clapping of hands: and that done, they did
repair to despatch common causes by themselves, as
they did before.

So his old age being thus entertained with such
honour, and with the love and good-will of every man,
as of a common father to them all: in the end a
sickness took him by the back, whereof he died.
So the Syracusans had a certain time appointed
them to prepare for his funerals, and their neighbours
also thereabouts to come unto it. By reason whereof his funeral was so much more honourably performed in all things, and specially for that the people
appointed the noblest young gentlemen of the city to
carry his coffin upon their shoulders, richly furnished
and set forth, whereon his body lay, and so did convey
him through the place, where the palace and castle of
the tyrant Dionysius had been, which then was razed to
the ground. There accompanied his body also many
thousands of people, all crowned with garlands of
flowers, and apparelled in their best apparel: so as it
seemed it had been the procession of some solemn
feast, and all their words were praisings and blessings
of the dead, with tears running down their cheeks,
which was a good testimony of the entire good-will
and love they did bear him, and that they did not
this as men that were glad to be discharged of the

honour they did him, neither for that it was so ordained: but for the just sorrow and grief they took for his death, and for very hearty good love they did bear him. And lastly, the coffin being put upon the stack of wood where it should be burnt, Demetrius one of the heralds that had the loudest voice, proclaimed the decree that was ordained by the people, the effect whereof was this. The people of Syracuse hath ordained, that this present body of Timoleon Corinthian, the son of Timodemus, should be buried at the charges of the common-weal, unto the sum of two hundred minas, and hath honoured his memory with plays and games of music, with running of horses, and with other exercises of the body, which shall be celebrated yearly on the day of his death for evermore: and this, because he did drive the tyrants out of Sicily, for that he over-came the barbarous people, and because he re-plenished many great cities with inhabitants again, which the wars had left desolate and uninhabited; and lastly, for that he had restored the Sicilians again to their liberty, and to live after their own laws. And afterwards, his tomb was built in the market-place, about the which, a certain time after, they builded certain cloisters and galleries to exercise the youth in, with exercise of their bodies, and the place so walled in, was called Timoleonteum: and so long as they did observe the laws and civil policy he stab-lished amongst them, they lived long time in great and continual prosperity.

THE LIFE OF PAULUS AEMILIUS

MANY (and the most part of historiographers) do write, that the house and family of the Aemilians in Rome, was always of the most ancient of the nobility, which they call patricians. Some writers affirm also, that the first of that house that gave name to all the posterity after, was Marcus, the son of Pythagoras the wise, whom King Numa for the sweetness and pleasant grace of his tongue, surnamed Marcus Aemilius: and those specially affirm it, that say King Numa was Pythagoras' scholar. Howsoever it was, the most part of this family that obtained honour and estimation for their virtue, were ever fortunate also in all their doings, saving Lucius Paulus only, who died in the battle of Cannae. But his misfortune doth bear manifest testimony of his wisdom and valiancy together. For he was forced to fight against his will, when he saw he could not bridle the rashness of his fellow Consul that would needs join battle, and to do as he did, saving that he fled not as the other, who being the first procurer of the battle, was the first that ran away: where he to the contrary, to his power did what he could to let him, and did stick by it, and fought it valiantly to the last gasp. This Aemilius left a daughter behind him called Aemilia, which was married unto Scipio the great: and a son, Paulus Aemilius, being the same man whose life we presently treat of. His youth fortunately fell out in a flourishing time of glory and honour, through the sundry virtues of many great and noble persons living in those days, among whom he made his name famous also: and it was not by that ordinary art and course, which the best esteemed young men of that age did take and follow. For he did not use to plead private men's causes in law, neither would creep into men's favour by fawning upon any of them: though he saw it a common practice and policy of men, to seek the people's favour and goodwills by such means. Moreover, he refused not that common course which other took, for that it was contrary to his nature, or that he could not frame with either of both, if he had been so disposed: but he rather sought to win reputation by his honesty, his valiantness, and upright dealing, as choosing that the better way than either of the other two, insomuch as in marvellous short time he passed all those that were of his age.

The first office of honour he sued for, was the office of Aedilis, in which suit he was preferred before twelve other that sued for the self same office: who were men of no small quality, for they all came afterwards to be Consuls. After this, he was chosen to be one of the number of the priests, whom the Romans call Augurs: who have the charge of all the divinations and soothsayings, in telling of things to come by flying of birds, and signs in the air. He was so careful, and took such pains to understand how the Romans did use the same, and with such diligence sought the observation of the ancient religion of the Romans in all holy matters: that where that priesthood was before esteemed but a title of honour, and desired for the name only, he brought it to pass, that it was the most honourable science, and best reputed of in Rome. Wherein he confirmed the philosophers' opinion, that religion is the knowledge how to serve God. For when he did anything belonging to his office of priesthood, he did it with great experience, judgement, and diligence, leaving all other thoughts, and without omitting any ancient ceremony, or adding to any new, contending oftentimes with his companions, in things which seemed light, and of small moment: declaring unto them, that though we

P.   4

do presume the gods are easy to be pacified, and
that they readily pardon all faults and scapes committed by negligence, yet if it were no more but for
respect of commonwealth's sake, they should not
slightly nor carelessly dissemble or pass over faults
committed in those matters.   For no man (saith he)
at the first that committeth any fault, doth alone
trouble the state of the commonwealth: but withal,
we must think he leaveth the grounds of civil government, that is not as careful to keep the institutions of
small matters, as also of the great.   So was he also
a severe captain, and strict observer of all martial
discipline, not seeking to win the soldiers' love by
flattery, when he was general in the field, as many
did in that time: neither corrupting them for a second
charge, by shewing himself gentle and courteous in
the first, unto those that served under him: but
himself did orderly shew them the very rules and
precepts of the discipline of wars, even as a priest
that should express the names and ceremonies of
some holy sacrifice, wherein were danger to omit any
part or parcel.   Howbeit, being terrible to execute
the law of arms upon rebellious and disobedient
soldiers, he kept up thereby the state of the common-
weal the better: judging to overcome the enemy
by force was but an accessory as a man may term it,
in respect of well training and ordering his citizens
by good discipline.

While the Romans were in wars against King
Antiochus surnamed the Great, in the south parts:
all the chiefest captains of Rome being employed that
ways, there fell out another in the neck of that, in
the west parts towards Spain, where they were all up
in arms.   Thither they sent Aemilius Praetor, not with
six axes as the other Praetors had borne before them,
but with twelve: so that under the name of Praetor,
he had the authority and dignity of a Consul.   He
twice overcame the barbarous people in main battle,
and slew a thirty thousand of them, and got this
victory through his great skill and wisdom, in choosing

the advantage of place and time to fight with his
enemies, even as they passed over a river; which
easily gave his soldiers the victory. Moreover, he took
there two hundred and fifty cities, all which did open
and gladly receive him in. So, leaving all that
country quiet and in good peace, and having received
their fealty by oath made between his hands, he
returned again to Rome, not enriched the value of a
drachma more than before. For then he took little
regard to his expenses, he spent so frankly, neither
was his purse his master, though his revenue was not
great to bear it out: as it appeared to the world after
his death, for all that he had was little enough to
satisfy his wife's jointure.

His first wife was Papiria, the daughter of a noble
Consul Papirius Maso, and after they had lived a long
time together, he was divorced from her, notwithstanding he had goodly children by her. For by her
he had that famous Scipio the second, and Fabius
Maximus. The just cause of the divorce between them
appeareth not to us in writing: but methinks the tale
that is told concerning the separation of a certain
marriage is true: that a certain Roman having forsaken his wife, her friends fell out with him, and asked
him: What fault doest thou find in her? is she not
honest of her body? is she not fair? doth she not
bring thee goodly children? But he putting forth
his foot, showed them his shoe, and answered them:
Is not this a goodly shoe? is it not finely made? and
is it not new? yet I dare say there is never a one of
you can tell where it wringeth me. For to say truly,
great and open faults are commonly occasions to make
husbands put away their wives: but yet oftentimes
household words run so between them (proceeding of
crooked conditions, or of diversity of natures, which
strangers are not privy unto) that in process of time
they do beget such a strange alteration of love and
minds in them, as one house can no longer hold them.
So Aemilius, having put away Papiria his first wife,
he married another that brought him two sons, which

he brought up with himself in his house, and gave his two first sons (to wit, Scipio the second, and Fabius Maximus) in adoption to two of the noblest and richest families of the city of Rome: the elder of the twain, unto Fabius Maximus, he that was five times Consul, and the younger unto the house of the Cornelians, whom the son of the great Scipio the African did adopt, being his cousin-german, and named him Scipio. Concerning his daughters, the son of Cato married the one, and Aelius Tubero the other, who was a marvellous honest man, and did more nobly maintain himself in his poverty, than any other Roman: for they were sixteen persons all of one name, and of the house of the Aelians, very near akin one to the other, who had all but one little house in the city, and a small farm in the country, wherewith they entertained themselves, and lived all together in one house, with their wives, and many little children. Amongst their wives, one of them was the daughter of Paulus Aemilius, after he had been twice Consul, and had triumphed twice, not being ashamed of her husband's poverty, but wondering at his virtue that made him poor. Whereas brethren and kinsmen, as the world goeth now, if they dwell not far asunder, and in other countries, not one near another, and that rivers part them not, or walls divide their lands, leaving great large wastes between them: they are never quiet, but still in quarrel one with another. Goodly examples doth this story lay before the wise, and well advised readers, to learn thereby how to frame their life, and wisely to behave themselves.

Now Aemilius, being chosen Consul, went to make war with the Ligurians, who dwelled in the Alps, and which otherwise are called Ligustines. These are very valiant and warlike men, and were very good soldiers at that time, by reason of their continual wars against the Romans, whose near neighbours they were. For they dwelt in the furthest part of Italy, that bordereth upon the great Alps, and the row of Alps, whereof the foot joineth to the Tuscan

Sea, and pointeth towards Africk, and are mingled
with the Gauls and Spaniards, neighbours unto the
sea-coast: who scouring all the Mediterranean Sea
at that time, unto the strait of Hercules' Pillars, did
with their little light pinnaces of pirates, let all the
traffic and intercourse of merchandise. Aemilius being
gone to seek them in their country, they tarried his
coming with an army of forty thousand men : nevertheless, though he had but eight thousand men in all,
and that they were five to one of his, yet he gave the
onset upon them, and overthrew them, and drave
them into their cities. Then he sent to offer them
peace, for the Romans would not altogether destroy
the Ligurians, because their country was as a rampier
or bulwark against the invasion of the Gauls, who lay
lurking for opportunity and occasion to invade Italy :
whereupon these Ligurians yielded themselves unto
him, and put all their forts and ships into his hands.
Aemilius delivered unto them their holds again,
without other hurt done unto them, saving that he
razed the walls of their fortifications: howbeit he
took all their ships from them, leaving them little
boats of three oars only, and no greater, and set all
the prisoners at liberty they had taken, both by sea
and by land, as well Romans as other, which were a
marvellous number. These were all the notable
acts he did worthy memory, in the first year of his
Consulship. Afterwards he oftentimes shewed himself very desirous to be Consul again, and did put forth
himself to sue for it: but when he was denied it, he
never after made suit for it again, but gave himself
only to study divine things, and to see his children
virtuously brought up, not only in the Roman tongue
which himself was taught, but also a little more curiously in the Greek tongue. For he did not only
retain grammarians, rhetoricians, and logicians, but
also painters, gravers of images, riders of horses, and
hunts of Greece about his children : and he himself
also (if no matters of common-wealth troubled him)
was ever with them in the school when they were at

their books, and also when they otherwise did exercise
themselves.   For he loved his children as much, or
more than any other Roman.

Now concerning the state of the commonwealth,
the Romans were at wars with King Perseus, and
they much blamed the captains they had sent thither
before, for that for lack of skill and courage, they had
so cowardly behaved themselves, as their enemies
laughed them to scorn: and they received more hurt
of them, than they did unto the king.   For not long
before, they had driven King Antiochus beyond
Mount Taurus, and made him forsake the rest of
Asia, and had shut him up within the borders of
Syria, who was glad that he had bought that country
with fifteen thousand talents, which he paid for a fine.
A little before also, they had overcome Philip, king
of Macedon, in Thessaly, and had delivered the
Grecians from the bondage of the Macedonians.   And
moreover, having overcome Hannibal (unto whom no
prince nor king that ever was in the world was comparable, either for his power or valiantness) they
thought this too great a dishonour to them, that this
war they had against King Perseus, should hold so
long of even hand with them, as if he had been an
enemy equal with the people of Rome: considering
also that they fought not against them, but with the
refuse and scattered people of the overthrown army
his father had lost before, and knew not that Philip
had left his army stronger, and more expert by reason
of his overthrow, than it was before: as I will
briefly rehearse the story from the beginning.

Antigonus, who was of the greatest power of all the
captains and successors of Alexander the Great,
having obtained for himself and his posterity the
title of a king, had a son called Demetrius, of whom
came Antigonus the second, that was surnamed
Gonatas, whose son was also called Demetrius, that
reigned no long time, but died, and left a young son
called Philip.   By reason whereof, the princes and
nobility of Macedon, fearing that the realm should be

left without heir: they preferred one Antigonus,
cousin to the last deceased king, and made him
marry the mother of Philip the less, giving him the
name at the first of the king's protector only, and
lieutenant-general of his majesty.   But after, when
they had found he was a good and wise prince, and a
good husband for the realm, they then gave him the
absolute name of a king, and surnamed him Doson, to
say, the giver: for he promised much and gave little.
After him reigned Philip, who in his green youth gave
more hope of himself, than any other of the kings
before: insomuch as they thought that one day he
would restore Macedon her ancient fame and glory,
and that he alone would pluck down the pride and
power of the Romans, who rose against all the world.
But after that he had lost a great battle, and was
overthrown by Titus Quintius Flamininus near unto
the city of Scotussa: then he began to quake for
fear, and to leave all to the mercy of the Romans,
thinking he escaped good cheap for any light ransom
or tribute the Romans should impose upon him.
Yet afterwards coming to understand himself, he
grew to disdain it much, thinking that to reign
through the favour of the Romans, was but to make
himself a slave, to seek to live in pleasure at his ease,
and not for a valiant and noble prince born.   Whereupon he set all his mind to study the discipline of
wars, and made his preparations as wisely and closely
as possibly he could.   For he left all his towns
along the sea-coast, and standing upon any highways, without any fortification at all, and in manner
desolate without people, to the end there might
appear no occasion of doubt or mistrust in him: and
in the meantime, in the high countries of his realm
far from great beaten ways, he levied a great number
of men of war, and replenished his towns and strongholds that lay scatteringly abroad, with armour and
weapon, money and men, providing for war, which
he kept as secretly as he could.   For he had provision
of armour in his armoury, to arm thirty thousand

men, and eight million bushels of corn safely locked
up in his forts and stronger places, and ready money,
as much as would serve to entertain ten thousand
strangers in pay, to defend his country for the space
of ten years. But before he could bring that to pass
he had purposed, he died for grief and sorrow, after
he knew he had unjustly put Demetrius the best of
his sons to death, upon the false accusation of the
worst, that was Perseus : who as he did inherit the
kingdom of his father by succession, so did he also
inherit his father's malice against the Romans. But
he had no shoulders to bear so heavy a burden, and
especially being as he was, a man of so vile and
wicked nature : for among many lewd and naughty
conditions he had, he was extreme covetous and
miserable. They say also, that he was not legitimate, because Philip's wife had taken him from
Gnathainion (a tailor's wife born at Argos) immediately after he was born, and did adopt the child to be
hers. And some think that this was the chiefest
cause why he practised to put Demetrius to death,
fearing lest this lawful son would seek occasion to
prove him a bastard.

Notwithstanding, simple though he was, and of
vile and base nature, he found the strength of his
kingdom so great, that he was contented to take upon
him to make war against the Romans, which he
maintained a long time, and fought against their
Consuls, that were their generals, and repulsed great
armies of theirs both by sea and land, and overcame
some. As Publius Licinius among other, the first
that invaded Macedon, was overthrown by him in a
battle of horsemen, where he slew at that time two
thousand five hundred good men of his, and took six
hundred prisoners. And their army by sea, riding
at anchor before the city of Oreus, he did suddenly set
upon, and took twenty great ships of burden, and all
that was in them, and sunk the rest, which were all
laden with corn : and took of all sorts besides, about
four and fifty foists, and galliots of fifty oars a-piece.

The second Consul and general he fought withal, was Hostilius, whom he repulsed, attempting by force to invade Macedon by way of the city of Elimia. Another time again, when he entered in by stealth upon the coast of Thessaly, he offered him battle, but the other durst not abide it. And as though this war troubled him nothing at all, and that he had cared little for the Romans, he went and fought a battle in the meantime with the Dardanians, where he slew ten thousand of those barbarous people, and brought a marvellous great spoil away with him. Moreover he procured the nation of the Gauls dwelling upon the river of Danubie, which they call Bastarnae (men very warlike, and excellent good horsemen) and did practise with the Illyrians also by means of their king Gentius, to make them join with him in this war: so that there ran a rumour, that for money he had gotten those Gauls to come down into Italy, from the high country of Gaul, all along the Adriatic Sea.

The Romans being advertised of these news, thought the time served not now to dispose their offices in wars any more by grace and favour unto those that sued for them: but contrariwise, that they should call some noble man that were very skilful and a wise captain, and could discreetly govern and perform things of great charge: as Paulus Aemilius, a man well stepped on in years, being three score year old, and yet of good power, by reason of the lusty young men his sons, and sons-in-law, besides a great number of his friends and kinsfolk. So all that bare great authority, did altogether with one consent counsel him to obey the people, which called him to the Consulship. At the beginning indeed he delayed the people much that came to importune him, and utterly denied them: saying, he was no meet man neither to desire, nor yet to take upon him any charge. Howbeit in the end, seeing the people did urge it upon him, by knocking continually at his gates, and calling him aloud in the streets, willing him to come into the market-place, and perceiving they were angry with him, because he refused it, he was content to be persuaded. And when he stood among them that sued for the Consulship, the people thought straight that he stood not there so much for desire of the office, as for that he put them in hope of assured victory, and happy success of this begun war: so great was their love towards him, and the good hope they had of him, that they chose him Consul again the second time. Wherefore so soon as he was chosen, they would not proceed to drawing of lots according to their custom, which of the two Consuls should happen to go into Macedon: but presently with a full and whole consent of them all, they gave him the whole charge of the wars of Macedon. So being Consul now, and appointed to make war upon King Perseus, all the people did honourably company him home unto his house: where a little girl (a daughter of his) called Tertia, being yet an infant, came weeping unto her father. He, making much of her, asked her why she wept. The poor girl answered, colling him about the neck, and kissing him: Alas, father, wote you what? our Perseus is dead. She meant it by a little whelp so called, which was her playfellow. In good hour, my girl, said he, I like the sign well. Thus doth Cicero the orator report of it in his book of divinations.

The Romans had a custom at that time, that such as were elected Consuls (after that they were openly proclaimed) should make an oration of thanks unto the people, for the honour and favour they had shewed him. The people then (according to the custom) being gathered together to hear Aemilius speak, he made this oration unto them. " That the first time he sued to be Consul, was in respect of himself, standing at that time in need of such honour: now he offered himself the second time unto it, for the good love he bare unto them, who stood in need of a general; wherefore he thought himself nothing bound nor beholding unto them now. And if they did

think also this war might be better followed by any
other, than by himself, he would presently with all
his heart resign the place.   Furthermore, if they had
any trust or confidence in him, that they thought him
a man sufficient to discharge it : then that they would
not speak nor meddle in any matter that concerned
his duty and the office of a general, saving only, that
they would be diligent (without any words) to do
whatsoever he commanded and should be necessary
for the war and service they took in hand.   For if
every man would be a commander, as they had been
heretofore, of those by whom they should be commanded ; then the world would more laugh them to
scorn in this service, than ever before had been
accustomed."   These words made the Romans very
obedient to him, and conceiving good hope to come,
being all of them very glad that they had refused
those ambitious flatterers that sued for the charge,
and had given it unto a man, that durst boldly and
frankly tell them the truth.   Mark how the Romans
by yielding unto reason and virtue, came to command
all other, and to make themselves the mightiest people
of the world.

Now that Paulus Aemilius setting forward to this
war, had wind at will, and fair passage to bring him
to his journey's end, I impute it to good fortune,
that so quickly and safely conveyed him to his camp.
But for the rest of his exploits he did in all this war,
part of them being performed by his own hardiness,
other by his wisdom and good counsel, other by the
diligence of his friends in serving him with good will,
other by his own resolute constancy and courage in
extremest danger, and last, by his marvellous skill in
determining at an instant what was to be done, I
cannot attribute any notable act or worthy service
unto this his good fortune they talk of so much, as
they may do in other captains' rioings.   Unless they
will say peradventure, that Perseus' covetousness and
misery was Aemilius' good fortune: for his miserable
fear of spending money, was the only cause and

destruction of the whole realm of Macedon, which
was in good state and hope of continuing in prosperity.
For there came down into the country of Macedon at
King Perseus' request, ten thousand Bastarnae a-
horseback, and as many footmen to them, who always
joined with them in battle, all mercenary soldiers,
depending upon pay and entertainment of wars, as
men that could not plough nor sow, nor traffic
merchandises by sea, nor skill of grazing to gain their
living with: and to be short, that had no other
occupation or merchandise, but to serve in the wars,
and to overcome those with whom they fought.
Furthermore, when they came to encamp and lodge
in the Maedica, near to the Macedonians, who saw
them so goodly great men, and so well trained and
exercised in handling all kind of weapons, so brave
and lusty in words and threats against their enemies:
they began to pluck up their hearts, and to look big,
imagining that the Romans would never abide them,
but would be afraid to look them in the face, and only
to see their march, it was so terrible and fearful.

But Perseus, after he had encouraged his men in
this sort, and had put them in such a hope and
jollity, when this barbarous supply came to ask him a
thousand crowns in hand for every captain, he was
so damped and troubled withal in his mind, casting
up the sum it came to, that his only covetousness
and misery made him return them back, and refuse
their service: not as one that meant to fight with the
Romans, but rather to spare his treasure, and to be
a husband for them, as if he should have given up a
straight account unto them of his charges in this
war, against whom he made it. And notwithstanding
also his enemies did teach him what he had to do,
considering that besides all other their warlike
furniture and munition, they had no less than a
hundred thousand fighting men lying in camp together, ready to execute the Consul's commandment:
yet he taking upon him to resist so puissant an army,
and to maintain the wars, which forced his enemies

to be at extreme charge in entertaining such
multitudes of men, and more than needed, hardly
would depart with his gold and silver, but kept it
safe locked up in his treasury, as if he had been
afraid to touch it, and had been none of his. And
he did not shew that he came of the noble race of
the kings of Lydia, and of Phoenicia, who gloried
to be rich : but shewed how by inheritance of blood
he challenged some part of the virtue of Philip, and
of Alexander, who both because they esteemed to
buy victory with money, not money with victory, did
many notable things, and thereby conquered the
world. Hereof came the common saying in old
time, that it was not Philip, but his gold and silver
that won the cities of Greece. And Alexander when
he went to conquer the Indies, seeing the Macedonians
carry with them all the wealth of Persia, which made
his camp very heavy, and slow to march : he himself
first of all set fire on his own carriage that conveyed
all his necessaries, and persuaded other to do the
like, that they might march more lightly and easily
on the journey. But Perseus contrarily would not
spend any part of his goods to save himself, his
children and realm, but rather yielded to be led
prisoner in triumph with a great ransom, to shew
the Romans how good a husband he had been for
them. For he did not only send away the Gauls
without giving them pay as he had promised, but
moreover having persuaded Gentius king of Illyria to
take his part in these wars, for the sum of three
hundred talents which he had promised to furnish
him with : he caused the money to be told, and put
up in bags by those whom Gentius sent to receive it.
Whereupon Gentius, thinking himself sure of the
money promised, committed a fond and foul part :
for he stayed the ambassadors the Romans sent
unto him, and committed them to prison. This part
being come to Perseus' ears, he thought now he
needed not hire him with money to be an enemy to
the Romans, considering he had waded so far as

that he had already done, was as a manifest sign of his ill-will towards them, and that it was too late to look back and repent him, now that his foul part had plunged him into certain wars, for an uncertain hope. So did he abuse the unfortunate king, and defrauded him of the three hundred talents he had promised him. And worse than this, shortly after he suffered Lucius Anicius the Roman Praetor, whom they sent against him with an army, to pluck king Gentius, his wife and children, out of his realm and kingdom, and to carry them prisoners with him.

Now when Aemilius was arrived in Macedon, to make war against such an enemy, he made no manner of reckoning of his person, but of the great preparation and power he had. For in one camp he had four thousand horsemen, and no less than forty thousand footmen, with the which army he had planted himself along the sea side, by the foot of the mount Olympus, in a place unpossible to be approached: and there he had so well fortified all the straits and passages unto him with fortifications of wood, that he thought himself to lie safe out of all danger, and imagined to dally with Aemilius, and by tract of time to eat him out with charge. Aemilius in the mean season lay not idle, but occupied his wits throughly, and left no means unattempted to put something in proof. And perceiving that his soldiers by overmuch licentious liberty (wherein by sufferance they lived before) were angry with delaying and lying still, and that they did busily occupy themselves in the general's office, saying this, and such a thing would be done that is not done: he took them up roundly, and commanded them they should meddle no more too curiously in matters that pertained not to them, and that they should take care for nothing else, but to see their armour and weapon ready to serve valiantly, and to use their swords after the Romans' fashion, when their general should appoint and command them. Wherefore, to make them more careful to look to themselves, he com-

manded those that watched, should have no spears nor
pikes, because they should be more wakeful, having no
long weapon to resist the enemy, if they were assaulted.

The greatest trouble his army had, was lack of
fresh water, because the water that ran to the sea
was very little, and marvellous foul by the sea side.
But Aemilius considering they were at the foot of the
mount Olympus (which is of a marvellous height, and
full of wood withal) conjectured, seeing the trees so
fresh and green, that there should be some little
pretty springs among them, which ran under the
ground. So he made them dig many holes and wells
along the mountain, which were straight filled with
fair water, being pent within ground before for lack
of breaking open the heads, which than ran down in
streams, and met together in sundry places. And
yet some do deny, that there is any meeting of waters
within the ground, from whence the springs do come:
and they say, that running out of the earth as they
do, it is not for that the water breaketh out by
any violence, or openeth in any place, as meeting
together in one place of long time: but that it
engendreth and riseth at the same time and place
where it runneth out, turning the substance into
water, which is a moist vapour, thickened and
made cold by the coldness of the earth, and so be-
cometh as stream, and runneth down. For, say they,
as women's breasts are not always full of milk, as milk
pans are that continually keep milk, but do of themselves convert the nutriment women take into milk,
and after cometh forth at their nipples : even so the
springs and watery places of the earth, from whence
the fountains come, have no meetings of hidden
waters, nor hollow places so capable readily to deliver
water from them, as one would draw it out of a pump
or cistern, from so many great brooks and deep
rivers : but by their natural coldness and moisture,
they wax thick, and put forth the vapour and air so
strong, that they turn it into water. And this is the
reason why the places where they dig and open the

earth, do put forth more abundance of water by opening the ground : like as women's breasts do give more milk when they are most drawn and sucked, because in a sort they do better feed the vapour within them, and convert it thereby into a running humour. Where to the contrary, those parts of the earth that are not digged, nor have no vent outward, are the more unable, and less meet to ingender water, having not that provocation and course to run, that causeth the bringing forth of moisture. Yet such as maintain this opinion, do give them occasion that love argument, to contrary them thus. Then we may say by like reason also, that in the bodies of beasts there is no blood long before, and that it engendreth upon a sudden, when they are hurt, by transferring of some spirit or flesh that readily changeth into some running liquor. And moreover, they are confuted by the common experience of those mine men, that dig in the mines for metal, or that undermine castles to win them: who when they dig any great depth, do many times meet in the bowels of the earth with running rivers, the water whereof is not engendred by little and little, as of necessity it should be, if it were true, that upon the present opening of the ground, the humour should immediately be created, but it falleth vehemently all at one time. And we see oftentimes that in cutting through a mountain or rock, suddenly there runneth out a great quantity of water. And thus much for this matter. Now to return to our history again.

Aemilius lay there a convenient time, and stirred not: and it is said there were never seen two so great armies one so near to the other, and to be so quiet. In the end, casting many things with himself, and devising sundry practices, he was informed of another way to enter into Macedon, through the country of Perrhaebia, over against the temple called Pythion, and the rock upon which it is built, where there lay no garrison : which gave him better hope to pass that way, for that it was not kept, than that he feared the narrowness and hardness of the way unto it. So he broke the matter to his council. Thereupon Scipio called Nasica (the son adopted of that great Scipio the African, who became afterwards a great man, and was president of the Senate or council) was the first man that offered himself to lead them whom it would please him to send to take that passage, and to assault their enemies behind. The second was Fabius Maximus, the eldest son of Aemilius, who being but a very young man, rose notwithstanding, and offered himself very willingly. Aemilius was very glad of their offers, and gave them not so many men as Polybius writeth, but so many as Nasica himself declareth in a letter of his he wrote to a king, where he reporteth all the story of this journey. There were three thousand Italians levied in Italy by the confederates of the Romans, who were not of the Roman legions, and in the left wing about five thousand. Besides those, Nasica took also one hundred and twenty men at arms, and about two hundred Cretans and Thracians mingled together, of those Harpalus had sent thither. With this number Nasica departed from the camp, and took his way toward the sea side, and lodged by the temple of Hercules, as if he had determined to do this feat by sea, to environ the camp of the enemies behind. But when the soldiers had supped, and that it was dark night, he made the captains of every band privy to his enterprise, and so marched all night a contrary way from the sea, until at length they came under the temple of Pythion, where he lodged to rest the soldiers that were sore travelled all night. In this place, the mount Olympus is above ten furlongs high, as appeared in a place engraven by him that measured it.

> Olympus mount is just by measure made with line,
> Twelve hundred seventy paces trod, as measure can assign,
> The measure being made right o'er against the place,
> Whereas Apollo's temple stands ybuilt with stately grace,
> Even from the level plot of that same country's plain
> Unto the top which all on high doth on the hill remain.

P.   5

And so Xenagoras the son of Eumelus,
In olden days by measure made, the same did find for us :
And did engrave it here in writing for to see,
When as he took his latest leave (Apollo god) of thee.

Yet the geometricians say, that there is no
mountain higher, nor sea deeper, than the length
of ten furlongs: so that I think this Xenagoras (in
my opinion) did not take his measure at adventure,
and by guess, but by true rules of the art and
instruments geometrical.

There Nasica rested all night. King Perseus perceiving in the meantime that Aemilius stirred not
from the place where he lay, mistrusted nothing his
practice, and the coming of Nasica who was at hand:
until such time as a traitor of Crete (stealing from
Nasica) did reveal unto him the pretended practice,
as also the Romans compassing of him about. He
wondered much at these news, howbeit he removed
not his camp from the place he lay in, but dispatched
one of his captains called Milo, with ten thousand
strangers, and two thousand Macedonians: and
straitly commanded him with all the possible speed
he could, to get the top of the hill before them.
Polybius saith, that the Romans came and gave
them an alarm, when they were sleeping. But
Nasica writeth, that there was a marvellous sharp
and terrible battle on the top of the mountain: and
said plainly, that a Thracian soldier coming towards
him, he threw his dart at him, and hitting him right
in the breast, slew him stark dead: and having
repulsed their enemies, Milo their captain shamefully running away in his coat without armour or
weapon, he followed him without any danger, and
so went down to the valley, with the safety of all
his company. This conflict fortuning thus, Perseus
raised his camp in great haste from the place where
he was, and being disappointed of his hope, he retired
in great fear, as one at his wits' end, and not
knowing how to determine. Yet was he constrained
either to stay, and encamp before the city of Pydna,

there to take the hazard of battle: or else to divide
his army into his cities and strongholds, and to
receive the wars within his own country, the which
being once crept in, could never be driven out again,
without great murder and bloodshed.   Hereupon his
friends did counsel him to choose rather the fortune
of battle: alleging unto him, that he was the stronger
in men a great way, and that the Macedonians would
fight lustily with all the courage they could, considering that they fought for the safety of their wives and
children, and also in the presence of their king, who
should both see every man's doing, and fight himself
in person also for them.   The king, moved by these
persuasions, determined to venture the chance of
battle.   So he pitched his camp and viewed the
situation of the places all about, and divided the
companies amongst his captains, purposing to give
a hot charge upon the enemies when they should
draw near.   The place and country was such, as
being all champion, there was a goodly valley to
range a battle of footmen in, and little pretty hills
also one depending upon another, which were very
commodious for archers, naked men, and such as
were lightly armed, to retire themselves unto being
distressed, and also to environ their enemies behind.
There were two small rivers also, Aeson and Leucus
that ran through the same, the which though they
were not very deep, being about the latter end of
summer, yet they would annoy the Romans notwithstanding.
    Now when Aemilius was joined with Nasica, he
marched on straight in battle array towards his
enemies.   But perceiving afar off their battle marched
in very good order, and the great multitude of men
placed in the same: he wondered to behold it, and suddenly stayed his army, considering with himself what he
had to do.   Then the young captains having charge
under him, desirous to fight it out presently, went unto
him to pray him to give the onset, but Nasica specially
above the rest, having good hope in the former good

luck he had at his first encounter. Aemilius smiling
answered him : So would I do, if I were as young as
thou ; but the sundry victories I have won heretofore, having taught me by experience the faults the
vanquished do commit, do forbid me to go so hotly
to work (before my soldiers have rested, which did
return but now) to assault an army set in such order
of battle.   When he had answered him thus, he commanded the first bands that were now in view of the
enemies, should embattle themselves, showing a
countenance to the enemy as though they would
fight ; and that those in the rearward should lodge in
the meantime, and fortify the camp.   So, bringing
the foremost men to be hindmost, by changing from
man to man before the enemies were aware of it, he
had broken his battle by little and little, and lodged
his men, fortified within the camp without any tumult
or noise, and the enemies never perceiving it.   But
when night came, and every man had supped, as
they were going to sleep and take their rest ; the moon
which was at the full, and of a great height, began to
darken and to change into many sorts of colours,
losing her light, until such time as she vanished away,
and was eclipsed altogether.   Then the Romans began
to make a noise with basons and pans, as their fashion
is to do in such a chance, thinking by this sound to
call her again, and to make her come to her light,
lifting up many torches lighted and firebrands into
the air.   The Macedonians on the other side did no
such matter within their camp, but were altogether
stricken with an horrible fear : and there ran straight
a whispering rumour through the people, that this
sign in the element signified the eclipse of the king.
For Aemilius was not ignorant of the diversities of the
eclipses, and he had heard say the cause is by reason
that the moon, making her ordinary course about the
world, (after certain revolutions of time) doth come to
enter into the round shadow of the earth, within the
which she remaineth hidden, until such time as having
passed the dark region of the shadow, she cometh

afterwards to recover her light which she taketh of the sun. Nevertheless, he being a godly devout man, so soon as he perceived the moon had recovered her former brightness again, he sacrificed eleven calves. And the next morning also by the break of day, making sacrifice to Hercules, he could never have any signs or tokens that promised him good luck, in sacrificing twenty oxen one after another : but at the one-and-twentieth he had signs that promised him victory, so he defended himself. Wherefore, after he had vowed a solemn sacrifice of a hundred oxen to Hercules, and also games of prizes at the weapons, he commanded his captains to put their men in readiness to fight ; and so sought to win time, tarrying till the sun came about in the afternoon towards the west, to the end that the Romans which were turned towards the east, should not have it in their faces when they were fighting. In the meantime, he reposed himself in his tent, which was all open behind towards the side that looked into the valley, where the camp of his enemies lay.

When it grew towards night, to make the enemies set upon his men, some say he used this policy. He made a horse be driven towards them without a bridle, and certain Romans followed him, as they would have taken him again : and this was the cause of procuring the skirmish. Other say, that the Thracians serving under the charge of Captain Alexander, did set upon certain foragers of the Romans, that brought forage into the camp : out of the which, seven hundred of the Ligurians ran suddenly to the rescue, and relief coming still from both armies, at the last the main battle followed after. Wherefore Aemilius like a wise general foreseeing by the danger of this skirmish, and the stirring of both camps, what the fury of the battle would come to, came out of his tent, and passing by the bands did encourage them, and prayed them to stick to it like men. In the meantime, Nasica thrusting himself into the place where the skirmish was hottest, perceived the army of the enemies marching

in battle, ready to join. The first that marched in
the vaward, were the Thracians, who seemed terrible
to look upon, as he writeth himself: for they were
mighty made men, and carried marvellous bright
targets of steel before them, their legs were armed
with greaves, and their thighs with tasses, their coats
were black, and marched shaking heavy halberds upon
their shoulders. Next unto these Thracians, there
followed them all the other strangers and soldiers
whom the king had hired, diversely armed and set
forth : for they were people of sundry nations gathered
together, among whom the Paeonians were mingled.
The third squadron was of Macedonians, and all of
them chosen men, as well for the flower of their youth,
as for the valiantness of their persons : and they were
all in goodly gilt armours, and brave purple cassocks
upon them, spick and span new. And at their backs
came after them the old bands to show themselves
out of the camp, with targets of copper, that made all
the plain to shine with the brightness of their steel and
copper. And all the hills and mountains thereabouts
did ring again like an echo, with the cry and noise of
so many fighting men, one encouraging another.

In this order they marched so fiercely with so great
heart-burning, and such swiftness, that the first
which were slain at the encounter, fell dead two
furlongs from the camp of the Romans. The charge
being given and the battle begun, Aemilius galloping
to the vaward of the battle, perceived that the captains
of the Macedonians which were in the first ranks,
had already thrust their pikes into the Romans'
targets, so as they could not come near them with
their swords : and that the other Macedonians
carrying their targets behind them, had now plucked
them before them, and did base their pikes all at
one time, and made a violent thrust into the targets
of the Romans. Which when he had considered,
and of what strength and force his wall and rank of
targets was, one joining so near another, and what
a terror it was to see a front of a battle with so

many armed pikes and steel heads: he was more
afraid and amazed withal, than with any sight he
ever saw before. Nevertheless he could wisely dissemble it at that time. And so passing by the companies of his horsemen, without either cuirass or
helmet upon his head, he shewed a noble cheerful
countenance unto them that fought. But on the
contrary side, Perseus the king of Macedon, as
Polybius writeth, so soon as the battle was begun,
withdrew himself, and got into the city of Pydna,
under pretence to go to do sacrifice unto Hercules:
who doth not accept the faint sacrifice of cowards,
neither doth receive their prayers, because they be
unreasonable. For it is no reason, that he that
shooteth not, should hit the white: nor that he
should win the victory, that bideth not the battle:
neither that he should have any good, that doeth
nothing toward it: nor that a naughty man should
be fortunate and prosper. The gods did favour
Aemilius' prayers, because he prayed for victory
with his sword in his hand, and fighting did call to
them for aid. Howbeit there is one Posidonius a
writer, who saith he was in that time, and moreover,
that he was at the battle: and he hath written an
history containing many books of the acts of King
Perseus, where he saith that it was not for faint
heart, nor under colour to sacrifice unto Hercules,
that Perseus went from the battle; but because he had
a stripe of a horse on the thigh the day before. Who
though he could not very well help himself, and that
all his friends sought to persuade him not to go to
the battle: yet he caused one of his horses to be
brought to him notwithstanding (which he commonly
used to ride up and down on) and taking his back,
rode into the battle unarmed, where an infinite
number of darts were thrown at him from both sides.
And among those, he had a blow with a dart that
hurt him somewhat, but it was overthwart, and not
with the point, and did hit him on the left side glancing
wise, with such a force that it rent his coat, and

rased his skin underneath, so as it left a mark behind
a long time after.   And this is all that Posidonius
writeth to defend and excuse Perseus.

The Romans having their hands full, and being
stayed by the battle of the Macedonians that they
could make no breach into them: there was a captain
of the Paelignians called Salvius, who took the ensign
of his band, and cast it among the press of his enemies.
Then all the Paelignians brake in upon them, with a
marvellous force and fury into that place: for all
Italians think it too great a shame and dishonour for
soldiers to lose or forsake their ensign.   Thus was
their marvellous force of both sides used in that place:
for the Paelignians proved to cut the Macedonians'
pikes with their swords, or else to make them give
back with their great targets, or to make a breach
into them, and to take the pikes with their hands.
But the Macedonians to the contrary, holding their
pikes fast with both hands, ran them through that
came near unto them: so that neither target nor
corslet could hold out the force and violence of the
push of their pikes, insomuch as they turned up the
heels of the Paelignians and Terracinians, who like
desperate beasts without reason, shutting in themselves among their enemies, ran wilfully upon their
own deaths, and their first rank were slain every man
of them.   Thereupon those that were behind gave
back a little, but fled not turning their backs, and only
retired giving back towards the mountain Olocrus.
Aemilius, seeing that, (as Posidonius writeth) rent his
arming coat from his back for anger, because that
some of his men gave back: others durst not front
the battle of the Macedonians, which was so strongly
embattled on every side, and so mured in with a wall
of pikes, presenting their armed heads on every side
a man could come, that it was impossible to break
into them, no not so much as to come near them only.
Yet notwithstanding, because the field was not
altogether plain and even, the battle that was large
in the front, could not always keep that wall, con-

tinuing their targets close one to another, but they were driven of necessity to break and open in many places, as it happeneth oft in great battles, according to the great force of the soldiers: that in one place they thrust forward, and in another they give back, and leave a hole. Wherefore Aemilius, suddenly taking the advantage of this occasion, divided his men into small companies, and commanded them they should quickly thrust in between their enemies, and occupy the places they saw void in the front of their enemies, and that they should set on them in that sort, and not with one whole continual charge, but occupying them here and there with divers companies in sundry places. Aemilius gave this charge unto the private captains of every band and their lieutenants, and the captains also gave the like charge unto their soldiers that could skilfully execute their commandment. For they went presently into those parts where they saw the places open, and being once entered in among them, some gave charge upon the flanks of the Macedonians, where they were all naked and unarmed: others set upon them behind: so that the strength of all the corps of the battle (which consisteth in keeping close together) being opened in this sort, was straight overthrown. Furthermore, when they came to fight man for man, or a few against a few: the Macedonians with their little short swords, came to strike upon the great shields of the Romans, which were very strong, and covered all their bodies down to the foot. And they, to the contrary, were driven of necessity to receive the blows of the strong heavy swords of the Romans, upon their little weak targets: so that what with their heaviness, and the vehement force wherewith the blows lighted upon them, there was no target nor corslet, but they passed it through, and ran them in. By reason whereof they could make no long resistance, whereupon they turned their backs and ran away.

But when they came to the squadron of the old beaten soldiers of the Macedonians, there was the

cruellest fight and most desperate service, where
they say that Marcus Cato (son of great Cato, and
son-in-law of Aemilius) shewing all the valiantness in
his person that a noble mind could possibly perform,
lost his sword which fell out of his hand.   But he
like a young man of noble courage, that had been
valiantly brought up in all discipline, and knew how
to follow the steps of his father (the noblest person
that ever man saw) was to shew then his value and
worthiness: and thought it more honour for him
there to die, than living to suffer his enemies to
enjoy any spoil of his.   So, by-and-by he ran into
the Roman army, to find out some of his friends,
whom he told what had befallen him, and prayed
them to help him to recover his sword: whereto
they agreed.   And being a good company of lusty
valiant soldiers together, they rushed straight in
among their enemies, at the place where he brought
them, and so did set upon them with such force
and fury, that they made a lane through the midst
of them, and with great slaughter and spilling
of blood, even by plain force, they cleared the way
still before them.   Now when the place was voided,
they sought for the sword, and in the end found it
with great ado, amongst a heap of other swords and
dead bodies, whereat they rejoiced marvellously.
Then singing a song of victory, they went again more
fiercely than before to give a charge upon their
enemies, who were not yet broken asunder: until
such time as at the length, the three thousand chosen
Macedonians fighting valiantly even to the last man,
and never forsaking their ranks, were all slain in the
place.   After whose overthrow, there was a great
slaughter of other also that fled: so that all the
valley and foot of the mountains thereabouts was
covered with dead bodies.   The next day after the
battle, when the Romans did pass over the river of
Leucus, they found it running all a-blood.   For it is
said there were slain at this field, of Perseus' men,
above five-and-twenty thousand: and of the Romans'

side, as Posidonius saith, not above six-score, or as
Nasica writeth, but four-score only.

And for so great an overthrow, it is reported it
was wonderful quickly done and executed.   For they
began to fight about three of the clock in the afternoon, and had won the victory before four, and all
the rest of the day they followed their enemies in
chase, an hundred and twenty furlongs from the
place where the battle was fought: so that it was
very late, and far forth night, before they returned
again into the camp.   So such as returned were
received with marvellous great joy of their pages
that went out with links and torches lighted, to bring
their masters into their tents, where their men had
made great bonfires, and decked them up with crowns
and garlands of laurel, saving the general's tent
only: who was very heavy, for that of his two sons
he brought with him to the wars, the younger could
not be found, which he loved best of the twain,
because he saw he was of a better nature than the
rest of his brethren.   For even then, being new
crept out of the shell as it were, he was marvellous
valiant and hardy, and desired honour wonderfully.
Now Aemilius thought he had been cast away, fearing
lest for lack of experience in the wars, and through
the rashness of his youth, he had put himself too far
in fight amongst the press of the enemies.   Hereupon the camp heard straight what sorrow Aemilius
was in, and how grievously he took it.   The Romans,
being set at supper, rose from their meat, and with
torchlight some ran to Aemilius' tent, other went
out of the camp to seek him among the dead bodies, if
they might know him: so all the camp was full of
sorrow and mourning, the valleys and hills all abouts
did ring again with the cries of those that called
Scipio aloud.   For even from his childhood he had
a natural gift in him, of all the rare and singular
parts required in a captain and wise governor of the
common weal above all the young men of his time.
At the last, when they were out of all hope of his

coming again, he happily returned from the chase
of the enemies, with two or three of his familiars
only, all bloodied with new blood (like a swift running
greyhound fleshed with the blood of the hare), having
pursued very far for joy of the victory.   It is that
Scipio which afterwards destroyed both the cities of
Carthage and Numantia, who was the greatest man
of war, and valiantest captain of the Romans in his
time, and of the greatest authority and reputation
among them.   Thus fortune deferring till another
time the execution of her spite, which she did bear to
so noble an exploit, suffered Aemilius for that time,
to take his full pleasure of that noble victory.

And as for Perseus, he fled first from the city of
Pydna unto the city of Pella, with his horsemen,
which were in manner all saved.   Whereupon the
footmen that saved themselves by flying, meeting
them by the way, called them traitors, cowards, and
villains: and worse than that, they turned them off
their horsebacks, and fought it out lustily with them.
Perseus seeing that, and fearing lest this mutiny
might turn to light on his neck, he turned his horse
out of the highway, and pulled off his purple coat,
and carried it before him, and took his diadem, fearing
to be known thereby: and because he might more
easily speak with his friends by the way, he lighted
afoot, and led his horse in his hand.   But such as
were about him, one made as though he would mend
the latchet of his shoe, another seemed to water his
horse, another as though he would drink: so that
one dragging after another in this sort, they all left
him at the last, and ran their way, not fearing the
enemies' fury so much, as their king's cruelty: who
being grieved with his misfortune, sought to lay the
fault of the overthrow upon all other but himself.
Now he being come into the city of Pella by night,
Euctus and Eudaeus, two of his treasurers, came unto
him, and speaking boldly (but out of time) presumed
to tell him the great fault he had committed, and
to counsel him what he should do.   The king was

so moved with their presumption, that with his own hands he stabbed his dagger in them both, and slew them outright. But after this fact, all his servants and friends refused him, and there only tarried with him but Evander Cretan, Archedamus Aetolian, and Neo Boeotian. And as for the mean soldiers, there were none that followed him but the Cretans, and yet it was not for the good will they did bear him, but for the love of his gold and silver, as bees that keep their hives for love of the honey. For he carried with him a great treasure, and gave them leave to spoil certain plate and vessel of gold and silver, to the value of fifty talents. But first of all, when he was come into the city of Amphipolis, and afterwards into the city of Galepsus, and that the fear was well blown over : he returned again to his old humour, which was born and bred with him, and that was, avarice and misery. For he made his complaint unto those that were about him, that he had unawares given to the soldiers of Crete, his plate and vessel of gold to be spoiled, being those which in old time belonged unto Alexander the Great : and prayed them with tears in his eyes that had the plate, they would be contented to change it for ready money. Now such as knew his nature, found straight this was but a fraud and a Cretan lie, to deceive the Cretans with : but those that trusted him, and did restore again the plate they had, did lose it every jot, for he never paid them penny for it. So he got of his friends the value of thirty talents, which his enemies soon after did take from him. And with that sum he went into the Isle of Samothracia, where he took the sanctuary and privilege of the temple of Castor and Pollux.

They say that the Macedonians of long continuance did naturally love their kings : but then seeing all their hope and expectation broken, their hearts failed them, and broke withal. For they all came and submitted themselves unto Aemilius, and made him lord of the whole realm of Macedon in two days : and this doth seem to confirm their words, who impute all Aemilius' doings unto his good fortune. And surely, the marvellous fortune he happened on in the city of Amphipolis doth confirm it much, which a man cannot ascribe otherwise but to the special grace of the gods. For one day beginning to do sacrifice, lightning fell from heaven, and set all the wood on fire upon the altar, and sanctified the sacrifice. But yet the miracle of his fame is more to be wondered at. For four days after Perseus had lost the battle, and that the city of Pella was taken, as the people of Rome were at the lists or shew-place, seeing horses run for games: suddenly there arose a rumour at the entering into the lists where the games were, how Aemilius had won a great battle of King Perseus, and had conquered all Macedon. This news was rife straight in every man's mouth, and there followed upon it a marvellous joy and great cheer in every corner, with shouts and clapping of hands, that continued all the day through the city of Rome. Afterwards they made diligent inquiry, how this rumour first came up, but no certain author could be known, and every man said they heard it spoken: so as in the end it came to nothing, and passed away in that sort for a time. But shortly after, there came letters, and certain news that made them wonder more than before, from whence the messenger came that reported the first news of it: which could be devised by no natural means, and yet proved true afterwards.

We do read also of a battle that was fought in Italy, near unto the river of Sagra, whereof news was brought the very same day unto Peloponnesus. And of another also in like manner that was fought in Asia against the Medes, before the city of Mycale: the news whereof came the same day unto the camp of the Grecians, lying before the city of Plataea. And in that great journey where the Romans overthrew the Tarquins and the army of the Latins: immediately after the battle was won, they saw two goodly young

men come newly from the camp, who brought news of
the victory to Rome, and they judged they were
Castor and Pollux.   The first man that spake to
them in the market-place before the fountain, where
they watered their horse being all of a white foam,
told them: that he wondered how they could so
quickly bring these news.   And they laughing came to
him, and took him softly by the beard with both their
hands, and even in the market-place his hair being
black before, was presently turned yellow.   This
miracle made them believe the report the man made,
who ever after was called Ahenobarbus, as you would
say, bearded as yellow as gold.   Another like matter
that happened in our time, maketh all such news
credible.   For when Antonius rebelled against the
Emperor Domitian, the city of Rome was in a
marvellous perplexity, because they looked for great
wars towards Germany.   But in this fear, there grew
a sudden rumour of victory, and it went currently
through Rome, that Antonius himself was slain, and
all his army overthrown, and not a man left alive.
This rumour was so rife, that many of the chiefest
men of Rome believed it, and did sacrifice thereupon
unto the gods, giving them thanks for the victory.
But when the matter came to sifting, who was the
first author of the rumour: no man could tell.   For
one put it over still to another, and it died so in the
end amongst the people, as in a bottomless matter,
for they could never bolt out any certain ground of
it: but even as it came flying into Rome, so went it
flying away again, no man can tell how.   Notwithstanding, Domitian holding on his journey to make
this war, met with posts that brought him letters for
the certain victory: and remembering the rumour of
the victory that ran before in Rome, he found it true,
that it was on the very same day the victory was
gotten, and the distance between Rome and the place
where the field was won, was above twenty thousand
furlongs off.   Every man in our time knoweth this to
be true.   But again to our history.

Cn. Octavius, lieutenant of the army of Aemilius by sea, came to anchor under the Isle of Samothracia, where he would not take Perseus by force out of the sanctuary where he was, for the reverence he did bear unto the gods Castor and Pollux: but he did besiege him in such sort, as he could not scape him, nor fly by sea out of the island. Yet he had secretly prac- tised with one Oroandes a Cretan, that had a brigantine, and was at a price with him for a sum of money to convey him away by night: but the Cretan served him a right Cretan's trick. For when he had taken aboard by night into his vessel all the king's treasure of gold and silver, he sent him word that he should not fail the next night following to come unto the pier by the temple of Ceres, with his wife, his children and servants, where indeed was no possibility to take shipping: but the next night following he hoised sail, and got him away. It was a pitiful thing that Perseus was driven to do and suffer at that time. For he came down in the night by ropes, out of a little straight window upon the walls, and not only himself, but his wife and little babes, who never knew before what flying and hardness meant. And yet he fetched a more grievous bitter sigh, when one told him on the pier, that he saw Oroandes the Cretan under sail in the main seas. Then day beginning to break, and seeing himself void of all hope, he ran with his wife for life to the wall, to recover the sanctuary again, before the Romans that saw him could overtake him. And as for his children, he had given them himself into the hands of one Ion, whom before he had marvellously loved, and who then did traitorously betray him: for he delivered his children unto the Romans. Which part was one of the chiefest causes that drave him (as a beast that will follow her little ones being taken from her) to yield himself into their hands that had his children. Now he had a special confidence in Scipio Nasica, and therefore he asked for him when he came to yield himself, but it was answered him, that he was not there. Then he began to lament his hard and miserable fortune every way. And in the end, considering how necessity enforced him, he yielded himself into the hands of Gnaeus Octavius, wherein he shewed plainly, that he had another vice in him more unmanly and vile than avarice : that was, a faint heart, and fear to die. But hereby he deprived himself of others' pity and compassion towards him, being that only thing which fortune cannot deny and take from the afflicted, and specially from them that have a noble heart. For he made request they would bring him unto the general Aemilius, who rose from his chair when he saw him come, and went to meet him with his friends, the water standing in his eyes, to meet a great king by fortune of war, and by the will of the gods, fallen into that most lamentable state. But he to the contrary, unmanly and shamefully behaved himself. For he fell down at his feet, and embraced his knees, and uttered such uncomely speech and vile requests, as Aemilius self could not abide to hear them : but knitting his brows against him, being heartily offended, he spake thus unto him. " Alas poor man, why dost thou discharge fortune of this fault, where thou mightest justly charge and accuse her to thy discharge, doing things, for the which every one judgeth thou hast deserved thy present misery, and art unworthy also of thy former honour ? why dost thou defame my victory, and blemish the glory of my doings, shewing thyself so base a man, as my honour is not great to overcome so unworthy an enemy ? The Romans have ever esteemed magnanimity, even in their greatest enemies : but dastardliness, though it be fortunate, yet is it hated of everybody." Notwithstanding, he took him up, and taking him by the hand, gave him into the custody of Aelius Tubero.

Then Aemilius went into his tent, and carried his sons and sons-in-law with him, and other men of quality, and specially the younger sort. And being set down, he continued a great space very pensive with himself, not speaking a word : insomuch that all the standers by wondered much at the matter. In the end, he began to enter into discourse and talk of fortune, and the unconstancy of these worldly things, and said unto them: "Is there any man living, my friends, who having fortune at will, should therefore boast and glory in the prosperity of his doings, for that he hath conquered a country, city, or realm: and not rather to fear the unconstancy of fortune? who laying before our eyes, and all those that profess arms at this present, so notable an example of the common frailty of men, doth plainly teach us to think, that there is nothing constant or perdurable in this world. For when is it, that men may think themselves assured, considering that when they have overcome others, then are they driven to mistrust fortune most, and to mingle fear and mistrust, with joy of victory: if they will wisely consider the common course of fatal destiny that altereth daily, sometime favouring one, otherwhile throwing down another? You see that in an hour's space we have trodden under our feet the house of Alexander the Great: who hath been the mightiest and most redoubted prince of the world. You see a king, that not long since was followed and accompanied, with many thousand soldiers of horsemen and footmen, brought at this present into such miserable extremity, that he is enforced to receive his meat and drink daily at the hands of his enemies. Should we have any better hope then, that fortune will always favour our doings, more than she doth his now, at this present? no, out of doubt. Therefore digesting this matter well, you young men I say, be not too brag nor foolish proud of this conquest and noble victory: but think what may happen hereafter, marking to what end fortune will turn the envy of this our present prosperity." Such were Aemilius' words to these young men, as it is reported, bridling by these and such like persuasions, the lusty bravery of this youth, even as with the bit and bridle of reason.

Afterwards he put his army into garrisons to

refresh them : and went himself in person in the
meantime to visit Greece, making it an honourable
progress, and also a commendable.   For as he passed
through the cities, he relieved the people, reformed
the government of their state, and ever gave them
some gift or present.   Unto some he gave corn,
which King Perseus had gathered for the wars :
and unto other he gave oils, meeting with so great
store of provision, that he rather lacked people to
give it unto, to receive it at his hands, than wanting
to give, there was so much.   As he passed by the city
of Delphi, he saw there a great pillar, four square,
of white stone, which they had set up, to put King
Perseus' image of gold upon it.   Whereupon he
commanded them to set up his in that place, saying :
it was reason the conquered should give place unto
the conquerors.   And being in the city of Olympia,
visiting the temple of Jupiter Olympian, he spake this
openly, which ever since hath been remembered :
that Phidias had rightly made Jupiter, as Homer had
described him.   Afterwards when the ten ambassadors were arrived that were sent from Rome to
establish with him the realm of Macedon, he
redelivered the Macedonians their country and towns
again, to live at liberty, according to their laws,
paying yearly to the Romans for tribute, a hundred
talents: where before they were wont to pay unto
their kings ten times as much.   And he made plays
and games of all sorts, and did celebrate sumptuous
sacrifices unto the gods.   He kept open court to all
comers, and made noble feasts, and defrayed the
whole charge thereof, with the treasure Perseus had
gathered together, sparing for no cost.   But through
his care and foresight there was such a special good
order taken, every man so courteously received and
welcomed, and so orderly marshalled at the table
according to their estate and calling, that the
Grecians wondered to see him so careful in matters
of sport and pleasure: and that he took as great
pains in his own person, to see that small matters

should be ordered as they ought, as he took regard
for discharge of more weighty causes.   But this was
a marvellous pleasure to him, to see that among such
sumptuous sights prepared to shew pleasure to the
persons invited, no sight nor stately show did so
delight them, as to enjoy the sight and company of
his person.   So he told them, that seemed to wonder
at his diligence and care in these matters : that to
order a feast well, required as great judgment and
discretion as to set a battle : to make the one fearful
to the enemies, and the other acceptable to his friends.
But men esteemed his bounty and magnanimity for
his best virtue and quality.   For he did not only
refuse to see the king's wonderful treasure of gold
and silver, but caused it to be told, and delivered
to the custody of the treasurers, to carry to the
coffers of store in Rome : and only suffered his sons
that were learned, to take the books of the king's
library.   When he did reward the soldiers for their
valiant service in this battle, he gave his son-in-law
Aelius Tubero a cup weighing five talents.   It is
the same Tubero we told you of before, who lived
with· sixteen other of his kin all in one house,
and of the only revenue they had of a little farm
in the country.   Some say, that cup was the first
piece of plate that ever came into the house of the
Aelians, and yet it came for honour and reward of
virtue : but before that time, neither themselves, nor
their wives, would ever have, or wear, any gold or
silver.

After he had very well ordered and disposed all
things, at the last he took leave of the Grecians, and
counselled the Macedonians to remember the liberty
the Romans had given them, and that they should be
careful to keep it, by their good government and concord together.   Then he departed from them, and
took his journey towards the country of Epirus,
having received commission from the Senate of Rome,
to suffer his soldiers who had done service in the
battle and overthrow of King Perseus, to spoil all the

cities of that country. Wherefore that he might surprise them on a sudden, and that they should mistrust nothing, he sent to all the cities that they should send him by a certain day, ten of the chiefest men of every city. Who when they were come, he commanded them to go and bring him by such a day, all the gold and silver they had within their cities, as well in their private houses as in their temples and churches, and gave unto every one of them a captain and garrison with them, as if it had been only to have received and searched for the gold and silver he demanded. But when the day appointed was come, the soldiers in divers places (and all at one time) set upon their enemies, and did rifle and spoil them of that they had, and made them also pay ransom every man : so as by this policy, there were taken and made slaves in one day, a hundred and fifty thousand persons, and threescore and ten cities spoiled and sacked every one. And yet when they came to divide the spoil of this general destruction of a whole realm by the poll, it came not to every soldier's part, above eleven silver drachms a-piece. Which made every one to wonder greatly, and to fear also the terror of the wars, to see the wealth and riches of so great a realm, to amount to so little for every man's share.

When Aemilius had done this fact against his own nature, which was very gentle and courteous : he went unto the seaside to the city of Oricum, and there embarked with his army bound for Italy. Where when he was arrived, he went up the river of Tiber against the stream, in King Perseus' chief galley, which had sixteen oars on a side, richly set out with the armour of the prisoners, rich clothes of purple colour, and other such spoils of the enemies : so that the Romans running out of Rome in multitudes of people to see this galley, and going side by side by her as they rowed softly, Aemilius took as great pleasure in it, as in any open games or feasts, or triumph that had been shewed indeed. But when the soldiers saw that the gold and silver of King Perseus'

treasure was not divided amongst them according
unto promise, and that they had a great deal less than
they looked for, they were marvellously offended, and
inwardly grudged Aemilius in their hearts. Nevertheless they durst not speak it openly, but did accuse
him, that he had been too strait unto them in this
war : and therefore they did shew no great desire, nor
forwardness, to procure him the honour of triumph.
Which Servius Galba understanding, that had been
an old enemy of his, notwithstanding he had the charge
of a thousand men under him in this war : he like an
envious viper told the people, how Aemilius had not
deserved the honour of triumph, and sowed seditious
words against him among the soldiers, to aggravate
their ill-will the more against him. Moreover, he
craved a day of the Tribunes of the people, to have
respite to bring forth such matter as they determined
to object against him : saying the time then was far
spent, the sun being but four hours high, and that
it would require longer time and leisure. The
Tribunes made him answer, that he should speak
then what he had to say against him, or otherwise
they would not grant him audience. Hereupon he
began to make a long oration in his dispraise, full of
railing words, and spent all the rest of the day in that
railing oration. Afterwards when night came on, the
Tribunes brake up the assembly, and the next morning the soldiers being encouraged by Galba's oration,
and having considered together, did flock about Galba,
in the mount of the Capitol, where the Tribunes had
given warning they would keep their assembly.

Now being broad day, Aemilius' triumph was referred to the most number of voices of the people,
and the first tribe flatly did deny his triumph. The
Senate, and the residue of the people hearing that,
were very sorry to see they did Aemilius so open
wrong and injury. The common people said nothing
to it, but seemed to be very sorry, howbeit they
sought no redress. The Lords of the Senate cried
out upon them, and said it was too much shame, and

exhorted one another to bridle the insolency and
boldness of these soldiers, who would grow in the end
to such tumult and disorder, that they would commit
all mischief and wickedness, if betimes they were not
looked to, and prevented, seeing they did so openly
stand against their general, seeking to deprive him
of the honour of his triumph and victory. So they
assembled a good company of them together, and
went up to the Capitol, and prayed the Tribunes they
would stay to take the voices of the people, until
they had acquainted them with such needful matter
as they had to open unto them. The Tribunes
granted to it, and silence was made. Then Marcus
Servilius, who had been Consul, and had fought
three-and-twenty combats of life and death in his
own person, and had always slain as many of his
enemies as challenged him man for man, rose up,
and spake in favour of Aemilius in this manner. " I
know now (said he) better than before, how noble
and worthy a captain Paulus Aemilius is, who hath
achieved such glory and honourable victory, with so
dishonourable and disobedient soldiers. And I can
but wonder that the people not long since rejoiced,
and made great account of the victories and triumphs
won upon the Illyrians and other nations of Africk :
and that now they should for spite envy his glory
(doing what lieth in them to hinder) to bring a
Macedonian king alive in a triumph, and to shew the
glory and greatness of King Philip and Alexander
the Great, subdued by the Romans' force and power.
What reason have ye, that not long since, upon a
flying rumour that Aemilius had won the battle against
Perseus, you straight made sacrifices to the gods
with great joy, praying them that you might be
witnesses of the truth thereof : and now that the
person himself whom ye made general is returned
home, and doth deliver you most assured victory,
you do frustrate the gods' most solemn thanks and
honour due to them, and do deprive your selves also
of your wonted glory in such a case ? as if you were

afeard to see the greatness of your prosperity, or that you meant to pardon a king, your slave and prisoner. And yet of the two, you have more reason to hinder the triumph, as pitying the king, than envying your captain. But the malice of the wicked, through your patience is grown to such an insolent audacity and boldness, that we see men present here before us, which never went from the smoke of the chimney, nor carried away any blows in the field, being crammed at home like women and house-doves: and yet they are so impudent and shameless, as they dare presume unreverently to your faces, to prate of the office and duty of a general of an army, and of the desert of triumph, before you I say, who by experience of many a sore cut and wound upon your bodies in the wars, have learned to know a good and valiant captain, from a vile and cowardly person." And speaking these words, he cast open his gown, and shewed before them all, the infinite scars and cuts he had received upon his breast: and then turning him behind, shewed all such places as were not fit to be seen openly, and so turned him again to Galba, and said unto him: " Thou mockest me for that I shew thee : but I rejoice before my countrymen and citizens that, for serving my country night and day a-horseback, I have these wounds upon me which thou seest. Now get thee about thy business, and receive their voices: and I will come after, noting them that are naughty and unthankful citizens, who like to be soothed with flattery, and not stoutly commanded, as behoveth a general in the war."

These words so reined the hard-headed soldiers with the curb of reason that all the other tribes agreed in one, and granted Aemilius triumph: the order and solemnity whereof was performed in this sort. First, the people having set up sundry scaffolds, as well in the lists and field (called *circus* by the Latins) where the games and common running of horses and chariots are made, as also about the market-place, and in other streets of the city, through

the which the show of the triumph should pass: they
all presented themselves in their best gowns to see
the magnificence and state thereof. All the temples
of the gods also were set wide open, hanged full of
garlands of flowers, and all perfumed within: and
there were set through all the quarters of the city,
numbers of sergeants and other officers holding
tipstaves in their hands to order the straggling people,
and to keep them up in corners and lanes' ends, that
they should not pester the streets, and hinder the
triumph. Furthermore, the sight of this triumph
was to continue three days, whereof the first was
scant sufficient to see the passing by of the images,
tables, and pictures, and statues of wonderful bigness,
all won and gotten of their enemies, and drawn in the
show upon two hundred and fifty chariots. The
second day, there were carried upon a number of
carts, all the fairest and richest armour of the
Macedonians, as well of copper as also of iron and
steel, all glistering bright, being newly furbished,
and artificially laid in order (and yet in such sort,
as if they had been cast in heaps one upon another,
without taking any care otherwise for the ordering
and laying of them) fair burganets upon targets:
habergeons, or brigantines, and corslets, upon greaves:
round targets of the Cretans, and javelins of the
Thracians, and arrows amongst the armed pikes: all
this armour and carriage, being bound one to another
so trimly (neither being too loose, nor too strait) that
one hitting against another, as they drew them upon
the carts through the city, they made such a sound
and noise, as it was fearful to hear it: so that the
only sight of these spoils of the captives being overcome, made the sight so much more terrible to behold it. After these carts laden with armour, there
followed three thousand men, which carried the ready
money in seven hundred and fifty vessels, which
weighed about three talents a-piece, and every one
of them were carried by four men: and there were
other that carried great bowls of silver, cups and

goblets fashioned like horns, and other pots to drink in, goodly to behold, as well for their bigness, as for their great and singular embossed works about them.

The third day early in the morning, the trumpets began to sound and set forwards, sounding no march nor sweet note, to beautify the triumph withal: but they blew out the brave alarm they sound at an assault, to give the soldiers courage for to fight. After them followed six-score goodly fat oxen, having all their horns gilt, and garlands of flowers and nose-gays about their heads, and there went by them certain young men, with aprons of needlework, girt about their middle, who led them to the sacrifice, and young boys with them also, that carried goodly basins of gold and silver, to cast and sprinkle the blood of the sacrifices about. And after these, followed those that carried all coins of gold divided by basins and vessels, and every one of them weighing three talents as they did before, that carried the great holy cup, which Aemilius had caused to be made of massy gold, set full of precious stones, weighing the weight of ten talents, to make an offering unto the gods. And next unto them went other that carried plate, made and wrought after antique fashion, and notable cups of the ancient kings of Macedon: as the cup called Antigonus', and another Seleucus': and to be short, all the whole cupboard of plate of gold and silver of King Perseus. And next came the chariot of his armour, in the which was all King Perseus' harness, and his royal band (they call a diadem) upon his armour. And a little space between them, followed next the king's children, whom they led prisoners, with the train of their schoolmasters and other officers, and their servants, weeping and lamenting: who held up their hands unto the people that looked upon them, and taught the king's young children to do the like, to ask mercy and grace at the people's hands. There were three pretty little children, two sons and a daughter

amongst them, whose tender years and lack of understanding, made them (poor souls) they could not feel
their present misery: which made the people so much
more to pity them, when they saw the poor little
infants, that they knew not the change of their hard
fortune: so that for the compassion they had of them,
they almost let the father pass without looking upon
him.   Many people's hearts did melt for very pity,
that the tears ran down their cheeks, so as this sight
brought both pleasure and sorrow together to the
lookers on, until they were past and gone a good way
out of sight.

King Perseus the father, followed after his children
and their train, and he was clothed in a black gown,
wearing a pair of slippers on his feet after his
country manner.   He shewed by his countenance his
troubled mind, oppressed with sorrow of his most
miserable state and fortune.   He was followed with
his kinsfolks, his familiar friends, his officers and
household servants, their faces disfigured by blubbering, shewing to the world by their lamenting tears,
and sorrowful eyes cast upon their unfortunate
master, how much they sorrowed and bewailed his
most hard and cruel fortune, little accounting of their
own misery.   The voice goeth that Perseus sent
unto Aemilius to entreat him, that he should not be
led through the city in the show and sight of the
triumph.   But Aemilius, mocking (as he deserved) his
cowardly faint heart, answered: As for that, it was
before, and is now in him, to do if he will: meaning
to let him understand thereby, that he might rather
choose to die, than living to receive such open shame.
Howbeit his heart would not serve him, he was so
cowardly, and made so effeminate, by a certain vain
hope he knew not what, that he was contented to
make one among his own spoils.   After all this, there
followed 400 princely crowns of gold, which the cities
and towns of Greece had purposely sent by their
ambassadors unto Aemilius, to honour his victory:
and next unto them, he came himself in his chariot

triumphing, which was passing sumptuously set forth
and adorned. It was a noble sight to behold: and yet
the person of himself only was worth the looking on,
without all that great pomp and magnificence. For
he was apparelled in a purple gown branched with
gold, and carried in his right hand a laurel bough, as
all his army did besides: the which being divided by
bands and companies, followed the triumphing chariot
of their captain, some of the soldiers singing songs
of victory, which the Romans use to sing in like
triumphs, mingling them with merry pleasant toys,
rejoicing at their captain. Other of them also did
sing songs of triumph, in the honour and praise of
Aemilius' noble conquest and victory. He was openly
praised, blessed, and honoured of everybody, and
neither hated nor envied of honest men, saving the
ordinary use of some god, whose property is always
to lessen or cut off some part of man's exceeding
prosperity and felicity, mingling with man's life the
sense and feeling of good and evil together: because
that no living person should pass all his time of life,
without some adversity or misfortune, but that such
(as Homer saith) should only think themselves happy,
to whom fortune hath equally sorted the good with
the evil.

And this I speak because Aemilius had four sons,
two of the which he gave in adoption unto the
families of Scipio and of Fabius, as we have said
before: and two other which he had by his second
wife, he brought up with him in his own house, and
were both yet very young. Of the which the one
died, being fourteen years of age, five days before his
father's triumph: and the other died also, three days
after the pomp of triumph, at twelve years of age.
When this sorrowful chance had befallen him, every
one in Rome did pity him in their hearts: but
fortune's spite and cruelty did more grieve and fear
them, to see her little regard towards him, to put into
a house of triumph (full of honour and glory, and of
sacrifices and joy) such a pitiful mourning, and

mingling of sorrows and lamentations of death, amongst such songs of triumph and victory.

Notwithstanding this, Aemilius taking things like a wise man, thought that he was not only to use constancy and magnanimity against the sword and pike of the enemy: but a like also against all adversity and enmity of spiteful fortune. So, he wisely weighed and considered his present misfortune, with his former prosperity: and finding his misfortune counterpoised with felicity, and his private griefs cut off with common joy, he gave no place to his sorrows and mischances, neither blemished any way the dignity of his triumph and victory. For when he had buried the eldest of his two last sons, he left not to make his triumphant entry, as you have heard before. And his second son also being deceased after his triumph, he caused the people to assemble, and in face of the whole city he made an oration, not like a discomforted man, but like one rather that did comfort his sorrowful countrymen for his mischance. He told them, "that concerning men's matters, never any thing did fear him: but for things above, he ever feared fortune, mistrusting her change and inconstancy, and specially in the last war, doubting for so great prosperity as could be wished, to be paid home with an after intolerable adversity, and sinister chance. For as I went (said he) I passed over the gulf of the Adriatic Sea, from Brindisium unto Corfu in one day. And from thence in five days after, I arrived in the city of Delphi, where I did sacrifice unto Apollo. And within five other days, I arrived in my camp, where I found mine army in Macedon. And after I had done the sacrifice, and due ceremonies for purifying of the same, I presently began to follow the purpose and cause of my coming: so as in fifteen days after, I made an honourable end of all those wars. But yet, mistrusting fortune always, seeing the prosperous course of my affairs, and considering that there were no other enemies, nor dangers I needed to fear: I feared sorely she

would change at my return, when I should be upon
the sea, bringing home so goodly and victorious an
army, with so many spoils, and so many princes
and kings taken prisoners. And yet when I was
safely arrived in the haven, and seeing all the city
at my return full of joy, and of feasts and sacrifices:
I still suspected fortune, knowing her manner well
enough, that she useth not to gratify men so frankly,
nor to grant them so great things clearly, without
some certain spark of envy waiting on them. Neither
did my mind being still occupied in fear of some thing
to happen to the commonwealth, shake off this
fear behind me: but that I saw, this home mishap
and misery lighted upon me, enforcing me with mine
own hands in these holy days of my triumph, to bury
my two young sons one after another, which I only
brought up with me, for the succession of my name
and house. Wherefore, methinks now I may say,
I am out of all danger, at the least touching my
chiefest and greatest misfortune, and do begin to
stablish myself with this assured hope, that this
good fortune henceforth shall remain with us evermore, without fear of other unlucky or sinister chance.
For she hath sufficiently countervailed the favourable
victory she gave you, with the envious mishap wherewith she hath plagued both me and mine: shewing
the conqueror and triumpher, as noble an example
of man's misery and weakness, as the party conquered,
that had been led in triumph. Saving that Perseus
yet, conquered as he is, hath this comfort left him:
to see his children living, and that the conqueror
Aemilius hath lost his."

And this was the sum of Aemilius' notable oration
he made unto the people of Rome, proceeding of a
noble and honourably disposed mind. And though
it pitied him in his heart to see the strange change
of King Perseus' fortune, and that he heartily desired
to help him, and to do him good: yet he could never
obtain other grace for him, but only to remove him
from the common prison (which the Romans called

Carcer) into a more cleanly and sweeter house: where
being straitly guarded and looked unto, he killed himself by abstinence from meat, as the most part of
historiographers do write.   Yet some writers tell a
marvellous strange tale, and manner of his death.
For they say the soldiers that guarded him, kept
him from sleep, watching him straitly when sleep
took him, and would not suffer him to shut his eyelids
(only upon malice they did bear him, because they
could not otherwise hurt him) keeping him awake
by force, not suffering him to take rest: until such
time as nature being forced to give over, he gave up
the ghost.   Two of his sons died also: but the third
called Alexander, became an excellent turner and
joiner, and was learned, and could speak the Roman
tongue very well, and did write it so trimly, that
afterwards he was chancellor to the magistrates of
Rome, and did wisely and discreetly behave himself
in his office.

Furthermore, they do add to this goodly conquest
of the realm of Macedon, that Aemilius conquered
another special good thing, that made him marvellously well liked of the common people: that is, that
he brought so much gold and silver unto the treasury
store of Rome, as the common people needed never
after to make contribution for anything, until the
very time and year that Hirtius and Pansa were
Consuls, which was about the beginning of the first
wars of Augustus and Antonius.   And yet Aemilius
had one singular good gift in him: that though the
people did greatly love and honour him, yet he ever
took part with the Senate and nobility, and did never
by word nor deed anything in favour of the people,
to flatter or please them, but in matters concerning
government, he did ever lean to the nobility and good
men.   And this did Appius afterwards cast in his
son's teeth, Scipio Afrieanus.   For both of them
being two of the chiefest men of their time, and contending together for the office of Censor: Appius
had about him, to favour his suit, all the Senate and

nobility, as of ancient time the family of the Appians
had ever held on their part. And Scipio Africanus,
though he was a great man of himself, yet he was
in all times favoured and beloved of the common
people. Whereupon when Appius saw him come
into the market-place, followed with men of small
quality and base condition, that had been slaves
before, but otherwise could skilfully handle such
practices, bring the people together, and by opportunity of cries and loud voices (if need were) obtain
what they would in the assemblies of the city: he
spake out aloud and said: O Paulus Aemilius, now
hast thou good cause to sigh and mourn in thy grave
where thou liest (if the dead do know what we do
here on earth) to see Aemilius a common sergeant,
and Licinius a prattling fellow, how they bring thy
son unto the dignity of a Censor. And as for Scipio,
he was always beloved of the common people, because
he did favour them in all things. But Aemilius also,
although he took ever the noblemen's part, he was
not therefore less beloved of the common people
than those that always flattered them, doing all
things as the people would, to please them: which
the common people did witness, as well by other
honours and offices they offered him, as in the dignity
of the Censor which they gave him. For it was the
holiest office of all other at that time, and of greatest
power and authority, specially for inquiry and reformation of every man's life and manners. For
he that was Censor, had authority to put any Senator
off the Council, and so degrade him, if he did not
worthily behave himself according to his place and
calling: and might name and declare any one of
the Senate, whom he thought to be most honest,
and fittest for the place again. Moreover, they might
by their authority, take from licentious young men,
their horse which was kept at the charge of the
commonweal. Furthermore, they be the sessors
of the people, and the muster-masters, keeping books
of the number of persons at every mustering. So

there appeared numbered in the register-book Aemilius made then of them, three hundred seven and thirty thousand, four hundred and two and fifty men, and Marcus Aemilius Lepidus named President of the Senate, who had that honour four times before, and did put off the Council three Senators, that were but mean men. And the like mean and moderation he and his companion, Marcius Philippus, kept, upon view and muster taken of the Roman horsemen.

And after he had ordered and disposed the greatest matters of his charge and office, he fell sick of a disease that at the beginning seemed very dangerous, but in the end there was no other danger, saving that it was a lingering disease, and hard to cure. So, following the counsel of physicians, who willed him to go to a city in Italy called Velia, he took sea and went thither, and continued there a long time, dwelling in pleasant houses upon the sea-side quietly and out of all noise. But during this time of his absence, the Romans wished for him many a time and oft. And when they were gathered together in the theatres, to see the plays and sports, they cried out divers times for him: whereby they shewed that they had a great desire to see him again. Time being come about when they used to make a solemn yearly sacrifice, and Aemilius finding himself also in good perfect health: he returned again to Rome, where he made the sacrifice with the other priests, all the people of Rome gathering about him, rejoicing much to see him. The next day after, he made another particular sacrifice, to give thanks unto the gods for recovery of his health. After the sacrifice was ended, he went home to his house, and sat him down to dinner: he suddenly fell into a raving (without any perseverance of sickness spied in him before, or any change or alteration in him) and his wits went from him in such sort, that he died within three days after, lacking no necessary thing, that an earthly man could have, to make him happy in this world. For he was even honoured at his funeral, and his virtue was

adorned with many goodly glorious ornaments, neither
with gold, silver, nor ivory, nor with other such
sumptuousness or magnificence of apparel, but with
the love and good-will of the people, all of them con-
fessing his virtue and well-doing: and this did not
only his natural countrymen perform in memory of
him, but his very enemies also. For all those that
met in Rome by chance at that time, that were either
come out of Spain, from Genoa, or out of Macedon,
all those that were young and strong, did willingly
put themselves under the coffin where his body lay,
to help to carry him to the church: and the old men
followed his body to accompany the same, calling
Aemilius the benefactor, saviour, and father of their
country. For he did not only entreat them gently,
and graciously, whom he had subdued: but all his
lifetime he was ever ready to pleasure them, and to
set forward their causes, even as they had been his
confederates, very friends, and near kinsmen. The
inventory of all his goods after his death, did scant
amount unto the sum of three hundred threescore
and ten thousand silver drachms, which his two sons
did inherit. But Scipio being the younger, left all
his right unto his elder brother Fabius, because he
was adopted into a very rich house, which was the
house of the great Scipio Africanus. Such they say
was Paulus Aemilius' conditions of life.

THE COMPARISON OF PAULUS
AEMILIUS WITH TIMOLEON

SITH these two men were such as the historiographers
have described them to be : it is certain, that com-
paring the one with the other, we shall find no great
odds or difference between them. For first of all,
the wars they made, have been against great and
famous enemies : the one against the Macedonians,
and the other against the Carthaginians, and both
their victories very notable. For the one of them
conquered the realm of Macedon, which he took from
the seventh king that reigned by succession from the
father to the son, since the time of the great Antigonus : and the other drove all the tyrants out of
Sicily, and restored the whole isle and cities therein,
unto their former liberty. Unless some will allege
perhaps that there was this difference between them,
that Aemilius fought against King Perseus, when he
had all his power whole and entire, and had fought
with the Romans many times before, and had the
better of them in all conflicts : where Timoleon set
upon Dionysius when he was in greatest despair,
and in manner utterly cast away. On the contrary
side, it may be objected for Timoleon, that he overcame many tyrants, and a mighty great army of the
Carthaginians, with a very small number of men, and
yet men of all sorts : not as Aemilius with a great
army of well-trained and expert soldiers in wars, but
with men gathered together at adventure of all sorts,
being mercenary hirelings, and men fighting for pay,
loose people, and unruly in wars, that would do but
what they listed. For where the goodly deeds are
like, and the means unequal : there we must confess
that the praise is due unto the general.

Both the one and the other kept their hands clean from corruption, in the charge which they took upon them. But it seemeth that Aemilius came so fashioned and prepared, by the good civil law, and moral discipline of his country: and that Timoleon came rawly thither, and afterwards fashioned himself to be that he was. And this is to be proved: for that all the Romans in that time were so civilly brought up, and exceeded all other in strait keeping the laws of their country; where to the contrary, there was not one of the captains of the Grecians that came then, or were sent into Sicily, but fell straight to corruption, when he had put his foot in Sicily, Dion only excepted: and yet they had a certain suspicion of him, that he aspired to the kingdom, and imagined in his head to establish a certain empire at Syracuse, like unto that of Lacedaemon. Timaeus the historiographer writeth, that the Syracusans sent Gylippus with shame back again into his country, for his unsatiable greedy covetousness, and for his great thefts, and bribes taken in his charge. Divers other have also written the great treasons and falsehoods Pharax Spartan, and Callippus Athenian did commit, both of them seeking to make themselves lords of Syracuse: and yet what men are they, and what means had they to have such a foolish vain hope and fancy in their heads? considering that the one did follow and serve Dionysius, after that he was driven out of Syracuse: and the other also was but a private captain of a band of footmen, of those that came in with Dion. Timoleon in contrary manner was sent, to be general of the Syracusans, upon their great instance and suit. And he having no need to seek or hunt after it, but only to keep the power and authority they did willingly put into his hands: so soon as he had destroyed and overthrown all such as would unjustly usurp the government, he did immediately of his own good-will, frankly resign up his office and charge. And sure, so is this a notable thing to be commended, and esteemed in Paulus Aemilius: who having conquered so great and rich a realm, he never increased his goods the value of one farthing, neither did see nor handle any money at all, although he was very liberal, and gave largely unto others.

I mean not in speaking this to upbraid or detect Timoleon, for that he accepted a fair house the Syracusans gave him in the city, and a goodly manor also in the country: for in such cases there is no dishonesty in receiving, but yet is it greater honesty to refuse than to take. But that virtue is most rare and singular, where we see they will receive nor take nothing, though they have justly deserved it. And if it be so, that the body is stronger and better compounded, which best abideth change of parching heat, and nipping cold: and that the mind is much more stronger and stable, that swelleth not up with pride of prosperity, nor droopeth for sorrow in adversity: then it appeareth, that Aemilius' virtue was so much more perfect, in that he shewed himself of no less grave and constant a mind, in the patience he endured for his loss and sorrow happened unto him, (losing at one time in manner, both his children), than he had done before, in all his triumph and greatest felicity. Where Timoleon to the contrary, having done a worthy act against his brother, could with no reason suppress the grief and sorrow he felt: but overcome with bitter grief and repentance, continued the space of twenty years together, and never durst once only shew his face again in the marketplace, nor deal any more in matters of the commonweal. Truly, for a man to beware to do evil, and to shun from evil, it is a very good and comely thing: so also to be sorry, and afraid of every reproach, and ill opinion of the world, it sheweth a simpleness of nature, and a good and well-disposed mind, but no manly courage.

THE LIVES OF AGIS AND CLEOMENES

Truly the fable of Ixion was not ill-devised against ambitious persons: who embracing a cloud for the goddess Juno, begot (as it is said) the Centaurs. For even so ambitious men, embracing glory for the true image of virtue, do never any act that is good nor perfect: but being carried away with divers fancies, and following others' humours with desire to please the people, they may as the herdmen in the tragedy of Sophocles (speaking of their cattle) say:

> We wait upon their beasts, though we their masters be,
> And wheresoever they become, there also follow we.

Such indeed are they compared to, that govern common weals, after people's lusts and fancy: who doubtless are as their servants obedient at call, because they only may enjoy the glorious title and name of an officer. For like as in a ship the mariners that stand in the prow, do better see before them, than the pilots that steer the helm in the poop, and yet look always back unto them to see what they command: even so, they that govern in the commonwealth for honour's sake, are no better than honourable slaves of the people, having no more but the bare name of a governor.

But indeed, the perfect good and honest man should never covet outward glory, but as a mean to bring him to noble attempts, whereby he might procure the better credit of his doings. And for a young man that coveteth honour by virtue, give him leave a little to glory in his well-doing: for as Theophrastus saith, virtue buddeth and flourisheth in youth, and taketh

fast root by praises given, as wit and courage groweth
in them. But overmuch praise is dangerous in every
person, but chiefly in ambitious governors. For if
they be men of great power, it makes them commit
many desperate parts: for they will not allow that
honour proceeds of virtue, but that honour is
virtue itself. But indeed they should say as Phocion
did unto Antipater, that requested an unlawful matter
of him: Thou canst not, said he, have Phocion a friend
and flatterer both. This, or the very like, may be
said unto the people: You cannot both have one, a
master and a servant, that can command and obey
together. Or else the mischief spoken of in the tale
of the dragon must needs happen, which was: the
tail on a time fell out with the head, and complained,
saying it would another while go before, and would
not always come behind. The head granted the tail,
which fell out very ill for it, not knowing how to
guide the head, and besides that the head thereby was
tormented every way, being compelled against nature
to follow that part and member, which could neither
hear, nor see how to guide it. The like matter have
we seen happen unto many, which in the adminis-
tration of the commonwealth, did seek to please the
humours of the multitude. For when they have once
put their heads under their girdles to please the
common people, which without cause and reason do
soon rebel: they can by no possible means afterwards
bridle their fury and insolency. Now the reason,
that made us to enter into discourse against the
ambition and vainglory amongst the people, was the
consideration I had of their great power, remembering
the misfortunes of Tiberius and Caius Gracchi: both
of the which coming of a noble house, and having been
marvellous well brought up, and managing also the
affairs of the commonwealth with a good desire, were
notwithstanding in the end cast away: not so much
through covetousness of glory, as for fear of dishonour, which came also of no base mind. For they
having received great pleasures and friendships of

the people, were ashamed to be indebted to them,
and therefore earnestly sought to exceed the people
in good-will, by new decrees and devices, which they
preferred for common benefit: and the people also
for their parts contended to honour them the more,
by how much they strived to shew themselves thank-
ful. So with like strife on either side, they to gratify
the common people, and the people also to honour
them, were unawares so entangled with public causes,
that they could no more follow the common proverb,
which saith :

> Although our deeds dissent from equity,
> Yet can we not desist with honesty.

This thou shalt easily find by the declaration of the
history. With these we do compare two other
popular men, both kings of Lacedaemon, Agis and
Cleomenes. For they as the Gracchi, seeking to
increase the power of the common people, and to
restore the just and honest government again of the
commonwealth of Lacedaemon, which of long time
had been out of use: did in like manner purchase
the hate of the nobility, which were loath to loose
any part of their wonted covetousness. Indeed these
two Laconians were no brethren born, but yet did
both follow one self course and form of government,
which had beginning in this sort.

After that covetousness of gold and silver crept
again into the city of Sparta, and with riches, covetousness also and misery, and by use, voluptuousness
and licentious life: Sparta then was void of all
honour and goodness, and was long time drowned in
shame and dishonour, until King Agis and Leonidas
came to reign there. Agis was of the house of the
Eurypontidae, the son of Eudamidas, the sixth of
lineal descent after Agesilaus, who had been the
greatest prince of all Greece in his time. This
Agesilaus had a son slain in Italy by the Messapians,
called Archidamus, before the city of Mandyrium.
Archidamus had issue two sons, Agis and Eudamidas

that was king, who succeeded his brother Agis, whom Antipater slew before the city of Megalopolis, and left no children behind him. Eudamidas begat Archidamus, which Archidamus begat another Eudamidas: which Eudamidas also begat Agis, whose life we now write of. Leonidas also, the son of Cleonymus, was of the other family of the Agiads, the eighth of succession after Pausanias, who slew Mardonius, the king's lieutenant-general of Persia, in a battle fought before the city of Plataea. This Pausanias had a son called Plistonax, and Plistonax also another, called Pausanias: who flying from Sparta unto the city of Tegea, his eldest son Agesipolis was made king in his father's room, who dying without issue, his younger brother Cleombrotus succeeded him in the kingdom. Cleombrotus had two sons, Agesipolis and Cleomenes: of the which, Agesipolis reigned not long king, and died without issue. Then Cleomenes his brother, who was king after him, had two sons, Acrotatus the elder, that died in his father's lifetime: and Cleonymus the younger which survived him, and was not king, but one Areus his nephew, the son of Acrotatus. This Areus died before the city of Corinth: who having another Acrotatus to his son, he succeeded him in the kingdom. He also died at a battle before the city of Megalopolis, and was slain there by the tyrant Aristodemus, leaving his wife great with child. She being brought to bed after his death of a son, whom Leonidas the son of Cleonymus taught and brought up: the child dying very young, the crown by his death was cast upon Leonidas himself. Howbeit his manners and conditions never liked the people. For though all men generally were corrupted through the commonwealth, and clean out of order: yet Leonidas of all other exceeded, deforming most the ancient Laconian life: because he had been long time brought up in princes' houses, and followed also Seleucus' court, from whence he had brought all the pride and pomp of those courts into Greece, where law and reason ruleth.

Agis on the contrary part did not only far excel Leonidas, in honour and magnanimity of mind: but all other almost also which had reigned in Sparta from the time of Agesilaus the Great. So that when Agis was not yet twenty years old, and being daintily brought up with the fineness of two women, his mother Agesistrata, and Archidamia his grandmother, which had more gold and silver, than all the Lacedaemonians else, he began to spurn against these womanish delights and pleasures, in making himself fair to be the better beliked, and to be fine and trim in his apparel, and to cast upon him a plain Spanish cape, taking pleasure in the diet, baths, and manner of the ancient Laconian life: and openly boasted besides, that he would not desire to be king, but only for the hope he had to restore the ancient Laconian life by his authority.

Then began the state of Lacedaemon first to be corrupted, and to leave her ancient discipline, when the Lacedaemonians having subdued the empire of the Athenians, stored themselves and country both, with plenty of gold and silver. But yet reserving still the lands left unto them by succession from their fathers, according unto Lycurgus' first ordinance and institution, for division of the lands amongst them: which ordinance, and equality being inviolably kept amongst them, did yet preserve the commonwealth from defamation of divers other notorious crimes: until the time of the authority of Epitadeus, one of the Ephors, a seditious man, and of proud conditions: who bitterly falling out with his own son, preferred a law, that every man might lawfully give his lands and goods whilst he lived, or after his death by testament, unto any man whom he liked or thought well of. Thus this man made this law to satisfy his anger, and others also did confirm it for covetousness' sake, and so overthrew a noble ordinance. For the rich men then began to buy lands of numbers, and so transferred it from the right and lawful heirs: whereby a few men in short time being made very rich, im-

mediately after there fell out great poverty in the
city of Sparta, which made all honest sciences to
cease, and brought in thereupon unlawful occupations,
who envied them that were wealthy. Therefore,
there remained not above seven hundred natural
citizens of Sparta in all, and of them, not above a
hundred that had lands and inheritance: for all the
rest were poor people in the city, and were of no
countenance nor calling, and besides that, went un-
willingly to the wars against their enemies, looking
every day for stir and change in the city.

Agis therefore thinking it a notable good act (as
indeed it was) to replenish the city of Sparta again,
and to bring in the old equality, he moved the matter
unto the citizens. He found the youth (against all
hope) to give good ear unto him, and very well given
unto virtue, easily changing their garments and life,
to recover their liberty again. But the oldest men,
which were now even rotten with covetousness and
corruption, they were afraid to return again to the
straight ordinances of Lycurgus, as a slave and run-
agate from his master, that trembleth when he is
brought back again unto him. Therefore they
reproved Agis, when he did lament before them their
present miserable state, and wish also for the former
ancient honour and true dignity of Sparta. Howbeit
Lysander the son of Libys, and Mandroclidas the son
of Ecphanes, and Agesilaus also, greatly commended
his noble desire, and persuaded him to go forward
withal. This Lysander was of great authority and
estimation amongst them in the city: Mandroclidas
was also very wise, and careful about any matter of
counsel, and with his wisdom and policy, very valiant:
Agesilaus in like manner, the king's uncle, and an
eloquent man, was very effeminate and covetous, and
yet pricked forward to give his furtherance to this
attempt as it appeared, by his son Hippomedon,
who was a notable good soldier, and could do very
much, by means of the love and good-will the young
men did bear him. But indeed, the secret cause that

brought Agesilaus to consent unto this practice, was
the greatness of his debt which he owed, of the
which he hoped to be discharged by changing of the
state and commonwealth.

Now when Agis had won him, he sought by his
means to draw his mother also unto the matter, which
was Agesilaus' sister. She could do very much by
the number of her friends, followers, and debtors in
the city, by whose means she ruled the most part of
the affairs of the city after her own pleasure. But
the young man Hippomedon making her privy unto it,
at the first she was amazed withal, and bade him hold
·his peace if he were wise, and not meddle in matters
unpossible and unprofitable. But when Agesilaus
had told her what a notable act it would be, and how
easily it might be brought to pass, with marvellous
great profit : and that King Agis began also to strain
her with great entreaty, that she should willingly
depart with her goods to win her son honour and
glory : who though he could not in money and riches
come to be like unto other kings (because the slaves
and factors only of the Kings Seleucus and Ptolemy,
had more money then all the kings of Sparta had
together that ever reigned), yet if in temperance,
thriftiness, and noble mind (exceeding all their
vanities) he could come to restore the Lacedæmonians again unto equality : that then indeed he
should be counted a noble king. These women
being stirred up with ambition by these persuasions
of the young man, seeing him so nobly bent,
as if by the gods their minds had secretly been
inflamed with the love of virtue : did presently alter
their minds in such sort, that they themselves did
prick forward Agis, and sent for their friends to pray
and entreat them to favour his enterprise : and
furthermore they brought on other women also,
knowing that the Lacedaemonians did ever hear and
believe their wives, suffering them to understand more
of the affairs of the state, than they themselves did
of their private estate at home. Herein is to be

considered, that the most part of the riches of Lacedaemon was in the hands of the women, and therefore they were against it, not only because thereby they were cut off from their fineness and excess, in the which being ignorant of the true good indeed, they put all their felicity : but also because they saw their honour and authority, which they had by their riches, clean trodden underfoot. Therefore they coming to Leonidas, they did persuade him to reprove Agis, because he was elder man than he, and to let that this enterprise went not forward. Leonidas did what he could in favour of the rich, but fearing the common people, who desired nothing but alteration, he durst not openly speak against him, but secretly he did the best he could to hinder Agis' practice : talking with the magistrates of the city, and accusing Agis unto them, he told them how he did offer the rich men's goods unto the poor, the division of their lands, and the abolishing of all debts, for reward to put the tyranny into his hands, and that thereby he got him a strong guard unto himself, but not many citizens unto Sparta.

This notwithstanding, King Agis having procured Lysander to be chosen one of the Ephors, he presently preferred his law unto the council. The articles whereof were these : That such as were in debt, should be cleared of all their debts, and that the lands also should be divided into equal parts : so that from the valley of Pellené unto Mount Taÿgetus, and unto the cities of Malea and Sellasia, there should be four thousand five hundred parts, and without those bounds, there should be in all the rest, fifteen thousand parts, the which should be distributed unto their neighbours meet to carry weapon : and the rest unto the natural Spartans. The number of them should be replenished with their neighbours and strangers in like manner, which should be very well brought up, and be able men besides to serve the commonwealth : all the which afterwards should be divided into fifteen companies, of the which, some should receive two hundred, and others four hundred men, and should live according to the old ancient institution observed by their ancestors.

This law being preferred unto the Senate, the Senators grew to divers opinions upon it. Whereupon Lysander himself assembled the great council of all the people, and there spake unto them himself, and Mandroclidas, and Agesilaus also, praying them not to suffer the honour of Sparta to be trodden underfoot, for the vanity of a few: but that they would remember the ancient oracles of the gods, warning them to beware of avarice, as of the plague and destruction of the commonwealth: and of the late oracle also brought unto them, from the temple of Pasiphaé. The temple and oracle of Pasiphaé, was famous at the city of Thalamae: and some say, that Pasiphaé was one of the daughters of Atlas, which was gotten with child by Jupiter, and was delivered of a son called Ammon. Other think that it was Cassandra, one of King Priamus' daughters that died there, which was surnamed Pasiphaé, because she gave all the answers and oracles of things to come. But Phylarchus writeth, that Daphné, the daughter of Amyclas, flying from Apollo that would have ravished her, was turned into a laurel tree, and honoured by Apollo with the gift of prophecy. So, they said that this oracle of the god commanded them, that the Spartans should again return unto their former ancient equality, stablished first by Lycurgus' law. When every man else had spoken, King Agis rising up, briefly speaking unto the people, said: that he would bestow great contributions for the reformation of this commonwealth, which he was desirous to restore again. For first of all, he would make common all his arable and pasture he had, and besides that, he would add too six hundred talents in ready money, and so much should his mother, grandmother, kinsmen and friends, all the which were the richest and wealthiest in Sparta.

When the people heard what he said, they mar-

velled much at the noble mind of this young king,
and were very glad of it, saying : that for three
hundred years' space together, the city of Sparta had
not so worthy a king as he.   But Leonidas contrarily
assayed with all his power he could to resist him,
thinking with himself, that if King Agis' purpose took
place, he should also be compelled to do as he did,
and yet he should have no thanks, but King Agis :
because that all the Spartans indifferently should be
compelled to make their goods in common, but the
honour should be his only that first began it.   So he
asked Agis, whether he thought Lycurgus had been a
good and just man or not.   Agis answered, that he
had been.   Then replied Leonidas : Did you ever see
that he had taken away and abolished any debts, or
had received strangers into the number of the citizens
of Sparta ?   Who contrarily thought his commonwealth imperfect, if all strangers were not banished
the city.   Agis again answered him : That he marvelled not that Leonidas being brought up in a
strange country, and also married there in a noble-
man's house, he should be ignorant of Lycurgus' laws,
who banishing gold and silver out of his city, did
therewithal exile debt and lending.   And for strangers,
he hated them that would not conform themselves
unto the manners and fashions of life which he
instituted, and those they were which he banished :
not for any ill-will he bare unto their persons, but
because he feared their manners of life, lest that
mingling them with the citizens, they should make
them run after vanity and covetousness to be rich.
For otherwise, Terpander, Thales, and Pherecydes,
which were all strangers, were marvellously reverenced and honoured in Sparta in old time, because
they did sing in their writings, the self same things
which Lycurgus had established in his laws.   And
thou thy self also dost commend Ecprepes, being one
of the Ephors, because he did cut with a hatchet the
two strings which Phrynis the musician had added
unto the cithern, more than the seven common

strings, and those also which did the like unto
Timotheus: and yet thou reprovest me, because I go
about to root out all excess and pride out of Sparta,
as though those men did not far off prevent that these
superfluous strings of the music, delighting the
citizens' minds too much with their songs, should not
cause them fall unto such trade and manner of life,
as should make the city at discord with itself.

After this contention, the common people did stick
unto King Agis, and the rich men followed Leonidas,
praying and persuading him not to forsake them : and
further, they did so entreat the Senators, in whom
consisteth the chief authority, to determine and
digest all matters before they be propounded unto
the people, that they overthrew the law, by the only
voice of one man more. Wherefore Lysander who
was yet in office, attempted to accuse Leonidas by
an ancient law, forbidding that none of the race of
Hercules should marry with any strange woman, nor
beget children of her : and said further, that no man
upon pain of death should dwell anywhere, but in
Sparta. When he had instructed others to object
these things against Leonidas, he with other of his
colleagues observed a sign in the element, the ceremony whereof was in this sort: Every ninth year,
the Ephors choosing a bright night without moonlight,
did sit down in some open place, and beheld the
stars in the element, to see if they saw any star
shoot from one place to another: if they did, then
they accused their kings that they had offended the gods,
and did deprive them of their kingdom, until some
oracle came from Delphi or Olympus, to restore
them again. Lysander then declaring that he had seen
a star fly in the element, did therefore accuse King
Leonidas, and brought forth witnesses against him :
how he had married a woman of Asia, the which one
of King Seleucus' lieutenants had given him in
marriage, and that he had two children by her : and
afterwards being forsaken of his wife that refused
him, he returned again into his country against his

will: and so had possessed the kingdom for lack of a lawful heir. So following his accusation in this manner against him, he allured Cleombrotus his son-in-law, being also of the king's blood, to make title to the crown. Leonidas being afraid of the success hereof, took sanctuary in the temple of Juno, surnamed Chalcioecos, and his daughter with him, who forsook her husband Cleombrotus. Leonidas then being cited to appear in person, and making default, they deposed him, and made Cleombrotus king.

In the meantime Lysander's office expired, and the new Ephors which succeeded him, did deliver Leonidas again, and accused Lysander and Mandroclidas, because against the law, they had abolished all debts, and had again made new division of lands. When they saw they were openly accused, they incensed both the kings, that joining together, they should make the Ephors' ordinances of no effect: declaring that their authority was only erected for the discord of the two kings, because they should give their voices unto that king that had the best judgment and reason, when the other would wilfully withstand both right and reason: and therefore, they two agreeing together, might lawfully do what they would, without controlment of any person: and that to resist the kings was a breaking of the law, sith that by right the Ephors had no other privilege and authority, but to be judges and arbitrators between them, when there was any cause of jar or controversy. Both the kings being carried away by this persuasion, went into the market-place accompanied with their friends, plucked the Ephors from their seats, and put others in their rooms, of the which Agesilaus was one. Furthermore, they armed a great number of young men, and opening the prisons, did set the prisoners at liberty: the which made their adversaries afraid of them, doubting some great murder would have followed upon it; howbeit no man had any hurt. For Agesilaus being bent to kill Leonidas, who fled unto the city of Tegea, and having also laid men in

P.   8

wait for him by the way: King Agis hearing of it, sent thither other friends of his in whom he put great confidence, and they did accompany Leonidas, and brought him safely unto the city of Tegea.

Thus their purpose taking effect, and no man contrarying them: one man only Agesilaus overthrew all, and dashed a noble Laconian law by a shameful vice, which was covetousness. For he being a great landed man, and having the best lands of any man in the country, and owing a great sum of money besides: would neither pay his debts nor let go his land. Wherefore he persuaded King Agis, that if he went about to stablish both together, he should raise a great uproar in the city, and withal, if he did first win them that were landed men, preferring at the beginning the cutting off of debts only: then that they would easily and willingly also accept the law for partition of lands. Lysander was also of this opinion: whereby King Agis and he both were deceived by Agesilaus' subtilty. So they commanded all the creditors to bring their bonds, obligations, and bills of debt (which the Lacedaemonians do call *claria*) into the market-place, and there laying them on a heap together, they did set fire of them. When the usurers and creditors saw their writings obligatory afire, they departed thence with heavy hearts: but Agesilaus mocking them said he never saw a brighter fire in his life. The people then requiring that the lands also should be presently divided, and the kings likewise commanding it: Agesilaus still interposing some cause of let, delayed time, until opportunity served that King Agis should go to the wars, for that the Achaeans their confederates had prayed aid of Lacedaemon, being bound thereunto by the league confirmed between them, because they looked daily that the Aetolians coming through the country of Megara, would invade Peloponnesus. Aratus general of the Achaeans had levied a great army to withstand their invasion, and had also written unto the Ephors, that they should send them aid.

Whereupon they presently sent King Agis, perceiving also the readiness and good-will of the soldiers which were appointed to go with him: for the most of them were young men and needy, who seeing themselves discharged of the fear of their debts, and hoping also at their return, that the lands likewise should be divided among them : they went with glad hearts, and were obedient to King Agis. So that the cities where through they passed, wondered how they came through Peloponnesus, from the one side to the other, very quietly, without noise or offence to any man. Likewise many Grecians calling to mind the ancient times, told one another, that it was a noble sight then to see the army of Lacedaemon, when they were led by Agesilaus, Lysander, and Leonidas, famous captains: sith now they saw so great obedience unto Agis by his soldiers, who was in manner the youngest man of all his camp: who also glorying to be content with little, to away with pains, and not to be more costly apparelled and armed than any private soldier he had: he won himself thereby a marvellous love of the people. Howbeit the rich men liked not this change, and were afraid lest Agis should give other people example to rise also, and to do the like with theirs, as he had done.

Agis meeting with Aratus by the city of Corinth, even as he was consulting whether he should fight with his enemy or not: shewed himself in his counsel, then no rash, but a resolute and valiant man. For he told him, that for his opinion he thought it better to fight, and not to suffer the war to come any farther, leaving the entry into Peloponnesus free to their enemy; nevertheless, that he would do what Aratus thought good, because he was the elder, and general also of the Achaeans, whom he came not to command, but to aid them. But Baton Sinopian writeth that King Agis would not fight, though Aratus was willing; howbeit he had not read that which Aratus had written for his excuse and justification, alleging there that the farmers and husbandmen having brought all

8—2

the corn into their barns, he thought it better to
suffer the enemies to come farther into the country,
rather than to hazard battle, to the loss of the whole
country of Peloponnesus, and that therefore he licensed
all the confederates to depart and break up his army.

So King Agis returned home again, greatly honoured
of them that served with him in his journey, finding
the city of Sparta then in great broil and trouble.
For Agesilaus at that time being one of the Ephors,
finding himself rid of the fear which before kept him
under, cared not what injury or mischief he did unto
any citizen, so he might get money. For amongst
other things, that very year he made them pay beyond
all reason the tallages and taxes due unto the commonwealth for thirteen months, adding too the thirteenth
month above the ordinary time of the year.   Wherefore perceiving every man hated him, and being afraid
of them he had offended: he kept soldiers about him,
armed with their swords, and so came down into the
market place among them. And for the two kings,
he made no account of the one: but of the other that
was Agis, he seemed outwardly to make good account,
rather for kindred's sake, than for his dignity of a king,
and furthermore gave it out abroad, that he would also
be one of the Ephors the next year following.   Whereupon, his enemies speedily to prevent the danger,
gathered force together, and openly brought King
Leonidas from Tegea, to restore him again to his
kingdom. The people were glad to see that, because
they were angry they had been mocked in that sort,
for that the lands were not divided according unto
promise.   Furthermore, Hippomedon was so well
beloved for his valiantness of every man, that entreating the people for his father Agesilaus, he saved his
life, and got him out of the city.

But for the two kings, Agis took sanctuary in the
temple of Juno Chalcioecos. And Cleombrotus the
other king fled into the temple of Neptune: for it
seemed that Leonidas being much more offended with
him, did let King Agis alone, and went against him

with certain soldiers armed. Then he sharply taunted him, that being his son-in-law, he had conspired against him to deprive him of his kingdom, and had driven him out of his country. But then Cleombrotus not having a word to say, sat still, and made him no answer. Whereupon his wife Chelonis, the daughter of Leonidas, who before was offended for the injury they did her father, and had left her husband Cleombrotus, that had usurped the kingdom from him, to serve her father in his adversity, and while he was in sanctuary took part with him also of his misery, and afterwards when he went unto the city of Tegea, wore blacks for sorrow, being offended with her husband: she contrarily then changing her anger with her husband's fortune and misery, became also an humble suitor with him, sitting down by him, and embracing him, having her two little sons on either side of them. All men wondering, and weeping for pity to see the goodness and natural love of this lady, who showing her mourning apparel, and hair of her head flaring about her eyes, bareheaded: she spake in this manner unto her father: "O father mine, this sorrowful garment and countenance is not for pity of Cleombrotus, but hath long remained with me, lamenting sore your former misery and exile: but now, which of the two should I rather choose, either to continue a mourner in this pitiful state, seeing you again restored to your kingdom, having overcome your enemies: or else putting on my princely apparel, to see my husband slain, unto whom you married me a maid? who if he cannot move you to take compassion on him, and to obtain mercy, by the tears of his wife and children: he shall then abide more bitter pain of his evil counsel, than that which you intend to make him suffer. For he shall see his wife die before him, whom he loveth more dearly than anything in the world. Also, with what face can I look upon other ladies, when I could never bring my father to pity by any intercession I could make for my husband, neither my husband, entreating him for my father: and that my hap is to be born a daughter and wife always most unfortunate, and despised of mine own? And for my husband, if he had any reason to do that he did, I then took it from him, by taking your part, and protesting against him: and contrarily, your self doth give him honest colour to excuse his fault, when he seeth in you the desire of the kingdom so great, that for the love thereof, you think it lawful to kill your sons-in-law, and also not to regard the children he hath gotten, for her sake."

Chelonis pitifully complaining in this sort, putting her face upon Cleombrotus' head, cast her swollen and blubbering eyes upon the standers-by. Wherefore Leonidas after he had talked a little with his friends, he commanded Cleombrotus to get him thence and to leave the city as an exile: and prayed his daughter for his sake to remain with him, and not to forsake her father, that did so dearly love her, as for her sake he had saved her husband's life. This notwithstanding, she would not yield to his request, but rising up with her husband, gave him one of his sons, and herself took the other in her arms: and then making her prayer before the altar of the goddess, she went as a banished woman away with her husband. And truly the example of her virtue was so famous, that if Cleombrotus' mind had not been too much blinded with vainglory, he had cause to think his exile far more happy, to enjoy the love of so noble a wife as he had, than for the kingdom which he possessed without her. Then Leonidas having banished King Cleombrotus out of the city, and removing the first Ephors, had substituted other in their place: he presently bethought him how he might craftily come by King Agis. First, he persuaded him to come out of the sanctuary, and to govern the kingdom safely with him, declaring unto him that his citizens had forgiven him all that was past, because they knew he was deceived, and subtly circumvented by Agesilaus' craft, being a young man, ambitious of honour. Agis would not leave the sanctuary for Leonidas' cunning persuasion, but mistrusted all that he said unto him. Wherefore Leonidas would no more beguile him with fair words. But Amphares, Demochares, and Arcesilaus, did oftentimes go to visit King Agis, and otherwhile also they got him out of the sanctuary with them unto the bath, and brought him back again into the temple, when he had bathed. But Amphares having borrowed not long before certain rich apparel and plate of Agesistrata, because he would not redeliver them again, he determined to betray King Agis, his mother and grandmother. And it is reported that he chiefly did serve Leonidas' turn, and provoked the Ephors (of which number he was one) against Agis.

Now therefore, Agis keeping all the rest of his time within the temple, saving when he went upon occasion to the bath: they determined to intercept him by the way, and to take him when he was out of the sanctuary. So they watched him one day when he bathed, and came and saluted him as their manner was, and seemed to accompany him, sporting, and being merry with him, as with a young man their familiar. But when they came to the turning of a street that went towards the prison, Amphares laying hold on him, being one of the Ephors, said unto him: I arrest thee Agis, and will bring thee before the Ephors, to give account of thy doings in the commonwealth. Then Demochares, which was a great mighty man, cast his gown over his ears, and pulled him forward: others also thrust him forward behind him, as they had agreed together. So no man being near them to help Agis, they got him into prison. Then came Leonidas incontinently with a great number of soldiers that were strangers, and beset the prison round about. The Ephors went into the prison, and sent unto some of the Senate to come unto them, whom they knew to be of their mind: then they commanded Agis, as if it had been judicially, to give account of the alteration he had made in the commonwealth. The young man laughed at their hypocrisy. But Amphares told him that it was no laughing sport, and that he should pay for his folly. Then another of the Ephors, seeming to deal more favourably with him, and to shew him a way how he might escape the condemnation for his fault, asked him if he had not been enticed into it by Agesilaus and Lysander. Agis answered, that no man compelled him, but that he only did it to follow the steps of the ancient Lycurgus, to bring the commonwealth unto the former estate of his grave ordinance and institution. Then the same Senator asked him again, if he did not repent him of that he had done. The young man boldly answered him, that he would never repent him of so wise and virtuous an enterprise, though he ventured his life for it. Then they condemned him to death, and commanded the sergeants to carry him into the Dechad, which was a place in the prison where they were strangled, that were condemned to die. Demochares perceiving the sergeants durst not lay hold of him, and likewise that the soldiers which were strangers, did abhor to commit such a fact contrary to the law of God and man, to lay violent hands upon the person of a king: he threatened and reviled them, and dragged Agis perforce into that place called the Dechad. Now the rumour ran straight through the city, that King Agis was taken, and a multitude of people were at the prison doors with lights and torches. Thither came also King Agis' mother and grandmother, shrieking out and praying that the king of Sparta might yet be heard and judged by the people. For this cause they hastened his death the sooner, and were afraid besides, lest the people in the night would take him out of their hands by force, if there came any more people thither.

Thus King Agis, being led to his death, spied a sergeant lamenting and weeping for him, unto whom he said: Good fellow, I pray thee weep not for me,

for I am an honester man than they that so shamefully
put me to death: and with those words he willingly
put his head into the halter. Amphares then going
out of the prison into the street, found Agesistrata
there, King Agis' mother, who straight fell down at
his feet: but he taking her up again, in old familiar
manner, as being her very friend, told her that they
should do King Agis no hurt, and that she might if
she would, go and see him. Then she prayed that
they would also let her mother in with her. Amphares
said, With a good-will: and so put them both into
the prison-house and made the doors be shut after them.
But when they were within, he first gave Archidamia
unto the sergeants to be put to death, who was a
marvellous old woman, and had lived more honourably
unto that age, than any lady or matron beside her
in the city. She being executed, he commanded
Agesistrata also to come in. Who when she saw
the body of her dead son laid on the ground, and
her mother also hanging on the gallows: she did
her self help the hangman to pluck her down, and
laid her body by her son's. Then having covered her
in decent manner, she laid her down on the ground
by the corpse of her son Agis, and kissing his cheek
said: Out, alas my son, thy great modesty, goodness,
and clemency, brought thee and us unto this death.
Then Amphares peeping in at the door to see what
was done, hearing what she said, came in withal in a
great rage, and said: I perceive that thou hast also been
of council with thy son, and sith it is so, thou shalt
also follow him. Then she rising also to be strangled,
said: The gods grant yet that this may profit Sparta.

This horrible murder being blown abroad in the
city, and the three dead bodies also brought out of
prison: the fear though it were great amongst the
people, could not keep them back from apparent
shew of grief, and manifest hate against Leonidas
and Amphares, thinking that there was never a more
wicked and crueller fact committed in Sparta, since
the Dorians came to dwell in Peloponnesus. For

the very enemies themselves in battle, would not
willingly lay hands upon the kings of Lacedaemon,
but did forbear as much as they could possible, both
for fear and reverence they bare unto their majesty.
For in many great battles and conflicts which the
Lacedaemonians had against the Grecians, there was
never any king of Lacedaemon slain, before Philip's
time, but Cleombrotus only, who was slain with a
dart at the battle of Leuctra. Some write also that
the Messenians hold opinion, that their Aristomenes
slew King Theopompus: howbeit the Lacedaemonians
said, that he was but hurt not slain. But hereof there
are divers opinions: but it is certain that Agis was
the first king whom the Ephors ever put to death:
for that he had laid a plot of a noble device, and
worthy of Sparta, being of that age when men do
easily pardon them that offend: and was rather to
be accused of his friends and enemies, because he
had saved Leonidas' life, and had trusted other men,
as the best-natured young man that could be.

Now Agis having suffered in this sort, Leonidas
was not quick enough to take Archidamus his brother
also, for he fled presently. Yet he brought Agis'
wife out of her house by force, with a little boy she
had by him, and married her unto his son Cleomenes,
who was yet under age to marry: fearing lest this
young lady should be bestowed elsewhere, being
indeed a great heir, and of a rich house, and the
daughter of Gylippus, called by her name Agiatis,
besides that she was the fairest woman at that time
in all Greece, and the virtuousest, and best conditioned.
Wherefore for divers respects she prayed she might
not be forced to it. But now being at length married
unto Cleomenes, she ever hated Leonidas to the
death, and yet was a good and loving wife unto her
young husband: who immediately after he was
married unto her, fell greatly in fancy with her, and
for compassion's sake (as it seemed) he thanked her
for the love she bare unto her first husband, and for
the loving remembrance she had of him: insomuch

as he himself many times would fall in talk of it, and would be inquisitive how things had passed, taking great pleasure to hear of Agis' wise council and purpose. For Cleomenes was as desirous of honour, and had as noble a mind as Agis, and was born also to temperance, and moderation of life, as Agis in like manner was: howbeit, he had not that shamefast modesty and lenity, which the other had, but was somewhat more stirring of nature, and readier to put any good matter in execution. So he thought it great honesty, to bring the citizens if he could, to be contented to live after an honest sort: but contrarily, he thought it no dishonesty to bring them unto good life by compulsion also.

Furthermore, the manners of the citizens of Sparta, giving themselves over to idleness and pleasure, did nothing like him at all: neither that the king did suffer the commonwealth to be ruled as they listed, so no man impeached his pleasure, and that they did let him alone: insomuch, no man regarding the profit of the commonwealth, every man was for himself, and his family. And contrarily, it was not lawful for any man to speak for the exercises of the youth, for their education in temperance, and for the restoring again of equality of life, the preferment whereof was the only cause of the late death of Agis. They say also, that Cleomenes being a young stripling, had heard some disputation of philosophy, when the philosopher Sphaerus, of the country of Borysthenes, came to Lacedaemon, and lovingly stayed there to teach young men and children. He was one of the chiefest scholars of Zeno Citian, and delighted (as it seemed) in Cleomenes' noble mind, and had a great desire to prick him forward unto honour. For, as it is reported that the ancient Leonidas being demanded what poet he thought Tyrtaeus to be, answered he was good to flatter young men's minds: for he set their hearts on fire by his verses, when they began to fight any battle, fearing no danger, they were so encouraged by them: so the Stoic discipline is somewhat dangerous, for the stout and valiant minds, which otherwise doth make them desperate: but when they are joined unto a grave and gentle nature, first it lifteth up his heart, and then maketh him taste the profit thereof.

Now Leonidas (the father of Cleomenes) being deceased, and he himself also come into the crown, finding that the citizens of Sparta at that time were very dissolute, that the rich men followed their pleasure and profit, taking no care for the common weal, that the poor men also for very want and need, went with no good life and courage to the wars, neither cared for the bringing up of their children, and that he himself had but the name of a king, and the Ephors the absolute authority to do what they listed: at his first coming to his kingdom, he determined to alter the whole state and government of the commonwealth. Who having a friend called Xenares, that had been his lover in his youth (which the Lacedæmonians called Empnistae, as much as inspired) he began to sound his opinion, asking what manner of man King Agis had been, and by what reason, and whose advice he had followed in his attempt for the reformation of the commonwealth. Xenares at the first did not willingly rehearse these things unto him, declaring everything what had passed. But when he found that Cleomenes was affected into King Agis' intent, and still desired to hear of it: then Xenares sharply and angrily reproved him, and told him he was not wise, nor well advised, and at length would no more come and talk with him as he was wont, yet making no man privy why he abstained from coming to him but told them that asked him, he knew a cause well enough why. Xenares now having thus refused him, and thinking all the rest would do the like: to bring this matter to pass, he took this resolution with himself. Because he thought he might the rather do it in war, than in peace, he set the city of Sparta and the Achaeans at variance together: who did themselves give the first occasion to be complained upon. For Aratus being the President and chief of all the

Achaeans, had practised a long time to bring all
Peloponnesus into one body : and had therefore only
sustained great troubles in wars, and at home in peace :
thinking that there was no other way to deliver them
from foreign wars. Now when he had won all the other
people to be of his opinion : there remained no more
but the Eleans, the Lacedaemonians, and a few of the
Arcadians, which were subject to the Lacedaemonians.
When King Leonidas was dead, Aratus began to invade the Arcadians, those specially that bordered upon
the Argives : to prove how the Lacedaemonians would
take it, making no account of Cleomenes, being but
a young king, and had no experience of wars.

Thereupon the Ephors sent Cleomenes unto Athenium
(a temple of Minerva hard by the city of Belbina) with
an army to take it : because it was a passage and
entry into the country of Laconia ; howbeit the place
at that time was in question betwixt the Megalopolitans
and the Lacedaemonians : Cleomenes got it, and
fortified it. Aratus making no complaint otherwise
of the matter, stole out one night with his army to
set upon the Tegeans and Orchomenians, hoping to
have taken those cities by treason. But the traitors
that were of his confederacy, their hearts failed them
when they should have gone about it : so that
Aratus returned, having lost his journey, thinking that
this secret attempt of his was not discovered. But
Cleomenes finely wrote unto him as his friend, and
asked him, whither he had led his army by night ?
Aratus returned answer again, that understanding
Cleomenes meant to fortify Belbina, he went forth
with his army, thinking to have let him. Cleomenes
wrote again unto him, and said he did not believe
that which he spake was true : howbeit he earnestly
requested him (if it were no trouble to him) to
advertise him why he brought scaling-ladders and
lights after him. Aratus smiling at this mock,
asked what this young man was. Democritus Lacedaemonian, being a banished man out of his country,
answered : If thou hast anything to do against the

Lacedaemonians, thou hadst need make haste, before
this young cockerel have on his spurs. Then Cleomenes
being in the field in the country of Arcadia, with a few
horsemen and three hundred footmen only: the Ephors
being afraid of wars, sent for him to return again.
His back was no sooner turned, obeying their commandment: but Aratus suddenly took the city of
Caphyae. Thereupon, the Ephors incontinently sent
Cleomenes back again with his army: who took the
fort of Methydrium, and burnt the borders of the
Argives. The Achaeans came against him with an
army of twenty thousand footmen, and a thousand
horsemen led by Aristomachus: Cleomenes met with
them by the City of Pallantium and offered battle.
But Aratus, quaking at the hardiness of this young
man, would not suffer Aristomachus to hazard battle,
but went his way, derided by the Achaeans, and despised
by the Lacedaemonians: who in all were not above
five thousand fighting men. Cleomenes' courage being
now lift up, and bravely speaking to his citizens: he
remembered them of a saying of one of their ancient
kings, that the Lacedaemonians never inquired what
number their enemies were, but where they were.

Shortly after, the Achaeans making war with the
Eleans, Cleomenes was sent to aid them, and met
with the army of the Achaians by the mountain
Lycaeon, as they were in their return: he setting upon
them, gave them the overthrow, slew a great number
of them, and took many also prisoners, that the
rumour ran through Greece, how Aratus self was slain.
Cleomenes wisely taking the occasion which this
victory gave him: he went straight to the city of
Mantinea, and taking it upon a sudden, when no man
knew of his coming, he put a strong garrison into it.
Now the Lacedaemonians' hearts failing them, and
resisting Cleomenes' enterprises, over-wearying them
with wars: he went about to send for Archidamus,
King Agis' brother, being then at Messené, unto whom
the kingdom of right belonged by the other house,
supposing that he should easily weaken the power of

the Ephors, by the authority of the two kings, if both of them joined together. Which when the murderers of King Agis understood, being afraid that Archidamus returning from exile, he would be revenged of them, they secretly received him into the city, and found the means to bring him into Sparta. But when they had him, they put him straight to death, whether it was unwitting to Cleomenes (as Phylarchus plainly testifieth) or else with his privity, suffering them to make him away, by persuasion of his friends. But it is a clear case, the city was burdened withal, because probable matter fell out that they had compelled Cleomenes to do it.

Nevertheless, he holding still his first determination, to alter the state of the commonwealth of Sparta, as soon as he could possible : he so fed the Ephors with money, that he brought them to be contented he should make war. He had also won many other citizens by the means of his mother Cratesiclea, who furnished him with money, that he lacked not to honour him withal : and further, married as it is reported (being otherwise not meant to marry) for her son's sake, unto one of the wealthiest men of all the city. So Cleomenes leading his army into the field, won a place within the territory of Megalopolis, called Leuctra. The Achaeans also being quickly come to their aid, led by Aratus : they straight fought a battle by the city self, where Cleomenes had the worst on the one side of his army. Howbeit Aratus would not suffer the Achaeans to follow them, because of bogs and quagmires, but sounded the retreat. But Lydiadas a Megalopolitan, being angry withal, caused the horsemen he had about him to follow the chase, who pursued so fiercely, that they came amongst vines, walls, and ditches, where he was driven to disperse his men, and yet could not get out. Cleomenes perceiving it, sent the light horsemen of the Tarentines and Cretans against him : of whom Lydiadas valiantly fighting was slain. Then the Lacedaemonians being courageous for this victory, came with great cries, and giving a fierce charge upon the Achaeans, overthrew their whole army, and slew a marvellous number of them: but yet Cleomenes, at their request, suffered them to take up the dead bodies of their men to bury them. For Lydiadas' corpse, he caused it to be brought unto him, and putting a purple robe upon it, and a crown on his head, sent it in this array unto the very gates of the city of Megalopolis. It was that self Lydiadas, who giving over the tyranny and government of Megalopolis, made it a popular state, and free city, and joined it to the Achaeans.

After this victory, Cleomenes that determined greater matters and attempts, persuaded himself that if he might once come to stablish the affairs of the commonwealth at Sparta to his mind, he might then easily overcome the Achaeans, brake with his father-in-law Megistonous, and told him that it was necessary to take away the authority of the Ephors, and to make division of the lands among the Spartans, and then being brought to equality, to encourage them to recover the empire of Greece again unto the Lacedaemonians, which their predecessors before them, held and enjoyed. Megistonous, granting his good-will and furtherance, joined two or three of his friends more unto him. It chanced at that time that one of the Ephors lying in the temple of Pasiphaé, had a marvellous dream in the night. For he thought he saw but one chair standing where the Ephors did use to sit to give audience, and that the other four which were wont to be there, were taken away: and that marvelling at it, he heard a voice out of the temple that said, that was the best for Sparta. He declaring this dream the next morning unto Cleomenes, it somewhat troubled him at the first, thinking that he came to feel him, for that he had heard some inkling of his intent. But when he persuaded himself that the other meant good faith, and lied not unto him, being bolder than before, he went forward with his purpose, and taking with him unto the camp all those Spartans which he suspected to be against his enterprise, he went and took the cities of Heraea and

Alsaea, confederates of the Achaeans, and victualled Orchomenus, and went and camped before the city of Mantinea. In fine, he so wearied and overharried the Lacedaemonians by long journeys, that at length they besought him he would let them remain in Arcadia, to repose themselves there. In the meantime, Cleomenes with his strangers which he had hired, returned again unto Sparta, and imparted his intent by the way unto them he trusted best, and marched at his own ease, that he might take the Ephors at supper.

When he came near unto the city, he sent Euryclidas before, into the hall of the Ephors, as though he brought them news out of the camp from him. After him, he sent also Therycion and Phoebis, and two other that had been brought up with him, whom the Lacedaemonians called the Samothracians, taking with them a few soldiers. Now whilst Euryclidas was talking with the Ephors, they also came in upon them with their swords drawn, and did set upon the Ephors. Agesilaus was hurt first of all, and falling down, made as though he had been slain, but by little and little he crept out of the hall, and got secretly unto a chapel consecrated unto Fear, the which was wont ever to be kept shut, but then by chance was left open: when he was come in, he shut the door fast to him. The other four of the Ephors were slain presently, and above ten more besides, which came to defend them. Furthermore, for them that sat still and stirred not, they killed not a man of them, neither did keep any man that was desirous to go out of the city: but moreover, they pardoned Agesilaus, who came the next morning out of the chapel of Fear.

Amongst the Lacedaemonians in the city of Sparta, there are not only temples of Fear and Death, but also of Laughter, and of many other such passions of the mind. They do worship Fear, not as other spirits and devils that are hurtful: but because they are persuaded that nothing preserveth a commonwealth

better than fear.   Wherefore the Ephors (as Aristotle
witnesseth) when they are created, do by public proclamation command all the Spartans to shave their
chins, and to obey the law, lest they should make
them feel the rigour of the law.   They brought in the
shaving of their chins, in my opinion, to inure young
men to obey the magistrates even in trifles.   Moreover it seems that men in old time did esteem
fortitude to be no taking away of fear, but rather a
fear and loathness to incur shame.   For commonly
those that are most afraid to offend the law, are in
the field most valiant against their enemy: and shun
no peril to win fame and honest reputation.   And
therefore it was wisely said of one,

> That fear cannot be without shamefastness:

And so Homer in a certain place made Helen say
unto King Priamus:

> Of truth I do confess dear father-in-law,
> You are the man of whom I stand in awe,
> And reverence most of all that ever I saw.

And in another place, speaking of the Grecian soldiers,
he saith thus:

> For fear of their captains they spake not a word.

For men do use to reverence them whom they fear.
And this was the cause why the chapel of Fear was
by the hall of the Ephors, having in manner a
princely and absolute authority.

The next morning Cleomenes banished by trumpet
fourscore citizens of Sparta, and overthrew all the
chairs of the Ephors but one only, the which he reserved for himself to sit in to give audience.   Then
calling the people to council, he gave them an account
of his doings, and told them that Lycurgus had joined
the Senators with the kings, and how the city had been
governed a long time by them, without help of any other
officers.   Notwithstanding, afterwards the city having
great wars with the Messenians, the kings being always
employed in that war, whereby they could not attend

the affairs of the commonwealth at home, did choose
certain of their friends to sit in judgment in their
steads to determine controversies of law: which were
called Ephors, and did govern long time as the king's
ministers, howbeit that afterwards, by little and little,
they took upon them absolute government by themselves.   And for manifest proof hereof, you see that
at this present time when the Ephors do send for the
king, the first and second time he refuseth to come,
but the third time he riseth and goeth unto them.
The first man that gave the Ephors this authority,
was Asteropus, one of the Ephors many years after
the first institution of the kings: and yet if they had
governed discreetly, peradventure they might have
continued longer.   But they licentiously abusing their
authority,   by   suppressing   the   lawful   governors
instituted of old time, taking upon them to banish
some of their kings, and putting other of them also
to death, without law and justice, and threatening
others that desire to restore that noble and former
blessed government unto Sparta again: all these
things, I say, are in nowise to be suffered any
longer.   And therefore, if it had been possible to
have banished all these plagues of the commonwealth
out of Sparta, brought from foreign nations: (I mean,
pleasures, pastimes, money, debts, and usuries, and
others yet more ancient, poverty and riches) he might
then have esteemed himself the happiest king that
ever was, if like a good physician he had cured his
country of that infection, without grief or sorrow.
But in that he was constrained to begin with blood, he
followed Lycurgus' example; who being neither king
nor other magistrate, but a private citizen only, taking
upon him the authority of the king, boldly came into
the marketplace with force and armed men, and made
King Charilaus, that then reigned, so afraid, that he was
driven to take sanctuary in one of the temples.   But
the king being a prince of a noble nature, and loving
the honour of his country, took part with Lycurgus,
adding to his advice and counsel, for the alteration

of the state of the government of the commonwealth, which he did confirm. Hereby then it appeareth, that Lycurgus saw it was a hard thing to alter the commonwealth without force and fear: the which he notwithstanding had used with as great modesty and discretion as might be possible, banishing them that were against the profit and wealth of Lacedaemon, giving all the lands of the country also to be equally divided amongst them, and setting all men clear that were in debt. And furthermore, that he would make a choice and proof of the strangers, to make them free citizens of Sparta whom he knew to be honest men, thereby to defend their city the better by force of arms: to the end that from henceforth we may no more see our country of Laconia spoiled by the Aetolians and Illyrians, for lack of men to defend themselves against them.

Then he began first himself to make all his goods common, and after him Megistonous his father-in-law, and consequently all his other friends. Then he caused the lands also to be divided, and ordained every banished man a part, whom he himself had exiled, promising that he would receive them again into the city, when he had established all things. So when he had replenished the number of the citizens of Sparta, with the choicest honest men their neighbours: he made four thousand footmen well armed, and taught them to use their pikes with both hands, instead of their darts with one hand, and to carry their targets with a good strong handle, and not buckled with a leather thong. Afterwards he took order for the education of children, and to restore the ancient Laconian discipline again: and did all these things in manner by the help of Sphaerus the philosopher, insomuch as he had quickly set up again schoolhouses for children, and also brought them to the old order of diet: and all, but a very few, without compulsion were willing to fall to their old institution of life. Then because the name of one king should not offend any man, he made his brother Euclidas king with him. But this was the first time that ever the two kings were of one house but then.

Furthermore, understanding that the Achaeans and Aratus were of opinion, that he durst not come out of Lacedaemon, for fear to leave it in peril of revolting, because of the late change and alteration in the commonwealth: he thought it an honourable attempt of him, to make his enemies see the readiness and good-will of his army. Thereupon he invaded the territories of the Megalopolitans, and brought away a great prey and booty, after he had done great hurt unto his enemies. Then having taken certain players and minstrels that came from Messené, he set up a stage within the enemies' country, made a game of forty minas for the victor, and sat a whole day to look upon them, for no pleasure he took in the sight of it, but more to despite the enemies withal, in making them see how much he was stronger than they, to make such a May-game in their own country, in despite of them. For of all the armies otherwise of the Grecians, or kings in all Greece, there was no army only but his, that was without players, minstrels, fools and jugglers: for his camp only was clean of such rabble and foolery, and all the young men fell to some exercise of their bodies, and the old men also to teach them. And if they chanced to have any vacant time, then they would pleasantly be one merry with another, in giving some pretty fine mock after the Laconian manner. And what profit they got by that kind of exercise, we have written it at large in Lycurgus' life.

But of all these things, the king himself was their schoolmaster and example, shewing himself very temperate of life, and plain without curiosity, no more than any private soldier of all his camp: the which were great helps unto him in his enterprises he made in Greece. For the Grecians having cause of suit and negotiation with other kings and princes, did not wonder so much at their pomp and riches, as they did abhor and detest their pride and insolency: so disdainfully they would answer them that had to do with them.   But contrarily when they went unto Cleomenes, who was a king in name and deed as they were, finding no purple robes nor stately mantles, nor rich-embroidered beds, nor a prince to be spoken to but by messengers, gentlemen ushers, and supplications, and yet with great ado: and seeing him also come plainly apparelled unto them, with a good countenance, and courteously answering the matters they came for: he thereby did marvellously win their hearts and good-wills, that when they returned home, they said he only was the worthy king, that came of the race of Hercules.

Now for his diet at his board, that was very straight and Laconian-like, keeping only three boards: and if he chanced to feast any ambassadors or other his friends that came to see him, he then added to two other boards, and besides, made his men to see that his fare should be amended, not with pastry and conserves, but with more store of meat, and some better wine than ordinary.   For he one day reproved one of his friends, that bidding strangers to supper, he gave them nothing but black broth, and brown bread only, according to the Laconian manner.   Nay, said he, we may not use strangers so hardly after our manner. The board being taken up, another little table was brought with three feet, whereupon they set a bowl of copper full of wine, and two silver cups of a pottle apiece, and certain other few silver pots besides: so every man drank what they listed, and no man was forced to drink more than he would.   Furthermore, there was no sport, nor any pleasant song sung to make the company merry, for it needed not.   For Cleomenes self would entertain them with some pretty questions or pleasant tale: whereby, as his talk was not severe and without pleasure, so was it also pleasant without insolency.   For he was of opinion, that to win men by gifts of money, as other kings and princes did, was but base and clownlike: but to seek their good-wills by courteous means and pleasantness, and therewith to mean good faith, that he thought most fit and honourable for a prince. For this was his mind, that there was no other difference betwixt a friend and a hireling: but that the one is won with money, and the other with civility and good entertainment.

The first therefore that received King Cleomenes into their city, were the Mantineans, who opened him the gates in the night, and helping him to drive out the garrison of the Achaeans, they yielded themselves unto him. But he referring them to the use and government of their own laws and liberty, departed from thence the same day, and went unto the city of Tegea. Shortly after, he compassed about Arcadia, and came unto Pherae in Arcadia determining one of the two, either to give the Achaeans battle, or to bring Aratus out of favour with the people, for that he had suffered him to spoil and destroy their country. Hyperbatas was at that time general of the Achaeans, but Aratus did bear all the sway and authority. Then the Achaeans coming into the field with all their people armed, and encamping by the city of Dymae, near unto the temple of Hecatombaeum; Cleomenes going thither, lay betwixt the city of Dymae that was against him, and the camp of his enemies, which men thought a very unwise part of him. Howbeit valiantly provoking the Achaeans, he procured them to the battle, overthrew them, made them fly, and slew a great number in the field, and took many of them also prisoners. Departing from thence, he went and set upon the city of Langon, and drave the garrison of the Achaeans out of it, and restored the city again unto the Eleans.

The Achaeans being then in very hard state, Aratus that of custom was wont to be their general (or at the least once in two years) refused now to take the charge, notwithstanding the Achaeans did specially pray and entreat him: the which was an ill act of him, to let another steer the rudder, in so dangerous a storm and tempest. Therefore the Achaeans sent

ambassadors unto Cleomenes to treat peace, unto
whom it seemed he gave a very sharp answer. After
that, he sent unto them, and willed them only to
resign the signiory of Greece unto him : and that
for all other matters he would deal reasonably with
them, and presently deliver them up their towns and
prisoners again, which he had taken of theirs. The
Achaeans being glad of peace with these conditions,
wrote unto Cleomenes that he should come unto the
city of Lerna, where the diet and general assembly
should be kept to consult thereupon. It chanced
then that Cleomenes marching thither, being very
hot, drank cold water, and fell on such a bleeding
withal, that his voice was taken from him, and he
almost stifled. Wherefore he sent the Achaeans
their chiefest prisoners home again, proroguing the
parliament till another time, and returned back to
Lacedaemon.

It is supposed certainly, that this let of his coming
to the diet, was the only cause of the utter destruction of Greece : the which otherwise was in good
way to have risen again, and to have been delivered
from the present miseries, and extreme pride and
covetousness of the Macedonians. For Aratus, either
for that he trusted not Cleomenes, or for that he was
afraid of his power, or that he otherwise envied
his honour and prosperity, to see him risen to
such incredible greatness in so short a time, and
thinking it also too great shame and dishonour
to him, to suffer this young man in a moment to
deprive him of his great honour and power which
he had possessed so long time, by the space of thirty
years together, ruling all Greece : first, he sought
by force to terrify the Achaeans, and to make them
break off from this peace. But in fine, finding that
they little regarded his threats, and that he could
not prevail with them, for that they were afraid of
Cleomenes' valiantness and courage, whose request
they thought reasonable, for that he sought but to
restore Peloponnesus into her former ancient estate

again: he fell then into a practice far unhonest for a Grecian, very infamous for himself, but most dishonourable for the former noble acts he had done. For he brought Antigonus into Greece, and in his age filled the country of Peloponnesus with Macedonians, whom he himself in his youth had driven thence, had taken from them the castle of Corinth, and had always been an enemy of the king's (but especially of Antigonus, of whom before he had spoken all the ill he could, as appeareth in his writings, saying that he took marvellous pains, and did put himself into many dangers, to deliver the city of Athens from the garrison of the Macedonians) and yet notwithstanding he brought them armed with his own hands, not into his country only, but into his own house, yea even into the ladies' chambers and closets: disdaining that the king of Lacedaemon, descending of the blood royal of Hercules (who setting up again the ancient manner of life of his country, did temper it as an instrument of music out of tune, and brought it to the good, ancient and sober discipline and Dorican life instituted by Lycurgus) should be called and written king of the Sicyonians, and of the Tritaeans. And furthermore, flying them that were contented with brown bread, and with the plain coarse capes of the Lacedaemonians, and that went about to take away riches (which was the chiefest matter they did accuse Cleomenes for) and to provide for the poor: he went and put himself and all Achaea unto crown and diadem, the purple robe, and proud imperious commandments of the Macedonians, fearing lest men should think that Cleomenes could command him. Furthermore his folly was such, that having garlands of flowers on his head, he did sacrifice unto Antigonus, and sing songs in praise of his honour, as if he had been a god, where he was but a rotten man consumed away. This that we have written of Aratus (who was endued with many noble virtues, and a worthy Grecian) is not so much to accuse him, as to make us see the frailty and weakness of man's

nature: the which, though it have never so excellent
virtues, cannot yet bring forth such perfect fruit, but
that it hath ever some maim and blemish.

Now when the Achaians were met again in the
city of Argos, to hold the session of their parliament
before prorogued, and Cleomenes also being come
from Tegea, to be at that parliament: every man
was in hope of good peace. But Aratus then, who
was agreed before of the chiefest articles of the
capitulations with Antigonus, fearing that Cleomenes
by fair words or force would bring the people to
grant that he desired, sent to let him understand,
that he should but come himself alone into the city,
and for safety of his person, they would give him
three hundred hostages: or otherwise, if he would
not leave his army, that then they would give him
audience without the city, in the place of exercises,
called Cyllarabium. When Cleomenes had heard
their answer, he told them that they had done him
wrong: for they should have advertised him of it
before he had taken his journey, and not now when
he was almost hard at their gates, to send him back
again, with a flea in his ear. Thereupon he wrote
a letter unto the council of the Achaeans, altogether
full of complaints against Aratus. On the other
side also, Aratus in his oration to the council,
inveighed with bitter words against Cleomenes.
Thereupon Cleomenes departing with speed, sent
a herald to proclaim wars against the Achaeans,
not in the city of Argos, but in the city of Aegion,
as Aratus writeth, meaning to set upon them being
unprovided. Hereupon all Achaea was in an uproar:
for divers cities did presently revolt against the
Achaeans, because the common people hoped after
the division of lands, and the discharging of their debts.
The noblemen also in many places were offended
with Aratus, because he practised to bring the
Macedonians into the country of Peloponnesus.
Cleomenes therefore hoping well for all these respects,
brought his army into Achaea, and at his first coming

took the city of Pellene, and drave out the garrison of the Achaeans: and after that, won also the cities of Pheneum, and Pentelium.

Now the Achaeans fearing some treason in Corinth and Sicyon, sent certain horsemen out of the city of Argos, to keep those cities. The Argives in the meantime, attending the celebration of the feast at the games Nemea, Cleomenes thinking (which fell out true) that if he went to Argos, he should find the city full of people that were come to see the feasts and games, and that assailing them upon the sudden, he should put them in a marvellous fear: brought his army in the night hard to the walls of the city of Argos, and at his first coming won a place they call Aspis, a very strong place above the theatre, and ill to come unto. The Argives were so amazed at it, that no man would take upon him to defend the city, but received Cleomenes' garrison, and gave him twenty hostages, promising thenceforth to be true confederates unto the Lacedaemonians, under his charge and conduct. The which doubtless won him great fame, and increased his power: for that the ancient kings of Lacedaemon, could never before, with any policy or device, win the city of Argos. For King Pyrrhus one of the most valiantest and warlikest princes that ever was, entering the city of Argos by force, could not keep it, but was slain there, and the most part of his army: whereby every man wondered greatly at the diligence and counsel of Cleomenes. And where every man did mock him before, when Cleomenes said that he would follow Solon and Lycurgus, in making the citizens' goods common, and discharging all debts: they were then clearly persuaded that he only was the cause and mean of that great change, which they saw in the courage of the Spartans: who were before so weak and out of heart, that they having no courage to defend themselves, the Aetolians entering Laconia with an army, took away at one time, fifty thousand slaves. Whereupon an old man of Sparta pleasantly said at that time, that their enemies had done them a great pleasure, to rid their country of Laconia of such a rabble of rascals. Shortly after, they being entered again into the former ancient discipline of Lycurgus, as if Lycurgus self had been alive to have trained them unto it: they showed themselves very valiant, and obedient also unto their magistrates, whereby they recovered again the commandment of all Greece, and the country also of Peloponnesus.

After Cleomenes had taken the city of Argos, the cities also of Cleonae, and Phlius, did yield themselves unto him. Aratus in the mean time remained at Corinth, and there did busily accuse them which were suspected to favour the Lacedæmonians. But when news was brought him that Argos was taken, and that he perceived also the city of Corinth did lean unto Cleomenes' part, and drave away the Achaians: he then calling the people to council in Corinth, secretly stole to one of the gates of the city, and causing his horse to be brought unto him, took his back, and galloped for life unto the city of Sicyon. When the Corinthians heard of it, they took their horsebacks also striving who should be there soonest, and posted in such haste unto Cleomenes at the city of Argos, that many of them (as Aratus writeth) killed their horses by the way: howbeit Cleomenes was very much offended with them, for that they had let him escape their hands. But Aratus saith further, that Megistonous came unto him from Cleomenes, and offered him a great sum of money to deliver him the castle of Corinth, wherein there was a great garrison of the Achaeans. But he answered again, that things were not in his power, but rather that he was subject to their power. Now Cleomenes departing from the city of Argos, overcame the Troezenians, the Epidaurians, and the Hermionians. After that, he came unto Corinth, and presently entrenched the castle there round about, and sending for Aratus' friends and factors, commanded them to keep his house and goods carefully for him, and sent

Tritymallus Messenian again unto him, to pray him to be contented that the castle might be kept indifferently betwixt the Achaeans and the Lacedaemonians, promising him privately to double the pension that King Ptolemy gave him. But Aratus refusing it, sent his son unto Antigonus with other hostages, and persuaded the Achaeans to deliver up the castle of Corinth, unto Antigonus' hands. Cleomenes, understanding it, entered with his army into the country of the Sicyonians, and destroyed it as he went, and took Aratus' goods and money of the gift of the Corinthians, by decree.

Now Antigonus in the mean time being passed the mountain of Geranea with a great power: Cleomenes determined not to fortify the isthmus or strait of Peloponnesus, but the ways of the mountains Onea, determining to keep every one of them against the Macedonians, with intent to consume them rather by time, than to fight a battle with an army, so good soldiers and well trained as they were. Cleomenes, following this determination, did put Antigonus to great trouble, because he had not in time provided for corn: and could not win the passage also by force, for that Cleomenes kept it with such guard and soldiers. Then Antigonus stealing secretly into the haven of Lechaeum, he was stoutly repulsed, and lost a number of his men: whereupon Cleomenes and his men being courageous for this victory, went quietly to supper. Antigonus on the other side fell into despair, to see himself brought by necessity into such hard terms. Wherefore he determined to go to the temple of Juno, and from thence to pass his army by sea into the city of Sicyon, the which required a long time, and great preparation. But the same night there came some of Aratus' friends of the Argives, who coming from Argos by sea, brought news that the Argives were rebelled against Cleomenes. The practiser of this rebellion, was one Aristoteles, who easily brought the people unto it, that were already offended with Cleomenes, that had promised to pass a law for the clearing of debts, but performed it not according to their expectation. Wherefore, Aratus with a thousand five hundred men which Antigonus gave him, went by sea unto Epidaurus. Howbeit Aristoteles tarried not his coming, but taking them of the city with him, went and besieged the garrison of the Lacedaemonians within the castle, being aided by Timoxenus, with the Achaeans that came from Sicyon.

Cleomenes receiving advertisement hereof, about the second watch of the night, sent for Megistonous in haste, and commanded him in anger speedily to go and aid their men that were in the city of Argos. For it was Megistonous himself that promised Cleomenes the fidelity of the Argives, and that kept him from driving them out of the city, which he suspected. So sending him away forthwith with two thousand men, he attended Antigonus, and comforted the Corinthians the best he could: advertising them that it was but a little mutiny of a few, that chanced in the city of Argos. Megistonous being come to Argos, and slain in battle, fighting for the Lacedaemonians in garrison there who (being in great distress, scant able to keep the castle against the enemies) sent sundry messengers unto Cleomenes, to pray him to send them immediate aid. Cleomenes then being afraid that the enemies having taken Argos, would stop his way to return back into his country, who having opportunity safely to spoil Laconia, and also to besiege the city self of Sparta, that had but a few men to defend it, he departed with his army from Corinth. Immediately after came Antigonus, and took it from him, and put a strong garrison into it. When Cleomenes came before the city of Argos, he scaled the walls, and breaking the vaults and arches of the place called Aspis, entered into the city, and joined with his garrison there, which yet resisted the Achaeans: and taking other parts of the same also, assaulted the walls, and cleared the streets in such sort, that not an enemy durst be seen, for fear of the archers of the Cretans. In the meantime, when he saw Antigonus afar off, coming down the hills into the valley with his footmen, and that his horsemen also came upon the spur into the city: despairing then that he could any longer keep it, he gathered all his men together, and safely going down by the walls retired without loss of any man. So, when in short time he had conquered much, and had almost won all within Peloponnesus: in shorter space also, he lost all again. For, of the confederates that were in his camp, some did presently forsake him: others also immediately after surrendered up the towns unto Antigonus.

Cleomenes being thus oppressed with the fortune of war, when he came back to Tegea with the rest of his army, news came to him in the night from Lacedaemon, which grieved him as much as the loss of all his conquests: for he was advertised of the death of his wife Agiatis, whom he loved so dearly, that in the midst of his chiefest prosperity and victories, he made often journeys to Sparta to see her. It could not but be a marvellous grief unto Cleomenes, who being a young man, had lost so virtuous and fair a young lady, so dearly beloved of him: and yet he gave not place unto his sorrow, neither did grief overcome his noble courage, but he used the self same voice, apparel, and countenance, that he did before. Then taking order with his private captains, about his affairs, and having provided also for the safety of the Tegeans: he went the next morning by break of day unto Sparta. After he had privately lamented the sorrow of his wife's death, with his mother and children: he presently bent his mind again to public causes. Now Cleomenes had sent unto Ptolemy king of Egypt, who had promised him aid, but upon demand to have his mother and children in pledge. So he was a long time before he would for shame make his mother privy unto it, and went oftentimes of purpose to let her understand it: but when he came he had not the heart to break it to her. She first suspecting a thing, asked Cleomenes' friends if her son had not somewhat to say unto her, that he durst not utter. Whereupon, in fine he gave the venture, and brake the matter to her. When she heard it, she fell a-laughing, and told him: Why, how cometh it to pass, that thou has kept it thus long, and wouldest not tell me? Come, come, said she, put me straight into a ship, and send me whither thou wilt, that this body of mine may do some good unto my country, before crooked age consume my life without profit. Then all things being prepared for their journey, they went by land, accompanied with the army, unto the head of Taenarum; where Cratesiclea being ready to embark, she took Cleomenes aside into the temple of Neptune, and embracing and kissing him, perceiving that his heart yearned for sorrow of her departure, she said unto him: O King of Lacedaemon, let no man see for shame when we come out of the temple, that we have wept and dishonoured Sparta. For that only is in our power; and for the rest, as it pleaseth the gods, so let it be. When she had spoken these words, and fashioned her countenance again, she went then to take her ship, with a little son of Cleomenes, and commanded the master of the ship to hoise sail. Now when she was arrived in Egypt, and understood that King Ptolemy received ambassadors from Antigonus, and were in talk to make peace with him: and hearing also that Cleomenes being requested by the Achaeans to make peace with them, durst not hearken to it, and end that war, without King Ptolemy's consent, and because of his mother: she wrote unto him, that he should not spare to do anything that should be expedient for the honour of Sparta, without fear of displeasing Ptolemy, or for regard of an old woman, and a young boy. Such was the noble mind of this worthy lady in her son Cleomenes' adversity.

Furthermore, Antigonus having taken the city of Tegea, and sacked the other cities of Orchomenus, and Mantinea: Cleomenes seeing himself brought to defend the borders only of Laconia, he did manumit all the Helots (which were the slaves of Lacedaemon), paying five Attica minas a man. With that money he made the sum of five hundred talents, and armed two thousand of these freed slaves after the Macedonian fashion to fight against the Leucaspides (to wit, the white shields of Antigonus): and then there fell into his mind a marvellous great enterprise, unlooked for of every man. The city of Megalopolis at that time being as great as Sparta, and having the aid of the Achaeans, and Antigonus at hand (whom the Achaeans as it seemed had brought in, chiefly at the request of the Megalopolitans) Cleomenes determining to sack this city, and knowing that to bring it to pass, nothing was more requisite than celerity: he commanded his soldiers to victual themselves for five days, and marching with the choice of all his army towards Sellasia, as though he had meant to have spoiled the Argives, suddenly turning from thence, he invaded the country of the Megalopolitans, and supping by Rhoeteum, went straight by Helicus unto the city. When he was come near unto it, he sent Panteus before with speed, with two bands of the Lacedaemonians, and commanded him to take a certain piece of the wall between two towers, which he knew was not kept nor guarded : and he followed him also with the rest of his army coming on fair and softly. When Panteus came thither, finding not only that place of the wall without guard or watch which Cleomenes had told him of, but also the most part of that side without defence : he took some part of the wall at his first coming, and manned it, and overthrew another piece of it also, putting them all to the sword that did defend it, and then came Cleomenes, and was within the city with his army, before the Megalopolitans knew of his coming.

At length, the citizens understanding that the city was taken, some fled in haste, conveying such light things as came to hand, in so great a fear : and the

others also arming themselves, ran together to resist
the enemies. But though they valiantly fought to
repulse them out of the city, and yet prevailed not:
they gave the rest leisure thereby to fly and save
themselves, so that there remained not behind above
a thousand men. For all the rest were fled with
their wives and children, into the city of Messené.
The most part of them also that fought with the
enemies, saved themselves, and very few were taken,
the chiefest whereof were Lysandridas, and Thearidas,
the noblest persons that were amongst the Megalopolitans: wherefore when the soldiers had taken
them, they brought them unto Cleomenes. Lysandridas, when he saw Cleomenes a good way off, cried
out aloud unto him: O King of Lacedaemon, this
day thou hast an occasion offered thee to do a more
famous princely act, than that which thou hast
already done, and that will make thy name also more
glorious. Cleomenes musing what he would request:
Well (quoth he) what is that thou requirest? One
thing I will tell thee beforehand, thou shalt not make
me restore your city to you again. Yet, quoth
Lysandridas, let me request thus much then, that
ye do not destroy it, but rather replenish it with
friends and confederates, which hereafter will be
true and faithful to you: and that shall you do,
giving the Megalopolitans their city again, and pre-
serving such a number of people as have forsaken it.
Cleomenes pausing a while, answered it was a hard
thing to believe that: but yet, quoth he, let honour
take place with us, before profit. After that he sent
a herald straight unto Messené unto them that were
fled thither, and told them that he was contented to
offer them their city again, so that they would become
good friends and confederates of the Lacedaemonians,
forsaking the alliance of the Achaeans. Philopoemen
would by no means suffer the Megalopolitans to
accept this gracious offer of Cleomenes, nor also to
leave their alliance with the Achaeans: telling them,
that he meant not to give them their city again, but

to take them also with their city: and therefore drave Thearidas and Lysandridas out of Messené, that moved this practice. It was that Philopoemen that afterwards was the chiefest man of the Achaeans, and that won such fame and honour among the Grecians, as we have particularly declared in his life.

This word being brought to Cleomenes, who had kept the city from spoiling until that time: he was then so thoroughly offended, that he gave the goods in prey to the soldiers, sent away their goodly tables, images, and pictures unto Sparta, and defaced the chiefest parts of the city, and then returned home again, being afraid of Antigonus, and the Achaeans. Howbeit they stirred not, because of the parliament that was kept at that time in the city of Aegium, where Aratus being in the pulpit for orations, and holding his gown a long time before his face, the people marvelling at it, willed him to tell what he ailed: he answered them, Megalopolis is taken, and razed by Cleomenes. The Achaeans being amazed at the suddenness of this great loss, straight broke off their parliament and assembly. But Antigonus thinking to aid them, sent presently for all his garrisons, who being long a-coming, he willed them to stay where they were, and he himself taking a few soldiers with him, went unto the city of Argos. Therefore the second enterprise of Cleomenes seemeth at the first sight a very rash and desperate attempt: howbeit Polybius writeth, that it was an attempt of great wisdom and policy. For Cleomenes understanding that the Macedonians were dispersed in garrisons in divers places, and that Antigonus lay all the winter in the city of Argos, with a certain number of footmen that were strangers: he invaded the country of the Argives with his army, persuading himself, that either Antigonus would for shame come and fight with him, or if he did not, that then he should put him in disgrace with the Argives: which indeed came so to pass. The Argives seeing their country spoiled by Cleomenes, were in a marvellous rage, and gathering together at Antigonus' lodging, they cried out unto him, either to go into the field and fight with the enemy: or else if he were afraid, to resign his office of General of Greece, unto others that were valianter than himself. But Antigonus like a wise and excellent captain, thinking it a dishonour to him rashly to put himself in danger, and his friends also, though he were provoked with many injuries and opprobrious words, would not go into the field, but stood constant in his first determination. Then Cleomenes having brought his army hard to the walls of the city of Argos, and spoiled and destroyed the country round about: without let or danger he safely returned home again.

Within a while after, Cleomenes being advertised that Antigonus was come unto Tegea, with intent to invade the country of Laconia: he going another way with his army (unwitting to his enemies), they wondered when they saw him in the morning by the city of Argos, spoiling their country, and cutting down their corn, not with sickles and knives as other do use, but with long poles in form of scythes, that the soldiers as they went sporting-wise, did overthrow and spoil it. But when they came to the place of exercises in the suburbs, called Cyllarabis, certain of the soldiers going about to have set it afire, Cleomenes would not suffer them, and told them, that what he had done at Megalopolis, it was rather angrily than honestly done. Now Antigonus, presently returning back again, being minded first to have gone directly to the city of Argos, but suddenly altering his mind, did camp upon the top of hills and mountains. Cleomenes seeming not to be afraid of him, sent heralds to him to desire the keys of the temple of Juno, and then after he had done sacrifice, he would depart his way. Thus mocking Antigonus, after he had sacrificed unto the goddess, under the temple that was shut up, he sent his army unto Phlius, and having driven away the garrison out of Oligyrtus, he came unto the city of Orchomenus, having not only encouraged his citizens, but gotten even amongst the enemies themselves, a fame also to be a noble captain, and worthy to manage great affairs. For every man judged him to be a skilful soldier, and a valiant captain, that with the power of one only city, did maintain war against the kingdom of Macedon, against all the people of Peloponnesus, and against the treasure of so great a king: and withal, not only to keep his own country of Laconia unfiled, but far otherwise to hurt his enemies' countries, and to take so many great cities of theirs.

But he that said first, that money was the sinew of all things, spake it chiefly in my opinion, in respect of the wars. Demades the Orator said on a time, when the Athenians commanded certain galleys should be put out of the arsenal into the sea, and presently rigged and armed with all possible speed, though they lacked money: He that rules the prow, must first see before him: meaning, munition and victuals must be provided, before the ships be set out. And it is reported also, that the ancient Archidamus, when the confederates of the Lacedaemonians at the beginning of the war at Peloponnesus required that they might be sessed at a certain rate, answered: The charges of war have no certain stint. For like as wrestlers that exercise their bodies continually in games, are better able to wrestle, and overthrow them, with time, that have no strength, but only art and sleight: even so King Antigonus, who by the greatness of his kingdom did defray the charge of this war, did weary and overcome Cleomenes at the length, because he lacked money both to pay the strangers that served him, and also to maintain his own citizens. For otherwise doubtless the time served his turn well, because the troubles, that fell upon Antigonus in his realm, did make him to be sent for home. For the barbarous people his neighbours, in his absence did spoil and destroy the realm of Macedon, and specially the Illyrians of the high country that came down then with a great army: whereupon the Macedonians

being spoiled and harried on all sides by them, they
sent post unto Antigonus, to pray him to come
home. If these letters had been brought him but a
little before the battle, as they came afterwards,
Antigonus had gone his way, and left the Achaeans.
But fortune, that always striketh the stroke in all
weightiest causes, gave such speed and favour unto
time, that immediately after the battle was fought at
Sellasia (where Cleomenes lost his army and city), the
very messengers arrived that came for Antigonus to
come home, the which made the overthrow of King
Cleomenes so much more lamentable. For if he had
delayed battle but two days longer, when the
Macedonians had been gone, he might have made
what peace he would with the Achaeans: but for lack
of money, he was driven (as Polybius writeth) to give
battle, with twenty thousand men, against thirty
thousand: where he shewed himself an excellent and
skilful captain, and where his citizens also fought like
valiant men, and the strangers in like case did shew
themselves good soldiers. But his only overthrow
was, by the manner of his enemies' weapons, and the
force of their battle of footmen.

But Phylarchus writeth, that treason was the
cause of his overthrow. For Antigonus had appointed
the Acarnanians, and the Illyrians which he had in
his army, to steal upon the wing of his enemies' army,
where Euclidas, King Cleomenes' brother was, to compass him in behind, whilst he did set the rest of his
men in battle. When Cleomenes was got up upon
some hill to look about him, to see the countenance
of the enemy, and seeing none of the Acarnanians,
nor of the Illyrians: he was then afraid of Antigonus,
that he went about some stratagem of war. Wherefore he called for Damoteles, whose charge was to
take heed of stratagems and secret ambushes, and
commanded him to look to the rearward of his army,
and to be very circumspect all about. Damoteles,
that was bribed before (as it is reported) with money,
told him that all was clear in the rearward, and bade

him look to overthrow his enemies before him.
Cleomenes trusting this report, set forward against
Antigonus, and in the end, his citizens of Sparta
which he had about him, gave such a fierce charge
upon the squadron of the Macedonian footmen, that
they drave them back five furlongs off. But in the
meantime, Euclidas his brother, in the other wing of
his army, being compassed in behind, Cleomenes
turning him back, and seeing the overthrow, cried out
aloud: Alas, good brother, thou art but slain, yet
thou diest valiantly, and honestly, and thy death
shall be a worthy example unto all posterity, and shall
be sung by the praises of the women of Sparta. So
Euclidas and his men being slain, the enemies came
straight to set upon Cleomenes' wing. Cleomenes
then seeing his men discouraged, and that they durst
no longer resist the enemy, fled, and saved himself.
Many of the strangers also that served him, were
slain at this battle: and of six thousand Spartans,
there were left alive but only two hundred.

Now Cleomenes being returned unto Sparta, the
citizens coming to see him, he gave them counsel to
yield themselves unto Antigonus the conqueror: and
for himself, if either alive or dead he could do anything for the honour and benefit of Sparta, that he
would willingly do it. The women of the city also,
coming unto them that flying had escaped with him,
when he saw them unarm the men, and bring them
drink to refresh them with: he also went home to his
own house. Then a maid of the house, which he had
taken in the city of Megalopolis (and whom he had
entertained ever since the death of his wife) came
unto him as her manner was, to refresh him coming
hot from the battle: howbeit he would not drink
though he was extreme dry, nor sit being very weary,
but armed as he was, laid his arm across upon a
pillar, and leaning his head upon it, reposed himself a
little, and casting in his mind all the ways that were
to be thought of, he took his friends with him, and
went to the haven of Gythium, and there having his

ships which he had appointed for the purpose, he
hoised sail, and departed his way. Immediately after
his departure, came Antigonus into the city of Sparta,
and courteously entreated the citizens and inhabitants
he found, and did offend no man, nor proudly despise
the ancient honour and dignity of Sparta : but
referring them to their own laws and government,
when he had sacrificed to the gods for his victory, he
departed from thence the third day, news being
brought him that the war was very great in Macedon,
and that the barbarous people did spoil his country.
Now a disease took him, whereof he died afterwards,
which appeared a tisick, mixed with a sore catarrh :
but yet he yielded not to his disease, and bare it out,
that fighting for his country, and obtaining a famous
victory, with great slaughter of the barbarous people,
he might yet die honourably, as indeed he did, by
Phylarchus' testimony, who saith, that with the
force of his voice, fiercely crying out in the midst of
his fight, he tare his lungs and lights, worse than they
were before.   Yet in the schools it is said, that after
he had won the battle, he was so joyful of it, that
crying out, O blessed day : he brake out into a great
bleeding at the mouth, and a great fever took him
withal, that he died of it.   Thus much touching
Antigonus.

Now Cleomenes departing out of the Isle of
Cythera, went and cast anchor in another island,
called Aegialia.   Then determining to sail over to the
city of Cyrené, Therycion, one of Cleomenes' friends
(a man that in wars shewed himself very valiant, but
a boaster besides of his own doings) took Cleomenes
aside, and said thus unto him : "Truly, O king, we
have lost an honourable occasion to die in battle,
though every man hath heard us vaunt and say, that
Antigonus should never overcome the King of Sparta
alive, but dead.   A second occasion yet is offered us
to die, with much less honour and fame notwithstanding, than the first.   Whither do we sail to no
purpose ?   Why do we fly the death at hand, and

seek it so far off? If it be no shame nor dishonour
for the posterity and race of Hercules to serve the
successors of Philip and Alexander: let us save then
our labour, and long dangerous sailing, and go yield
ourselves unto Antigonus, who in likelihood will
better use us than Ptolemy, because the Macedonians
are far more noble persons than the Egyptians. And
if we disdain to be commanded by them which have
overcome us in battle, why then will we make him
lord of us, that hath not overcome us: instead of one,
to make us inferior unto both, flying Antigonus, and
serving King Ptolemy? Can we say that we go into
Egypt, in respect to see your mother there? A joyful
sight no doubt, when she shall shew King Ptolemy's
wives her son, that before was a king, a prisoner, and
fugitive now. Were it not better for us, that having
yet Laconia our country in sight, and our swords besides in our own hands, to deliver us from this great
misery, and so doing to excuse ourselves unto them
that are slain at Sellasia, for defence of Sparta, than
cowardly losing our time in Egypt, to inquire whom
Antigonus left his lieutenant and governor in Lacedaemon?" Therycion ending his oration, Cleomenes
answered him thus: "Dost thou think it a glory for
thee to seek death, which is the easiest matter, and
the presentest unto any man, that can be: and yet,
wretch that thou art, thou fliest now more cowardly
and shamefully, than from the battle? For divers
valiant men, and far better than ourselves, have often
yielded unto their enemies, either by some misfortune,
or compelled by greater number and multitude of men:
but he, say I, that submitteth himself unto pain and
misery, reproach and praise of men, he cannot but
confess that he is overcome by his own unhappiness.
For, when a man will willingly kill himself, he must
not do it to be rid of pains and labour, but it must
have an honourable respect and action. For, to live
or die for his own respect, that cannot but be dishonourable: the which now thou persuadest me unto,
to make me fly this present misery we are in, without

any honour or profit in our death.   And therefore, I
am of opinion, that we should not yet cast off the
hope we have to serve our country in time to come:
but when all hope faileth us, then we may easily make
ourselves away when we list."   Thereunto Therycion
gave no answer, but as soon as he found opportunity
to slip from Cleomenes, he went to the seaside, and
slew himself.

Cleomenes hoising sail from the Isle of Aegialia,
went into Africk, and was brought by the king's
servants unto the city of Alexandria.   King Ptolemy
at his first coming, gave Cleomenes no special good,
but indifferent entertainment: but after that he had
shewed himself to be of great wisdom and judgment,
and that Ptolemy saw in the simplicity of his Laconian
life he had also a noble disposition and courage,
nothing degenerating from the princely race and blood
of Hercules, and that he yielded not to his adversity:
he took more delight in his company, than in all the
company of his flatterers and hangers on him: and
then repented him greatly, that he had made no more
account of him before, but had suffered him to be
overthrown by Antigonus, who through the victory of
him, had marvellously enlarged his honour and power.
Then he began to comfort Cleomenes, and doing him
as great honour as could be, promised that he would
send him with ships and money into Greece, and put
him again into his kingdom: and further, gave him
an annual pension in the meantime, of four-and-
twenty talents, with the which he simply and soberly
entertained himself and his men about him: and
bestowed all the rest upon his countrymen that came
out of Greece into Egypt.

But now, old King Ptolemy deceasing before he
could perform the promise he made unto Cleomenes, to send him into Greece: the realm falling
then into great lasciviousness, drunkenness, and into
the government of women, his case and misery was
clean forgotten.   For the young king his son was so
given over to women and wine, that when he was

most sober, and in his best wits, he most disposed himself to make feasts and sacrifices, and to have the tabor playing in his Court, to gather people together, like a stage-player or juggler, whilst one Agathoclea, his leman and her mother, and Oenanthes a bawd, did rule all the affairs of the state. But when he came to be king, it appeared he had need of Cleomenes: because he was afraid of his brother Magas, who by his mother's means, was very well esteemed of among soldiers. Wherefore he called Cleomenes to him, and made him of his privy-council, where he devised by practice, which way to kill his brother. All other his friends that were of counsel with him, did counsel him to do it: but Cleomenes only vehemently dissuaded him from it, and told him, that if it were possible, rather more brethren should be begotten unto the king for the safety of his person, and for dividing of the affairs of the kingdom between them. Amongst the king's familiars that was chiefest about him, there was one Sosibius that said unto Cleomenes: so long as his brother Magas lived, the soldiers that be strangers, whom the king entertained, would never be true to him. Cleomenes answered him, For that matter there was no danger: for saith he, of those hired strangers, there are three thousand Peloponnesians, which he knew at the twinkling of an eye, would be at his commandment, to come with their armour and weapon where he would appoint them. These words of Cleomenes at that time shewed his faith and good-will he bare unto the king, and the force he was of besides. But afterwards, Ptolemy's fearfulness increasing his mistrust: (as it commonly happeneth, that they that lack wit, think it the best safety to be fearful of every wagging of a straw, and to mistrust every man) the remembrance of Cleomenes' words made him much suspected of the courtiers, understanding that he could do so much with the soldiers that were strangers: insomuch as some of them said: See (meaning Cleomenes), there is a lion amongst sheep. Indeed, considering his

fashions and behaviour, they might well say so of
him : for he would look through his fingers as though
he saw nothing, and yet saw all what they did.

In fine, he required an army and ships of the king :
and understanding also that Antigonus was dead,
and that the Achaeans and Aetolians were at great
wars together, and that the affairs of his country did
call him home, all Peloponnesus being in arms and
uproar, he prayed that they would license him to
depart with his friends. But never a man would
give ear unto him, and the king also heard nothing of
it, because he was continually entertained among ladies,
with banquets, dancing, and masques. But Sosibius
that ruled all the realm, thought that to keep Cleomenes against his will, were a hard thing, and also
dangerous : and to let him go also, knowing that he
was a valiant man, and of a stirring mind, and one
that knew the vices and imperfections of their government : he thought that also no safe way, sith no gifts
nor presents that could be offered him, could soften
him. For as the holy bull (which they call in Egypt
Apis), that is full fed in goodly pasture, doth yet
desire to follow his natural course and liberty, to run
and leap at his pleasure, and plainly sheweth that it
is a grief to him to be kept still by the priest : even
so the courtly pleasures did nothing delight Cleomenes,
but as Homer writeth of Achilles :

> It irked his noble heart to sit at home in slothful rest,
> When martial matters were in hand, the which he liked best.

Now Cleomenes standing in these terms, there
arrived in Alexandria one Nicagoras Messenian, who
maliced Cleomenes in his heart, but yet shewed as
though he loved him. This Nicagoras on a time had
sold Cleomenes certain land, but was not paid for it,
either because he had no present money, or else by
occasion of the wars which gave him no leisure to
make payment. Cleomenes one day by chance walking upon the sands, he saw Nicagoras landing out of
his ship, being newly arrived, and knowing him, he

courteously welcomed him, and asked what wind had
brought him into Egypt. Nicagoras, gently saluting
him again, told him that he had brought the king
excellent horse of service. Cleomenes smiling, told
him, Thou hadst been better have brought him some
courtesans and dancers, for they would have pleased
the king better. Nicagoras faintly laughed at his
answer, but within few days after he did put him in
remembrance of the land he sold him, and prayed
him then that he would help him to money, telling
him that he would not have pressed him for it,
but that he had sustained loss by merchandise.
Cleomenes answered him, that all his pension was
spent he had of the king. Nicagoras being offended
with this answer, he went and told Sosibius of the
mock Cleomenes gave the king. Sosibius was glad
of this occasion, but yet desiring further matter to
make the king offended with Cleomenes, he persuaded
Nicagoras to write a letter to the king against
Cleomenes, as though he had conspired to take the
city of Cyrené, if the king had given him ships,
money, and men of war.

When Nicagoras had written this letter, he took
ship, and hoised sail. Four days after his departure,
Sosibius brought his letter to the king, as though he
had but newly received it. The king upon sight of it
was so offended with Cleomenes, that he gave present
order he should be shut up in a great house, where
he should have his ordinary diet allowed him,
howbeit that he should keep his house. This grieved
Cleomenes much, but yet he was worse afraid of that
which was to come, by this occasion: Ptolemy the
son of Chrysermus, one of the king's familiars, who
had oftentimes before been very conversant and
familiar with Cleomenes, and did frankly talk together
in all matters: Cleomenes one day sent for him, to
pray him to come unto him. Ptolemy came at his
request, and familiarly discoursing together, went
about to dissuade him from all the suspicions he had,
and excused the king also for that he had done unto

him: so taking his leave he left him, not thinking that
Cleomenes followed him (as he did) to the gate, where
he sharply took up the soldiers, saying, that they
were very negligent and careless in looking to such a
fearful beast as he was, and so ill to be taken, if he
once escaped their hands. Cleomenes heard what
he said, and went into his lodging again, Ptolemy
knowing nothing that he was behind him: and
reported the very words again unto his friends. Then
all the Spartans converting their good hope into
anger, determined to be revenged of the injury Ptolemy
had done them, and to die like noble Spartans, not
tarrying till they should be brought to the shambles
like fat wethers to be sold and killed. For it would
be a great shame and dishonour unto Cleomenes,
having refused to make peace with Antigonus, a noble
prince and warrior, to tarry the king's pleasure till
he had left his drunkenness and dancing, and then to
come and put him to death.

They being fully resolved hereof, as you have heard:
King Ptolemy by chance went unto the city of
Canobus, and first they gave out in Alexandria, that
the king minded to set Cleomenes at liberty. Then
Cleomenes' friends observing the custom of the kings
of Egypt, when they meant to set a prisoner at
liberty (which was, to send the prisoners' meat, and
presents before to their supper) did send unto him
such manner of presents, and so deceived the soldiers
that had the keeping of him, saying, that they brought
those presents from the king. For Cleomenes himself
did sacrifice unto the gods, and sent unto the soldiers
that kept him, part of those presents that were sent
unto him, and supping with his friends that night,
made merry with them, every man being crowned
with garlands. Some say, that he made the more
haste to execute his enterprise, sooner than he would
have done, by means of one of his men that was privy
unto his conspiracy: who went every night to visit a
woman, his concubine, and therefore was afraid lest
he would bewray them. Cleomenes about noon, per-

ceiving the soldiers had taken in their cups, and that
they were asleep: he put on his coat, and unripping
it on the right shoulder, went out of the house with
his sword drawn in his hand, accompanied with his
friends, following him in that sort, which were thirty
in all. Amongst them there was one called Hippotas,
who being lame, went very lively out with them at the
first: but when he saw they went fair and softly
because of him, he prayed them to kill him, because
they should not hinder their enterprise for a lame
man, that could do them no service. Notwithstanding,
by chance they met with a townsman a-horseback,
that came hard by their door, whom a-they plucked
from his horse, and cast Hippotas upon him: and
then ran through the city, and cried to the people,
Liberty! Liberty!

Now the people had no other courage in them, but
only commended Cleomenes, and wondered at his
valiantness: but otherwise to follow him, or to further
his enterprise, not a man of them had any heart in
them. Thus running up and down the town, they
met with Ptolemy (the same whom we said before
was the son of Chrysermus) as he came out of the
court: whereupon three of them setting on him slew
him presently. There was also another Ptolemy that
was governor and lieutenant of the city of Alexandria:
who hearing a rumour of this stir, came unto them in
his coach. They went and met him, and first having
driven away his guard and soldiers that went before
him, they plucked him out of his coach, and slew him
also. After that they went towards the castle, with
intent to set all the prisoners there at liberty to take
their part. Howbeit the jailers that kept them had
so strongly locked up the prison doors, that Cleomenes
was repulsed, and put by his purpose. Thus wandering up and down the city, no man neither came to
join with him, nor to resist him, for every man fled
for fear of him. Wherefore at length being weary
with going up and down, he turned him to his friends,
and said unto them: It is no marvel though women

command such a cowardly people, that fly in this sort from their liberty. Thereupon he prayed them all to die like men, and like those that were brought up with him, and that were worthy of the fame of his so noble deeds. Then the first man that made himself be slain, was Hippotas, who died of a wound one of the young men of his company gave him with a sword at his request. After him every man slew themselves, one after another, without any fear at all, saving Panteus, who was the first man that entered the city of Megalopolis. He was a fair young man, and had been very well brought up in the Laconian discipline, and· better than any man of his years. Cleomenes did love him dearly, and commanded him that when he should see he were dead, and all the rest also, that then he should kill himself last of all. Now they all being laid on the ground, he searched them one after another with the point of his sword, to see if there were any of them yet left alive : and when he had pricked Cleomenes on the heel amongst others, and saw that he did yet knit his brows, he kissed him, and sat down by· him. Then perceiving that he had yielded up the ghost, embracing him when he was dead, he also slew himself, and fell upon him.

Thus Cleomenes having reigned king of Sparta sixteen years, being the same manner of man we have described him to be : he ended his days in this sort as ye hear. Now, his death being presently bruited through the city, Cratesiclea his mother, though otherwise she had a noble mind, did notwithstanding a little forget her greatness, through the extreme sorrow she felt for the death of her son : and so embracing Cleomenes' sons, she fell to bitter lamentation. But the eldest of his sons (no man mistrusting any such matter) found means to get out of her hands, and running up to the top of the house, cast himself headlong down to the ground, that his head was all broken and splitted, yet died not, but was taken up crying, and angry with them, that they would not suffer him to die. This news being brought to King Ptolemy, he commanded they should first flay Cleomenes, and then hang up his body, and also, that they should put his children, his mother, and all her women waiting on her to death: among the which was Panteus' wife, one of the fairest and courteousest women in her time. They had not been long married before, when these mischiefs lighted upon them, at what time their love was then in greatest force. Her parents then would not let her depart, and embark with her husband, but had locked her up, and kept her at home by force. Howbeit shortly after she found the means to get her a horse, and some money, and stole away in the night, and galloped towards the haven of Taenarum, where finding a ship ready bound for Egypt, she embarked, and went to seek her husband, with whom she gladly and lovingly led her life, forsaking her own country, to live in a strange realm. Now when the sergeants came to take Cratesiclea to put her to death, Panteus' wife led her by the arm, carrying up her train, and did comfort her, although Cratesiclea otherwise was not afraid to die, but only asked this favour, that she might die before her little children. This notwithstanding, when they came to the place of execution, the hangman first slew her children before her eyes, and then herself afterwards, who in such great grief and sorrow, said no more but thus: Alas, my poor children, what is become of you? And Panteus' wife also, being a mighty tall woman, girding her clothes to her, took up the slain bodies one after another, and wrapped them up in such things as she could get, speaking never a word, nor shewing any sign or token of grief. And in fine, having prepared herself to die, and plucked off her attire herself, without suffering any other to come near her, or to see her, but the hangman that was appointed to strike off her head: in this sort she died as constantly as the stoutest man living could have done, and had so covered her body, that no man needed after her death to touch her: so careful was she to her end, to keep her honesty, which she had always kept in her life, and in her death was mindful of her honour, wherewith she decked her body in her lifetime.

Thus these Lacedaemonian ladies playing their parts in this pitiful tragedy, contending at the time of death, even with the courage of the slain Spartans their countrymen, which of them should die most constantly: left a manifest proof and testimony, that fortune hath no power over fortitude and courage. Shortly after, those that were appointed to keep the body of King Cleomenes that hung upon the cross, they spied a great serpent wreathed about his head, that covered all his face, insomuch as no ravening fowl durst come near him to eat of it: whereupon the king fell into a superstitious fear, being afraid that he had offended the gods. Hereupon, the ladies in his court began to make many sacrifices of purification, for the clearing of this sin: persuading themselves, that they had put a man to death, beloved of the gods, and that he had something more in him than a man. The Alexandrians thereupon went to the place of execution, and made their prayers unto Cleomenes, as unto a demigod, calling him the son of the gods: until that the learned men brought them from that error, declaring unto them, that like as of oxen being dead and rotten, there breed bees, and of horse also come wasps, and of asses likewise beetles: even so men's bodies, when the marrow melteth and gathereth together, do bring forth serpents. The which coming to the knowledge of the ancients in old time, of all other beasts they did consecrate the dragon to kings and princes, as proper unto man.

THE LIVES OF TIBERIUS AND CAIUS GRACCHI

Now that we have declared unto you the history of the lives of these two Grecians, Agis and Cleomenes aforesaid: we must also write the history of two Romans, the which is no less lamentable for the troubles and calamities that chanced unto Tiberius and Caius, both of them the sons of Tiberius Gracchus. He having been twice Consul, and once Censor, and having had the honour of two triumphs, had notwithstanding more honour and fame only for his valiantness, for the which he was thought worthy to marry with Cornelia, the daughter of Scipio, who overcame Hannibal after the death of his father: though while he lived he was never his friend, but rather his enemy. It is reported, that Tiberius on a time found two snakes in his bed, and that the sooth-sayers and wizards having considered the signification thereof, did forbid him to kill them both, and also to let them both escape, but one only: assuring him that if he killed the male, he should not live long after: and if he killed the female, that then his wife Cornelia should die. Tiberius then loving his wife dearly, thinking it meeter for him also, that he being the elder of both, and she yet a young woman, should die before her: he slew the male, and let the female escape. Howbeit he died soon after, leaving twelve children alive, all of them begotten of Cornelia. Cornelia after the death of her husband, taking upon her the rule of her house and children, led such a chaste life, was so good to her children, and of so noble a mind that every man thought Tiberius a wise man for that he died, and left her behind him. She remaining widow, King Ptolemy made suit unto her, and would have made her his wife and queen. But she refused, and in her widowhood lost all her children, but one daughter (whom she bestowed upon the younger Scipio African) and Tiberius, and Caius, whose lives we presently write. Those she so carefully brought up, that they being become more civil, and better conditioned, than any other Romans in their time: every man judged, that education prevailed more in them, than nature. For, as in the favours and pictures of Castor and Pollux, there is a certain difference discerned, whereby a man may know that the one was made for wrestling, and the other for running: even so between these two young brethren, amongst other the great likeness between them, being both happily born to be valiant, to be temperate, to be liberal, to be learned, and to be nobly minded, there grew notwithstanding great difference in their actions and doings in the commonwealth: the which I think convenient to declare, before I proceed any farther.

First of all, for the favour of the face, the look and moving of the body, Tiberius was much more mild and tractable, and Caius more hot and earnest. For the first in his orations was very modest, and kept his place: and the other of all the Romans was the first that in his oration jetted up and down the pulpit, and that plucked his gown over his shoulders: as they write of Cleon Athenian, that he was the first of all orators that opened his gown, and clapped his hand on his thigh in his oration. Furthermore, Caius' words, and the vehemence of his persuasion, were terrible and full of passion, but Tiberius' words in contrary manner, were mild, moved men more to compassion, being very proper, and excellently applied, where Caius' words were full of fineness and curiosity. The like difference also was between them in their fare and diet. For Tiberius always kept a convenient ordinary: and Caius also in respect of other Romans, lived very temperately, but in respect of his brother's fare, curiously and superfluously : insomuch as Drusus on a time reproved him, because he had bought certain dolphins of silver, to the value of a thousand two hundred and fifty drachmas for every pound weight. And now, as touching the manners and natural disposition of them both agreeing with the diversity of their tongues, the one being mild and plausible, and the other hot and choleric : insomuch that otherwhile forgetting himself in his oration, against his will he would be very earnest, and strain his voice beyond his compass, and so with great uncomeliness confound his words. Yet finding his own fault, he devised this remedy. He had a servant called Licinius, a good wise man, who with an instrument of music he had, by the which they teach men to rise and fall in their tunes, when he was in his oration, he ever stood behind him : and when he perceived that his master's voice was a little too loud, and that through choler he exceeded his ordinary speech : he played a soft stop behind him, at the sound whereof Caius immediately fell from his extremity, and easily came to himself again.

And here was the diversity between them. Otherwise, for their hardiness against their enemies, the justice unto their tenants, the care and pains in their offices of charge, and also their continency against voluptuousness : in all these they were both alike. For age, Tiberius was elder by nine years, by reason whereof their several authority and doings in the commonwealth fell out at sundry times. And this was one of the chiefest causes why their doings prospered not, because they had not both authority in one self time, neither could they join their power together : the which if it had met at one self time, had been of great force, and peradventure invincible. Wherefore we must write particularly of them both, but first of all we must begin with the elder.

He, when he came to man's estate, had such a name and estimation, that immediately they made

him fellow, in the college of the priests, which at
Rome are called Augurs: (being those that have the
charge to consider of signs and predictions of things
to come) more for his valiantness, than for nobility.
The same doth Appius Claudius witness unto us, one
that hath been both Consul and Censor, and also
President of the Senate, and of greater authority
than any man in his time.   This Appius at a supper
when all·the Augurs were together, after he had
saluted Tiberius, and made very much of him, he
offered him his daughter in marriage. Tiberius was
very glad of the offer, and therewithal the marriage
was presently concluded between them.   Thereupon
Appius coming home to ·his house, at the threshold
of his door he called aloud for his wife, and told her:
Antistia, I have bestowed our daughter Claudia. She
wondering at it, O gods, said she, and what needed
all this haste? what couldst thou have done more,
if thou hadst got her Tiberius Gracchus for her
husband?   I know that some refer this history unto
Tiberius, father of these two men we write of, and
unto Scipio the African: but the most part of writers
agree with that we write at this present.   And
Polybius himself also writeth, that after the death
of Scipio African, his friends being met together,
they chose Tiberius before all the other young men
of the city, to marry him unto Cornelia, being free,
and unpromised, or bestowed upon any man by her
father.   Now Tiberius the younger being in the wars
in Africk under Scipio the second, who had married
his sister: lying in his tent with him, he found his
captain endued with many noble gifts of nature, to
allure men's hearts to desire to follow his valiantness:
So in a short time he did excel all the young men
of his time, as well in obedience as in the valiantness
of his person: insomuch that he was the first man
that scaled the walls of the enemies, as Fannius
reporteth, who saith that he scaled the walls with
him, and did help him in that valiant enterprise.   So
that being present, all the camp were in love with

him: and when he was absent, every man wished
for him again.

After this war was ended, he was chosen Treasurer,
and it was his chance to go against the Numantines,
with Caius Mancinus one of the Consuls, who was
an honest man, but yet had the worst luck of any
captain the Romans had. Notwithstanding, Tiberius'
wisdom and valiantness, in this extreme ill-luck of
his captain, did not only appear with great glory to
him, but also most wonderful the great obedience
and reverence he bare unto his captain; though his
misfortunes did so trouble and grieve him, that he
could not tell himself, whether he was captain or not.
For when he was overthrown in great foughten fields,
he departed in the night, and left his camp. The
Numantines hearing of it, first took his camp, and
then ran after them that fled, and setting upon the
rearward, slew them, and environed all his army, so
that they were driven into straight and narrow places,
where out they could by no means escape. Thereupon Mancinus despairing that he could get out by
force, he sent a herald to the enemies to treat of
peace. The Numantines made answer, that they
would trust no man but Tiberius only, and therefore
they willed he should be sent unto them. They
desired that, partly for the love they bare unto the
virtues of the young man, because there was no talk
of any other in all this war but of him: and partly
also, as remembering his father Tiberius, who making
wars in Spain, and having there subdued many
nations, he granted the Numantines peace, the which
he caused the Romans afterwards to confirm and
ratify. Hereupon Tiberius was sent to speak with
them, and partly obtaining that he desired, and partly
also granting them that they required: he concluded
peace with them, whereby assuredly he saved the
lives of twenty thousand Roman Citizens, besides
slaves and other stragglers that willingly followed
the camp.

This notwithstanding, the Numantines took the spoil

of all the goods they found in the Romans' camp,
among the which they found Tiberius' books of account
touching the money disbursed of the treasure in his
charge. Tiberius being marvellous desirous to have
his books again, returned back to Numantia with two
or three of his friends only; though the army of the
Romans were gone far on their way. So coming to
the town, he spoke unto the governors of the city,
and prayed them to redeliver him his books of
account, because his malicious enemies should not
accuse him, calling him to account for his doings.
The Numantines were very glad of this good hap, and
prayed them to come into the town. He standing
still in doubt with himself what to do, whether he
should go into the town or not: the governors of
the city came to him, and taking him by the hand,
prayed he would think they were not his enemies,
but good friends, and that he would trust them.
Whereupon Tiberius thought best to yield to their
persuasion, being desirous also to have his books
again, and the rather, for fear of offending the
Numantines, if he should have denied and mistrusted
them. When he was brought into the city, they provided his dinner, and were very earnest with him,
entreating him to dine with them. Then they gave
him his books again, and offered him moreover to
take what he would of all the spoils they had got in
the camp of the Romans. Howbeit of all that he
would take nothing but frankincense, which he used,
when he did any sacrifice for his country: and then
taking his leave of them, with thanks he returned.

When he was returned to Rome, all this peace
concluded was utterly misliked, as dishonourable to
the majesty of the empire of Rome. Yet the
parents and friends of them that had served in this
war, making the greatest part of the people: they
gathered about Tiberius, saying that what faults were
committed in this service, they were to impute it unto
the Consul Mancinus, and not unto Tiberius, who
had saved such a number of Romans' lives. Notwith-

standing, they that were offended with this dishonourable peace, would that therein they should follow the
example of their forefathers in the like case. For
they sent back their captains naked unto their
enemies, because they were contented the Samnites
should spoil them of that they had, to escape with
life. Moreover, they did not only send them the
captains and Consuls, but all those also that bare
any office in the field, and had consented unto that
condition : to the end they might lay all the perjury
and breach of peace upon them. Herein therefore
did manifestly appear the love and good-will the
people did bear unto Tiberius. For they gave order,
that the Consul Mancinus should be sent naked and
bound unto the Numantines, and for Tiberius' sake
they pardoned all the rest. I think Scipio, who bare
great sway at that time in Rome, and was a man of
greatest account, did help him at that pinch : who
notwithstanding was ill thought of, because he did
not also save the Consul Mancinus, and confirm the
peace concluded with the Numantines, considering it
was made by Tiberius his friend and kinsman. But
these mislikings grew chiefly through the ambition of
Tiberius' friends, and certain learned men, which
stirred him up against Scipio. But yet it fell not
out to open malice between them, neither followed
there any hurt upon it. And surely I am persuaded,
that Tiberius had not fallen into those troubles he
did afterwards, if Scipio African had been present,
when he passed those things he preferred. But
Scipio was then in wars at the siege of Numantia,
when Tiberius upon this occasion passed these laws.

When the Romans in old time had overcome any
of their neighbours, for ransom they took oftentimes
a great deal of their land from them, part whereof
they sold by the crier, for the benefit of the commonwealth, and part also they reserved to their state as
domain, which afterwards was let out to farm for a
small rent yearly, to the poor citizens that had no
lands. Howbeit the rich men enhanced the rents,

and so began to thrust out the poor men. Thereupon was an ordinance made, that no citizen of Rome should have above five hundred acres of land. This law for a time did bridle the covetousness of the rich men, and did ease the poor also that dwelt in the country, upon the farms they had taken up of the commonwealth, and so lived with their own, or with that their ancestors had from the beginning. But by process of time, their rich neighbours, by names of other men, got their farms over their heads, and in the end, the most of them were openly seen in it in their own names. Whereupon, the poor people, being thus turned out of all, went but with faint courage afterwards to the war, nor cared any more for bringing up of children: so that in short time, the freemen left Italy, and slaves and barbarous people did replenish it, whom the rich men made to plough those lands, which they had taken from the Romans. Caius Laelius, one of Scipio's friends, gave an attempt to reform this abuse: but because the chiefest of the city were against him, fearing it would break out to some uproar, he desisted from his purpose, and therefore he was called Laelius the Wise. But Tiberius being chosen Tribune, he did forthwith prefer the reformation aforesaid, being allured unto it (as divers writers report) by Diophanes the Orator, and Blossius the Philosopher: of the which, Diophanes was banished from the city of Mytilene, and Blossius the Italian from the city of Cumae, who was scholar and familiar unto Antipater of Tarsus at Rome, by whom he was honoured by certain works of philosophy he dedicated unto him. And some also do accuse their mother Cornelia, who did twit her sons in the teeth, that the Romans did yet call her Scipio's mother-in-law, and not the mother of the Gracchi. Other say it was Spurius Postumius, a companion of Tiberius, and one that contended with him in eloquence. For Tiberius returning from the wars, and finding him far beyond him in fame and reputation, and well beloved of

every one: he sought to excel him by attempting this
noble enterprise, and of so great expectation.   His
own brother Caius in a certain book wrote, that as
he went to the wars of Numantia, passing through
Tuscany, he found the country in manner uninhabited:
and they that did follow the plough, or keep beasts,
were the most of them slaves, and barbarous people,
come out of a strange country.   Whereupon ever
after it ran in his mind to bring this enterprise to
pass, which brought great troubles to their house.
But in fine, it was the people only that most set his
heart on fire to covet honour, and that hastened his
determination: first bringing him to it by bills set up
on every wall, in every porch, and upon the tombs,
praying him by them to cause the poor citizens of
Rome to have their lands restored, which were
belonging to the commonwealth.

This notwithstanding, he himself made not the
law alone of his own head, but did it by the counsel
and advice of the chiefest men of Rome, for virtue
and estimation: among the which, Crassus the
High-bishop was one, and Mucius Scaevola the
lawyer, that then was Consul, and Appius Claudius
his father-in-law.   And truly it seemeth, that never
law was made with greater favour, than that which
he preferred against so great injustice, and avarice.
For those that should have been punished for
transgressing the law, and should have had the lands
taken from them by force, which they unjustly kept
against the law of Rome, and that should also have
been amerced for it: he ordained that they should
be paid by the commonwealth to the value of the
lands, which they held unjustly, and so should
leave them to the poor citizens again that had no
land, and lacked help and relief.   Now, though the
reformation established by this law, was done with
such great favour: the people notwithstanding were
contented, and would forget all that was past, so that
they might have no more wrong offered them in time
to come.   But the rich men, and men of great

possessions, hated the law for their avarice, and for spite and self-will (which would not let them yield) they were at deadly feud with the lawyer that had preferred the law, and sought by all device they could to dissuade the people from it: telling them that Tiberius brought in this law Agraria again, to disturb the commonwealth, and to make some alteration in the state. But they prevailed not. For Tiberius defending the matter, which of itself was good and just, with such eloquence as might have justified an evil cause, was invincible: and no man was able to argue against him to confute him, when speaking in the behalf of the poor citizens of Rome (the people being gathered round about the pulpit for orations), he told them, that the wild beasts through Italy had their dens and caves of abode, and that the men that fought and were slain for their country, had nothing else but air and light, and so were compelled to wander up and down with their wives and children, having no resting-place nor house to put their heads in: and that the captains do but mock their soldiers, when they encourage them in battle to fight valiantly for the graves, the temples, their own houses, and their predecessors. For, said he, of such a number of poor citizens as there be, there cannot a man of them shew any ancient house or tomb of their ancestors: because the poor men do go to the wars, and be slain for the rich men's pleasures and wealth: besides, they falsely call them lords of the earth, where they have not a handful of ground, that is theirs.

These and such other like words being uttered before all the people with such vehemency and troth, did so move the common people withal, and put them in such a rage, that there was no adversary of his able to withstand him. Therefore, leaving to contrary and deny the law by argument, the rich men did put all their trust in Marcus Octavius, colleague and fellow Tribune with Tiberius in office, who was a grave and wise young man, and Tiberius' very familiar friend.

So that the first time they came to him, to oppose him against the confirmation of this law, he prayed them to hold him excused, because Tiberius was his very friend. But in the end, being compelled unto it through the great number of the rich men that were importunate with him, he did withstand Tiberius' law, the which was enough to overthrow it. For if any one of the Tribunes speak against it, though all the other pass with it, he overthroweth it : because they all can do nothing, if one of them be against it. Tiberius being very much offended with it, proceeded no further in this first favourable law, and in a rage preferred another more grateful to the common people, as also more extreme against the rich. In that law he ordained, that whosoever had any lands contrary to the ancient laws of Rome, that he should presently depart from them. But thereupon there fell out continual brawls in the pulpit for orations, against Octavius : in the which, though they were very earnest and vehement one against another, yet there passed no foul words from them (how hot soever they were one with another), that should shame his companion. Whereby it appeareth, that to be well brought up, breedeth such a stay and knowledge in a man, not only in things of pleasure to make him regard his credit, both in word and deed : but in passion and anger also, and in their greatest ambition of glory. Thereupon Tiberius finding that this law among others touched Octavius, because he enjoyed a great deal of land that was the commonwealth's : he prayed him secretly to contend no more against him, promising him to give him of his own, the value of those lands which he should be driven to forsake, although he was not very able to perform it. But when he saw Octavius would not be persuaded, he then preferred a law, that all magistrates and officers should cease their authority, till the law were either passed, or rejected, by voices of the people : and thereupon he set his own seal upon the doors of the temple of Saturn, where the coffers of the treasure lay, because the Treasurers

themselves, during that time, should neither take out
nor put in anything, upon great penalties to be for-
feited by the Praetors or any other magistrate of
authority, that should break this order. Hereupon,
all the magistrates fearing this penalty, did leave to
exercise their office for the time. But then the rich
men that were of great livings, changed their apparel,
and walked very sadly up and down the market-place,
and laid secret wait to take Tiberius, having hired
men to kill him: which caused Tiberius himself,
openly before them all, to wear a short dagger under
his long gown, properly called in Latin, *dolon*.

When the day came that this law should be
established, Tiberius called the people to give their
voices: and the rich men on the other side, they took
away the pots by force, wherein the papers of men's
voices were thrown, so that there was like to fall out
great stir upon it. For the faction of Tiberius was
the stronger side, by the number of people that were
gathered about him for that purpose: had it not been
for Manlius and Fulvius, both the which had been
Consuls, who went unto him, and besought him with
the tears in their eyes, and holding up their hands,
that he would let the law alone. Tiberius thereupon,
foreseeing the instant danger of some great mischief,
as also for the reverence he bare unto two such noble
persons, he stayed a little, and asked them what they
would have him to do. They made answer, that
they were not able to counsel him in a matter of so
great weight, but they prayed him notwithstanding,
he would be contented to refer it to the judgment of
the Senate. Thereupon he granted them presently.
But afterwards perceiving that the Senate sat upon it,
and had determined nothing, because the rich men
were of too great authority: he entered into another
device that was neither honest nor meet, which was,
to deprive Octavius of his Tribuneship, knowing that
otherwise he could not possibly come to pass the law
But before he took that course, he openly entreated
him in the face of the people with courteous words,

and took him by the hand, and prayed him to stand
no more against him, and to do the people this
pleasure, which required a matter just and reasonable,
and only requested this small recompense for the
great pains they took·in service abroad for their
country. Octavius denied him plainly. Then said
Tiberius openly, that both of them being brethren in
one self place and authority, and contrary one to
another in a matter of so great weight, this contention
could not be possibly ended, without civil war : and
that he could see no way to remedy it, unless one of
them two were deposed from their office.   Thereupon
he bade Octavius begin first with him, and he would
rise from the bench with a good-will, and become a
private man, if the people were so contented. Octavius
would do nothing in it. Tiberius then replied, that
he would be doing with him, if he altered not his mind,
upon a better breath and consideration : and so dismissed the assembly for that day.

The next morning the people being again assembled,
Tiberius going up to his seat, attempted again to
persuade Octavius to leave off. In fine, finding him
still a man unremovable, he referred the matter to
the voice of the people, whether they were contented
Octavius should be deposed from his office.   Now
there were five-and-thirty tribes of the people, of the
which seventeen of them had already passed their
voices against Octavius, so that there remained but
one tribe more to put him out of his office. Then
Tiberius made them stay for proceeding any further,
and prayed Octavius again, embracing him before all
the people, with all the entreaty possible : that for
self-will sake he would not suffer such an open shame
to be done unto him, as to be put out of his office :
neither also to make him the occasion and instrument
of so pitiful a deed. They say that Octavius at this
last entreaty was somewhat moved and won by his
persuasions, and that weeping, he stayed a long time,
and made no answer. But when he looked upon the
rich men that stood in a great company together, he

was ashamed (I think) to have their ill-wills, and rather betook himself to the loss of his office, and so bade Tiberius do what he would. Thereupon he being deprived by voices of the people, Tiberius commanded one of his enfranchised bondmen to pull him out of the pulpit for orations: for he used his enfranchised bondmen instead of sergeants. This made the sight so much more lamentable, to see Octavius thus shamefully plucked away by force. Yea furthermore, the common people would have run upon him, but the rich men came to rescue him, and would not suffer him to do him further hurt. So Octavius saved himself running away alone, after he had been rescued thus from the fury of the people. Moreover, there was a faithful servant of Octavius, who stepping before his master to save him from hurt, had his eyes pulled out, against Tiberius' mind, who ran to the rescue with all speed when he heard the noise.

After that, the law Agraria passed for division of lands, and three commissioners were appointed to make inquiry and distribution thereof. The commissioners appointed were these: Tiberius himself, Appius Claudius his father-in-law, and Caius Gracchus his brother: who was not at that time in Rome, but in the camp with Scipio African, at the siege of the city of Numantia. Thus Tiberius very quietly passed over these matters, and no man durst withstand him: and furthermore, he substituted in Octavius' place no man of quality, but only one of his followers, called Mucius. Wherewith the noblemen were so sore offended with him, that fearing the increase of his greatness, they being in the Senate-house did what they could possible to do him despite and shame. For when Tiberius demanded a tent at the charge of the commonwealth, when he should go abroad to make division of these lands, as they usually granted unto others, that many times went in far meaner commissions: they flatly denied him, and through the procurement of P. Nasica (who being a great landed man in his country, shewed himself in this action his mortal enemy, taking it grievously to be compelled to depart from his land) only granted him nine of their oboli a day, for his ordinary allowance. But the people on the other side were all in an uproar against the rich : insomuch as one of Tiberius' friends being dead upon the sudden, upon whose body being dead there appeared very ill signs, the common people ran suddenly to his burial, and cried out that he was poisoned. And so taking up the bier, whereon his body lay, upon their shoulders, they were present at the fire of his funerals, where immediately appeared certain signs to make them suspect, that indeed there was vehement cause of presumption he was poisoned. For his belly burst, whereout there issued such abundance of corrupt humours, that they put out the first fire, and made them fetch another, the which also they could not make to burn, until that they were compelled to carry the body into some other place, where notwithstanding they had much ado to make it burn. Tiberius seeing that, to make the common people mutiny the more, he put on mourning apparel, and brought his sons before them, and besought the people to be good unto them and their mother, as one that despaired of his health and safety.

About that time died Attalus, surnamed Philopater, and Eudemus Pergamenian brought his will to Rome, in the which he made the people of Rome his heirs. Wherefore Tiberius, still to increase the good-will of the common people towards him, preferred a law immediately, that the ready-money that came by the inheritance of this king should be distributed among the poor citizens, on whose lot it should fall to have any part of the division of the lands of the commonwealth, to furnish them towards house, and to set up their tillage. Furthermore, he said, that concerning the towns and cities of the kingdom of Attalus, the Senate had nothing to do to take any order with them, but that the people were to dispose of them,

and that he himself would put it out.   That made him
again more hated of the Senate than before, insomuch
as there was one Pompey a Senator, that standing
up, said, that he was next neighbour unto Tiberius,
and that by reason of his neighbourhood he knew that
Eudemus Pergamenian had given him one of King
Attalus' royal bands, with a purple gown besides, for
a token that he should one day be king of Rome.
And Quintus Metellus also reproved him, for that his
father being Censor, the Romans having supped in
the town, and repairing every man home to his house,
they did put out their torches and lights, because men
seeing them return, they should not think they tarried
too long in company banqueting: and that in contrary
manner, the seditious and needy rabble of the common
people did light his son home, and accompany him all
night long up and down the town.

At that time there was one Titus Annius, a man
that had no goodness nor honesty in him, howbeit
taken for a great reasoner, and for a subtle questioner
and answerer. He provoked Tiberius to answer him,
whether he had not committed a shameful fact to his
companion and brother Tribune, to defame him, that
by the laws of Rome should have been holy, and
untouched. The people took this provocation very
angrily, and Tiberius also coming out, and having
assembled the people, commanded them to bring this
Annius before him, that he might be endited in the
marketplace. But he finding himself far inferior unto
Tiberius, both in dignity and eloquence, ran to his fine
subtile questions, to take a man at his word: and
prayed Tiberius before he did proceed to his accusation, that he would first answer him to a question he
would ask him. Tiberius bade him say what he
would. So silence being made, Annius asked him:
If thou wouldst defame me, and offer me injury,
and that I called one of thy companions to help me,
and he should rise to take my part, and anger thee:
wouldst thou therefore put him out of his office? It
is reported that Tiberius was so gravelled with this

question, that though he was one of the readiest speakers, and the boldest in his orations of any man: yet at that time he held his peace, and had no power to speak, and therefore he presently dismissed the assembly.

Afterwards, understanding that of all the things he did, the deposing of Octavius from his office was thought (not only of the nobility, but of the common people also) as foul and wilful a part as ever he played, for that thereby he had embased, and utterly overthrown the dignity of the Tribunes, the which was always had in great veneration until that present time: to excuse himself therefore, he made an excellent oration to the people, whereby shall appear unto you some special points thereof, to discern the better the force and effect of his eloquence. "The Tribuneship," said he, "indeed was a holy and sacred thing, as particularly consecrated to the people, and established for their benefit and safety: where contrariwise, if the Tribune do offer the people any wrong, he thereby minisheth their power, and taketh away the means from them to declare their wills by voices, besides that he doth also embase his own authority, leaving to do the thing for the which his authority first was given him. Or otherwise we could not choose but suffer a Tribune, if it pleased him, to overthrow the Capitol, or to set fire on the arsenal: and yet notwithstanding this wicked part, if it were committed, he should be Tribune of the people still, though a lewd Tribune. But when he goeth about to take away the authority and power of the people, then he is no more a Tribune. Were not this against all reason, think you, that a Tribune when he list, may take a Consul, and commit him to prison: and that the people should not withstand the authority of the Tribune who gave him the same, when he would use his authority to the prejudice of the people? for the people are they that do choose both Consul and Tribune. Furthermore, the kingly dignity (because in the same is contained the absolute

12—2

authority and power of all other kinds of magistrates
and offices together) is consecrated with very great
and holy ceremonies, drawing very near unto the god-
head: and yet the people expulsed King Tarquin,
because he used his authority with cruelty, and for
the injury he offered one man only, the most ancient
rule and government (by the which the foundation of
Rome was first laid) was utterly abolished. And who
is there in all the city of Rome to be reckoned so
holy as the Vestal Nuns, which have the custody and
keeping. of the everlasting fire ? and yet if any of
these be taken in fornication, she is buried alive for
her offence : for when they are not holy to the gods,
they lose the liberty they have, in respect of serving
the gods. Even so also it is unmeet, that the
Tribune if he offend the people, should for the
people's sake be reverenced any more, seeing that
through his own folly he hath deprived himself of
that authority they gave him. And if it be so that
he was chosen Tribune by the most part of the tribes
of the people: then by greater reason is he justly
deprived, that by all the whole tribes together is
forsaken and deposed. There is nothing more holy
nor inviolate than things offered up unto the gods:
and yet it was never seen that any man did forbid
the people to take them, to remove and transport
them from place to place, as they thought good.
Even so, they may as lawfully transfer the office of
the Tribune unto any other, as any other offering
consecrated to the gods. Furthermore, it is manifest
that any officer or magistrate may lawfully depose
himself: for, it hath been often seen, that men in
office have deprived themselves, or otherwise have
sued to be discharged."

This was the effect of Tiberius' purgation. Now
his friends perceiving the threats the rich and noble
men gave out against him, they wished him for the
safety of his person, to make suit to be Tribune again
the next year. Whereupon he began to flatter the
common people again afresh, by new laws which he

preferred: by the which he took away the time and number of years prescribed when every citizen of Rome was bound to go to the wars being called, and his name billed. He made it lawful also for men to appeal from sentence of the judges unto the people, and thrust in also amongst the Senators (which then had absolute authority to judge among themselves) a like number of the Roman knights, and by this means sought to weaken and embase the authority of the Senate, increasing also the power of the people, more of malice than any reason, or for any justice or benefit to the commonwealth. Furthermore, when it came to the gathering of the voices of the people for the confirmation of his new laws, finding that his enemies were the stronger in the assembly, because all the people were not yet come together: he fell a-quarrelling with his brethren the Tribunes, always to win time, and yet in the end brake up the assembly, commanding them to return the next morning. There he would be the first man in the market-place apparelled all in black, his face beblubbered with tears, and looking heavily upon the matter, praying the people assembled to have compassion upon him, saying, that he was afraid lest his enemies would come in the night, and overthrow his house to kill him. Thereupon the people were so moved withal, that many of them came and brought their tents, and lay about his house to watch it.

At the break of the day, the keeper of the chickens, by signs of the which they do divine of things to come, brought them unto him, and cast them down meat before them. None of them would come out of the cage but one only, and yet with much ado, shaking the cage: and when it came out, it would eat no meat, but only lift up her left wing, and put forth her leg, and so ran into the cage again. This sign made Tiberius remember another he had had before. He had a marvellous fair helmet and very rich, which he wore in the wars: under it were crept two snakes unawares to any, and laid eggs, and hatched them. This made

Tiberius wonder the more, because of the ill signs of
the chickens: notwithstanding, he went out of his
house, when he heard that the people were assembled
in the Capitol, but as he went out, he hit his foot such
a blow against a stone at the threshold of the door,
that he brake the nail of his great toe, which fell in
such a bleeding, that it bled through his shoe. Again,
he had not gone far, but he saw upon the top of a
house on his left hand, a couple of ravens fighting
together : and notwithstanding that there passed a
great number of people by, yet a stone which one of
these ravens cast from them, came and fell hard at
Tiberius' foot. The fall thereof stayed the stoutest
man he had about him. But Blossius the philosopher
of Cumae that did accompany him, told him it were a
great shame for him, and enough to kill the hearts of
all his followers: that Tiberius being the son of Gracchus, and nephew of Scipio the African, and the chief
man besides of all the people's side, for fear of a raven,
should not obey his citizens that called him: and
how that his enemies and ill-willers would not make
a laughing sport of it, but would plainly tell the
people that this was a trick of a tyrant that reigned
indeed, and that for pride and disdain did abuse
the people's good-wills. Furthermore, divers messengers came unto him, and said that his friends
that were in the Capitol, sent to pray him to make
haste, for all went well with him. When he came
thither, he was honourably received : for the people
seeing him coming, cried out for joy to welcome him.
and when he was gotten up to his seat, they shewed
themselves both careful and loving towards him,
looking warily that none came near him, but such as
they knew well.

While Mucius began again to call the tribes of the
people to give their voices, he could not proceed
according to the accustomed order in the like case,
for the great noise the hindmost people made, thrusting forward, and being driven back, and one mingling
with another. In the meantime Fulvius Flaccus, one

of the Senators, got up into a place where all the
people might see him, and when he saw that his voice
could not be heard of Tiberius, he made a sign with
his hand that he had some matter of great importance
to tell him.   Tiberius straight bade him make a lane
through the press.   So, with much ado, Fulvius came
at length unto him, and told him, that the rich men
in open Senate, when they could not frame the
Consul to their wills, determined themselves to come
and kill him, having a great number of their friends,
and bondmen armed for the purpose.

Tiberius immediately declared this conspiracy unto
his friends and followers : who straight girt their long
gowns unto them, and brake the sergeant's javelins
which they carried in their hands to make room
among the people, and took the truncheons of the
same to resist those that would set upon them.   The
people also that stood furthest off, marvelled at it,
and asked what the matter was.   Tiberius by a sign
to tell them the danger he was in, laid both his
hands on his head, because they could not hear his
voice for the great noise they made.   His enemies
seeing the sign he gave, ran presently to the Senate,
crying out, that Tiberius required a royal band or
diadem of the people, and that it was an evident sign,
because they saw him clap his hands upon his head.
This tale troubled all the company.   Whereupon
Nasica besought the Consul, chief of the Senate, to
help the commonwealth, and to take away this tyrant.
The Consul gently answered again, that he would
use no force, neither put any citizen to death, but
lawfully condemned : as also he would not receive
Tiberius, nor protect him, if the people, by his
persuasion or commandment, should commit any act
contrary to the law.   Nasica then rising in anger,
Sith the matter is so, said he, that the Consul
regardeth not the commonwealth : all you then, that
will defend the authority of the law, follow me.
Thereupon he cast the skirt of his gown over his
head, and went straight to the Capitol.   They that

followed him also took their gowns, and wrapped them about their arms, and laid at as many as they might, to make them give way: and yet very few of the people durst meet with such states as they were to stay them, because they were the chiefest men of the city, but every man flying from them, they fell one on another's neck for haste.   They that followed them had brought from home great levers and clubs, and as they went, they took up feet of trestles and chairs, which the people had overthrown and broken, running away, and hied them apace to meet with Tiberius, striking at them that stood in their way: so that in short space they had dispersed all the common people, and many were slain flying.   Tiberius seeing that, betook him to his legs to save himself, but as he was flying, one took him by the gown and stayed him: but he leaving his gown behind him, ran in his coat, and running fell upon them that were down before. So, as he was rising up again, the first man that struck him, and that was plainly seen strike him, was one of the Tribunes his brethren, called Publius Satureius: who gave him a great rap on the head with the foot of a chair, and the second blow he had was given him by Lucius Rufus that boasted of it, as if he had done a notable act.   In this tumult there were slain above three hundred men, and were all killed with staves and stones, and not one man hurt with any iron.

This was the first sedition among the citizens of Rome, that fell out with murder and bloodshed, since the expulsion of the kings.   But for all other former dissensions (which were no trifles) they were easily pacified, either party giving place to other: the Senate for fear of the commoners, and the people for reverence they bare to the Senate.   And it seemeth, that Tiberius himself would easily have yielded also, if they had proceeded by fair means and persuasion, so they had meant good faith, and would have killed no man: for at that time he had not in all above three thousand men of the people about him.   But surely it seems this conspiracy was executed against him, more for very spite and malice the rich men did bear him, than for any other apparent cause they presupposed against him. For proof hereof may be alleged the barbarous cruelty they used to his body being dead. For they would not suffer his own brother to have his body to bury it by night, who made earnest suit unto them for it: but they threw him amongst the other bodies into the river. And yet this was not the worst. For, some of his friends they banished without form of law, and others they put to death, which they could meet withal. Among the which they slew Diophanes the Orator, and one Caius Villius, whom they enclosed in a pipe among snakes and serpents, and put him to death in this sort. Blossius also, the philosopher of Cumae, was brought before the Consuls, and examined about this matter: who boldly confessed unto them, that he did as much as Tiberius commanded him. When Nasica did ask him, And what if he had commanded thee to set fire on the Capitol? he made him answer, that Tiberius would never have given him any such commandment. And when divers others also were still in hand with him about that question: But if he had commanded thee? I would sure have done it, said he: for he would never have commanded me to have done it, if it had not been for the commodity of the people. Thus he escaped at that time, and afterwards fled into Asia unto Aristonicus, whom misfortune having overthrown, he slew himself.

Now, the Senate to pacify the people at that present time, did no more withstand the law Agraria, for division of the lands of the commonwealth, but suffered the people to appoint another commissioner for that purpose, in Tiberius' place. Thereupon Publius Crassus was chosen, being allied unto Tiberius, for Caius Gracchus (Tiberius' brother) had married his daughter Licinia. Yet Cornelius Nepos saith, that it was not Crassus' daughter Caius married, but the daughter of Brutus, that triumphed

for the Lusitanians. Howbeit the best writers and
authority agree with that we write.   But whatsoever
was done, the people were marvellously offended with
his death, and men might easily perceive, that they
looked but for time and opportunity to be revenged,
and did presently threaten Nasica to accuse him.
Whereupon the Senate fearing some trouble towards
him, devised a way upon no occasion, to send him
into Asia.   For the common people did not dissemble
the malice they bare him when they met him, but were
very round with him, and called him tyrant, and
murderer, excommunicate, and wicked man, that had
imbrued his hands in the blood of the holy Tribune,
and within the most sacred temple of all the city.
So in the end he was enforced to forsake Rome,
though by his office he was bound to solemnise all
the greatest sacrifices, because he was then chief
Bishop of Rome.   Thus, travelling out of his country
like a mean man, and troubled in his mind, he died
shortly after, not far from the city of Pergamum.
Truly it is not greatly to be wondered at, though the
people so much hated Nasica, considering that Scipio
the African himself (whom the people of Rome for
juster causes had loved better than any man else
whatsoever) was like to have lost all the people's
good-wills they bare him, because that being at the
siege of Numantia, when news was brought him of
Tiberius' death, he rang out this verse of Homer :

> Such end upon him ever light,
> Which in such doings doth delight.

Furthermore, being asked in the assembly of the
people, by Caius and Fulvius, what he thought of
Tiberius' death : he answered them, that he did not
like his doings.   After that the people handled him
very churlishly, and did ever break off his oration,
which they never did before: and he himself also
would revile the people even in the assembly.
   Now Caius Gracchus at the first because he feared
the enemies of his dead brother, or otherwise for

that he sought means to make them more hated of
the people : he absented himself for a time out of the
common assembly, and kept at home and meddled
not, as a man contented to live meanly, without
busying himself in the commonwealth : insomuch as
he made men think and report both, that he did
utterly mislike those matters which his brother had
preferred.   Howbeit he was then but a young man,
and nine years younger than his brother Tiberius,
who was not thirty year old when he was slain.   But
in process of time, he made his manners and conditions (by little and little) appear, who hated sloth and
curiosity, and was least of all given unto any covetous
mind of getting : for he gave himself to be eloquent,
as preparing him wings afterwards to practise in the
commonwealth.   So that it appeared plainly, that
when time came, he would not stand still, and look
on.   When one Vettius a friend of his was sued, he
took upon him to defend his cause in court.   The
people that were present, and heard him speak, they
leaped for joy to see him : for he had such an eloquent
tongue, that all the orators besides were but children
to him.   Hereupon the rich men began to be afraid
again, and whispered among themselves, that it be-
hoved them to beware he came not to be Tribune.   It
chanced so that he was chosen Treasurer, and it was
his fortune to go into the Isle of Sardinia, with the
Consul Orestes.   His enemies were glad of that, and
he himself was not sorry for it.   For he was a martial
man, and as skilful in arms as he was else an excellent orator : but yet he was afraid to come into
the pulpit for orations, and misliked to deal in matters
of state, albeit he could not altogether deny the
people, and his friends that prayed his furtherance.
For this cause therefore he was very glad of this
voyage, that he might absent himself for a time out
of Rome : though divers were of opinion, that he was
more popular, and desirous of the common people's
good-will and favour, than his brother had been
before him.   But indeed he was clean contrary ; for

it appeared that at the first he was drawn rather against his will, than of any special desire he had to deal in the commonwealth. Cicero the Orator also saith, that Caius was bent altogether to fly from office in the commonwealth, and to live quietly as a private man. But Tiberius (Caius' brother) appeared to him in his sleep, and calling him by his name, said unto him : Brother, why dost thou prolong time, for thou canst not possibly escape ? For we were both predestined to one manner of life and death, for procuring the benefit of the people.

Now when Caius arrived in Sardinia, he shewed all the proofs that might be in a valiant man, and excelled all the young men of his age, in hardiness against his enemies, in justice to his inferiors, and in love and obedience towards the Consul his captain : but in temperance, sobriety, and in painfulness, he excelled all them that were older than he. The winter by chance fell out very sharp, and full of sickness in Sardinia : whereupon the Consul sent unto the cities to help his soldiers with some clothes : but the towns sent in post to Rome, to pray the senate they might be discharged of that burden. The Senate found their allegation reasonable, whereupon they wrote to the Consul to find some other means to clothe his people. The Consul could make no other shift for them, and so the poor soldiers in the meantime smarted for it. But Caius Gracchus went himself unto the cities and so persuaded them, that they of themselves sent to the Romans' camp such things as they lacked. This being carried to Rome, it was thought straight it was a pretty beginning to creep into the people's favour, and indeed it made the Senate also afraid. In the neck of that, there arrived ambassadors of Africk at Rome, sent from King Micipsa, who told the Senate that the king their master, for Caius Gracchus sake, had sent their army corn into Sardinia. The Senators were so offended withal, that they thrust the ambassadors out of the Senate, and so gave order that other soldiers should

be sent in their places that were in Sardinia: and
that Orestes should still remain Consul there, meaning also to continue Caius their Treasurer. But
when he heard of it, he straight took sea, and returned to Rome in choler. When men saw Caius
returned to Rome unlooked for, he was reproved for it
not only by his enemies, but by the common people
also: who thought his return very strange before his
captain, under whom he was Treasurer. He being
accused hereof before the Censors, prayed he might
be heard. So, answering his accusation, he so turned
the people's minds that heard him, that they all said
he had open wrong. For he told them, that he
had served twelve years in the wars, where others
were enforced to remain but ten years: and that he
had continued Treasurer under his captain, the space
of three years, where the law gave him liberty to
return at the end of the year. And that he alone of
all men else that had been in the wars, had carried
his purse full, and brought it home empty: where
others having drunk the wine which they carried
thither in vessels, had afterwards brought them home
full of gold and silver.

Afterwards they went about to accuse him as
accessory to a conspiracy, that was revealed in the
city of Fregellae. But having cleared all that
suspicion, and being discharged, he presently made
suit to be Tribune: wherein he had all the men of
quality his sworn enemies. On the other side also
he had so great favour of the common people, that
there came men out of all parts of Italy to be at his
election, and that such a number of them, as there
was no lodging to be had for them all. Furthermore,
the field of Mars not being large enough to hold such
a multitude of people, there were that gave their voices
upon the top of houses. Now the noblemen could no
otherwise let the people of their will, nor prevent
Caius of his hope, but where he thought to be the
first Tribune, he was only pronounced the fourth.
But when he was once possessed officer, he became

immediately the chief man, because he was as
eloquent as any man of his time. And furthermore,
he had a large occasion of calamity offered him:
which made him bold to speak, bewailing the death
of his brother. For what matter soever he spake of,
he always fell in talk of that, remembering them what
matters had passed: and laying before them the
examples of their ancestors, who in old time had
made war with the Faliscans, by the means of one
Genucius, Tribune of the people, unto whom they
had offered injury: who also did condemn Caius
Veturius to death, because that he only would not give
a Tribune place, coming through the market-place:
Where these, said he, that standing before you in
sight, have slain my brother Tiberius with staves,
and have dragged his body from the mount of the
Capitol, all the city over, to throw it into the river:
and with him also have most cruelly slain all his
friends they could come by, without any law or justice
at all. And yet by an ancient custom of long time
observed in this city of Rome, when any man is
accused of treason, and that of duty he must appear
at the time appointed him, they do notwithstanding
in the morning send a trumpet to his house, to
summon him to appear: and moreover the judges
were not wont to condemn him, before this ceremony
was performed: so careful and respective were our
predecessors, where it touched the life of any Roman.

Now Caius having first stirred up the people with
these persuasions (for he had a marvellous loud voice)
he preferred two laws.

The first, that he that had once been put out of
office by the people, should never after be capable
of any other office.

The second, that if any Consul had banished any
citizen without lawful accusation, the sentence and
hearing of the matter should pertain to the people.

The first of these two laws did plainly defame
Octavius, whom Tiberius his brother had by the
people deposed from the Tribuneship. The second

also touched Popillius, who being Praetor, had banished his brother Tiberius' friends: whereupon he stayed not the trial, but willingly exiled himself out of Italy. And touching the first law, Caius himself did afterwards revoke it, declaring unto the people, that he had saved Octavius at the request of his mother Cornelia. The people were very glad of it, and confirmed it, honouring her no less for respect of her sons, than also for Scipio's sake her father. For afterwards they cast her image in brass, and set it up with this inscription: Cornelia the mother of the Gracchi. Many common matters are found written touching Cornelia his mother, and eloquently pleaded in her behalf, by Caius against her adversaries. As when he said unto one of them: How darest thou presume to speak evil of Cornelia, that had Tiberius to her son? And the other party also that slandered her, being a man of evil fame: And art thou so impudent, said he, to shew thy face before Cornelia? Hast thou brought forth children as she hath done? And yet it is well known to all men in Rome, that she being but a woman, hath lived in chastity longer than thou that art a man. Thus were Caius' words sharp and stinging, and many suchlike are to be gathered out of his writings.

Furthermore he made many other laws afterwards to increase the people's authority, and to embase the Senate's greatness.

The first was, for the restoring of the colonies to Rome, in dividing the lands of the commonwealth unto the poor citizens that should inhabit there.

The other, that they should apparel the soldiers at the charge of the commonwealth, and that it should not be deducted out of their pay: and also that no citizen should be billed to serve in the wars, under seventeen years of age at the least.

Another law was, for their confederates of Italy: that through all Italy they should have as free voices in the election of any magistrate, as the natural citizens of Rome itself.

Another setting a reasonable price of the corn that should be distributed unto the poor people.

Another touching judgment, whereby he did greatly minish the authority of the Senate. For before, the Senators were only judges of all matters, the which made them to be the more honoured and feared of the people, and the Roman knights: and now he joined three hundred Roman knights unto the other three hundred Senators, and brought it so to pass, that all matters judicial should be equally judged, among those six hundred men. After he had passed this law, it is reported he was very curious in observing all other things, but this one thing especially: that where all other orators speaking to the people turned them towards the palace where the Senators sat, and to that side of the market-place which is called Comitium: he in contrary manner when he made his oration, turned him outwards towards the other side of the market-place, and after that kept it constantly, and never failed. Thus, by a little turning and altering of his look only, he removed a great matter. For he so transferred all the government of the commonwealth from the Senate, unto the judgment of the people: to teach the orators by his example, that in their orations they should behold the people, not the Senate.

Now, the people having not only confirmed the law he made touching the judges, but given him also full power and authority to choose among the Roman knights such judges as he liked of: he found thereby he had absolute power in his own hands, insomuch as the Senators themselves did ask counsel of him. So did he ever give good counsel, and did prefer matters meet for their honour. As amongst others, the law he made touching certain wheat that Fabius Vicepraetor had sent out of Spain: which was a good and honourable act. He persuaded the Senate that the corn might be sold, and so to send back again the money thereof unto the towns and cities from whence the corn came: and therewithal to punish

Fabius for that he made the empire of Rome hateful
and intolerable unto the provinces and subjects of
the same. This matter won him great love and
commendation of all the provinces subject to Rome.
Furthermore, he made laws for the restoring of
the decayed towns, for mending of highways, for
building of garners for provision of corn. And to
bring all these things to pass, he himself took upon
him the only care and enterprise, being never wearied
with any pains taken in ordering of so great affairs.
For he followed all those things so earnestly and
effectually, as if he had had but one matter in hand :
insomuch that they who most hated and feared him,
wondered most to see his diligence and quick despatch
in matters. The people also wondered much to
behold him only, seeing always such a number of
labourers, artificers, ambassadors, officers, soldiers,
and learned men, whom he easily satisfied and
despatched, keeping still his state, and yet using
great courtesy and civility, entertaining every one
of them privately : so that he made his accusers to
be found liars, that said he was a stately man,
and very cruel. Thus he won the good-will of the
common people, being more popular and familiar in
his conversation and deeds, than he was otherwise
in his orations.

But the greatest pains and care he took upon him
was in seeing the highways mended, the which he
would have as well done as profitably done. For
he would cast the causeways by the line in the softest
ground in the fields, and then would pave them with
hard stone, and cast a great deal of gravel upon it,
which he caused to be brought thither. When he
found any low or watery places which the rivers
had eaten into, he raised them up, or else made
bridges over them, with an even height equal to either
side of the causeway : so that all his work carried
a goodly level withal even by the line or plummet,
which was a pleasure to behold it. Furthermore,
he divided these highways by miles, every mile

P. 13

containing eight furlongs, and at every mile's end
he set up a stone for a mark. At either end also
of these highways thus paved, he set certain stones
of convenient height, a pretty way asunder, to help
the travellers by to take their horsebacks again
without any help.

The people for these things highly praising and ex-
tolling him, and being ready to make shew of their
love and good-will to him any manner of way: he
told them openly one day in his oration, that he had
a request to make unto them, the which if it would
please them to grant him, he would think they
did him a marvellous pleasure: and if they denied
him also, he cared not much. Then every man
thought it was the Consulship he meant to ask, and
that he would sue to be Tribune and Consul together.
But when the day came to choose the Consuls, every
man looking attentively what he would do: they
marvelled when they saw him come down the field
of Mars, and brought Caius Fannius with his friends,
to further his suit for the Consulship. Therein he
served Fannius' turn, for he was presently chosen
Consul: and Caius Gracchus was the second time
chosen Tribune again, not of his own suit, but by the
good-will of the people. Caius perceiving that the
Senators were his open enemies, and that Fannius
the Consul was but a slack friend unto him, he
began again to curry favour with the common people,
and to prefer new laws, setting forth the law of the
colonies, that they should send of the poor citizens
to replenish the cities of Tarentum and Capua, and
that they should grant all the Latins the freedom of
Rome. The Senate perceiving his power grew great,
and that in the end he would be so strong that they
could not withstand him: they devised a new and
strange way to pluck the people's good-will from him,
in granting them things not altogether very honest.
There was one of the Tribunes, a brother in office
with Caius called Livius Drusus, a man nobly born,
and as well brought up as any other Roman: who

for wealth and eloquence was not inferior to the greatest men of estimation in Rome. The chiefest Senators went unto him, and persuaded him to take part with them against Caius, not to use any force or violence against the people to withstand them in anything, but contrarily to grant them those things which were more honesty for them to deny them with their ill-will.

Livius, offering to pleasure the Senate with his authority, preferred laws neither honourable nor profitable to the commonwealth and were to no other end, but contending with Caius, who should most flatter the people of them two, as players do in their common plays, to shew the people pastime. Whereby the Senate shewed that they did not so much mislike Caius' doings, as for the desire they had to overthrow him and his great credit with the people. For where Caius preferred but the replenishing of the two cities, and desired to send the honestest citizens thither: they objected against him, that he did corrupt the common people. On the other side also they favoured Drusus, who preferred a law that they should replenish twelve colonies, and should send to every one of them three thousand of the poorest citizens. And where they hated Caius for that he had charged the poor citizens with an annual rent for the lands that were divided unto them: Livius in contrary manner did please them by disburdening them of that rent and payment, letting them have the lands scot-free. Furthermore also, where Caius did anger the people, because he gave all the Latins the freedom of Rome to give their voices in choosing of magistrates as freely as the natural Romans: when Drusus on the other side had preferred a law that thenceforth no Roman should whip any soldier of the Latins with rods to the wars, they liked the law, and passed it. Livius also, in every law he put forth, said in all his orations, that he did it by the counsel of the Senate, who were very careful for the profit of the people: and this was

13—2

all the good he did in his office unto the commonwealth. For by his means the people were better
pleased with the Senate, and where they did before
hate all the noblemen of the Senate, Livius took
away that malice, when the people saw that all that
he propounded, was for the preferment and benefit of
the commonwealth, with the consent and furtherance
of the Senate.

The only thing also that persuaded the people to
think that Drusus meant uprightly, and that he only
respected the profit of the common people was: that
he never preferred any law for himself, or for his own
benefit. For in the restoring of these colonies which
he preferred, he always sent other commissioners,
and gave them the charge of it, and would never
finger any money himself: where Caius took upon
him the charge and care of all things himself, and
especially of the greatest matters. Rubrius also
another Tribune, having preferred a law for the re-
edifying and replenishing of Carthage again with
people, the which Scipio had razed and destroyed:
it was Caius' hap to be· appointed one of the commissioners for it. Whereupon he took ship and
sailed into Africk. Drusus in the meantime taking
occasion of his absence, did as much as might be to
seek the favour of the common people, and specially
by accusing Fulvius, who was one of the best friends
Caius had, and whom they had also chosen commissioner with him for the division of these lands
among the citizens, whom they sent to replenish these
colonies. This Fulvius was a seditious man, and
therefore marvellously hated of the Senate, and
withal suspected also of them that took part with the
people, that he secretly practised to make their
confederates of Italy to rebel. But yet they had no
evident proof of it to justify it against him, more
than that which he himself did verify, because he
seemed to be offended with the peace and quietness
they enjoyed. And this was one of the chiefest
causes of Caius' overthrow, because that Fulvius

was partly hated for his sake. For when Scipio
African was found dead one morning in his house,
without any manifest cause how he should come
to his death so suddenly (saving that there appeared certain blind marks of stripes on his body
that had been given him: as we have declared at
large in his life): the most part of the suspicion of his
death was laid to Fulvius, being his mortal enemy,
and because the same day they had been at great
words together in the pulpit for orations. So was
Caius Gracchus also partly suspected for it. Howsoever it was, such a horrible murder as this, of so
famous and worthy a man as any was in Rome, was
yet notwithstanding never revenged, neither any
inquiry made of it: because the common people
would not suffer the accusation to go forward, fearing
lest Caius would be found in fault, if the matter
should go forward. But this was a great while
before.

Now Caius at that time being in Africk about the
re-edifying and replenishing of the city of Carthage
again, the which he named Junonia: the voice goeth
that he had many ill signs and tokens appeared unto
him. For the staff of his ensign was broken with a
vehement blast of wind, and with the force of the
ensign-bearer that held it fast on the other side.
There came a flaw of wind also that carried away the
sacrifices upon the altars and blew them quite out of
the circuit which was marked out for the compass of
the city. Furthermore, the wolves came and took
away the marks which they had set down to limit the
bounds of their circuit, and carried them quite away.
This notwithstanding, Caius having despatched all
things in the space of three-score and ten days, he
returned incontinently to Rome, understanding that
Fulvius was oppressed by Drusus, and that those
matters required his presence. For Lucius Hostilius
that was all in all for the nobility, and a man of great
credit with the Senate, being the year before put by
the Consulship, by Caius' practice, who caused

Fannius to be chosen : he had good hope this year to
speed, for the great number of friends that furthered
his suit.   So that if he could obtain it, he was fully
bent to set Caius beside the saddle, and the rather,
because his estimation and countenance he was wont
to have among the people, began now to decay, for
that they were full of such devices as his were :
because there were divers others that preferred the
like to please the people withal, and yet with the
Senate's great good-will and favour.

So Caius being returned to Rome, he removed from
his house, and where before he dwelt in Mount
Palatine, he came now to take a house under the
market-place, to shew himself thereby the lowlier and
more popular, because many of the meaner sort of
people dwelt thereabouts.   Then he purposed to go
forward with the rest of his laws, and to make the
people to establish them, a great number of people
repairing to Rome out of all parts, for the furtherance
thereof.   Howbeit the Senate counselled the Consul
Fannius to make proclamation, that all those which
were no natural Romans, resident and abiding within
the city self of Rome : that they should depart out of
Rome.   Besides all this, there was a strange proclamation made, and never seen before : that none of
all the friends and confederates of the Romans, for
certain days should come into Rome.   But Caius on
the other side set up bills on every post accusing the
Consul for making so wicked a proclamation : and
further, promised the confederates of Rome to aid
them, if they would remain there against the Consul's
proclamation.   But yet he performed it not.   For
when he saw one of Fannius' sergeants carry a friend
of his to prison, he held on his way, and would see
nothing, neither did he help him : either of likelihood
because he feared his credit with the people, which
began to decay, or else because he was loth (as he
said) to pick any quarrel with his enemies, which
sought it of him.   Furthermore, he chanced to fall at
variance with his brethren the Tribunes, about this

occasion. The people were to see the pastime of the
sword-players or fencers at the sharp, within the very
market-place, and there were divers of the officers
that, to see the sport, did set up scaffolds round about,
to take money for the standing. Caius commanded
them to take them down again, because the poor men
might see the sport without any cost. But not a man
of them would yield to it. Wherefore he stayed till
the night before the pastime should be, and then he
took all his labourers he had under him, and went and
overthrew the scaffolds every one of them: so that
the next morning all the market-place was clear for
the common people, to see the pastime at their
pleasure. For this fact of his, the people thanked
him marvellously, and took him for a worthy man.
Howbeit his brethren the Tribunes were very much
offended with him, and took him for a bold presumptu-
ous man. This seemeth to be the chief cause why
he was put from his third Tribuneship, where he had
the most voices of his side: because his colleagues, to
be revenged of the part he had played them, of malice
and spite, made false report of the voices. Howbeit
there is no great troth in this. It is true that he was
very angry with this repulse, and it is reported he
spake somewhat too proudly to his enemies, that
were merry with the matter, and laughed him to
scorn: that they laughed a Sardonian's laugh, not
knowing how darkly his deeds had wrapt them in.
Furthermore, his enemies having chosen Opimius
Consul, they began immediately to revoke divers of
Caius' laws: as among the rest, his doings at Carthage
for the re-edifying of that city, procuring thus all the
ways they could to anger him, because they might
have just occasion of anger to kill him. Caius notwithstanding did patiently bear it at the first: but
afterwards his friends, and especially Fulvius, did
encourage him so, that he began again to gather men
to resist the Consul. And it is reported also, that
Cornelia his mother did help him in it, secretly hiring
a great number of strangers which she sent unto

Rome, as if they had been reapers, or harvest men. And this is that she wrote secretly in her letter unto her son in ciphers. And yet other write to the contrary, that she was very angry he did attempt those things. When the day came that they should proceed to the revocation of his laws, both parties met by break of day at the Capitol. There when the Consul Opimius had done sacrifice, one of Caius' sergeants called Quintus Antyllius, carrying the entrails of the beast sacrificed, said unto Fulvius, and others of his tribe that were about him: Give place to honest men, vile citizens that ye be. Some say also, that besides these injurious words, in scorn and contempt he held out his naked arm to make them ashamed. Whereupon they slew him presently in the field with great bodkins to write with, which they had purposely made for that intent. So the common people were marvellously offended for this murder, and the chief men of both sides also were diversly affected. For Caius was very sorry for it, and bitterly reproved them that were about him, saying, that they had given their enemies the occasion they looked for, to set upon them. Opimius the Consul in contrary manner, taking this occasion, rose upon it, and did stir up the people to be revenged.

But there fell a shower of rain at that time that parted them. The next morning the Consul having assembled the Senate by break of day, as he was despatching causes within, some had taken the body of Antyllius and laid it naked upon the bier, and so carried it through the market-place (as it was agreed upon before amongst them) and brought it to the Senate door: where they began to make great moan and lamentation, Opimius knowing the meaning of it, but yet he dissembled it, and seemed to wonder at it. Whereupon the Senators went out to see what it was, and finding this bier in the market-place, some fell a-weeping for him that was dead, others cried out that it was a shameful act, and in no wise to be suffered. But on the other side, this did revive the old grudge and malice of the people, for the wickedness of the ambitious noblemen: who having themselves before slain Tiberius Gracchus that was Tribune, and within the Capitol itself, and had also cast his body into the river, did now make an honourable shew openly in the market-place, of the body of the sergeant Antyllius (who though he were wrongfully slain, yet had himself given them the cause that slew him, to do that they did) and all the whole Senate were about the bier to bewail his death, and to honour the funerals of a hireling, to make the people also kill him, that was only left the protector and defender of the people. After this, they went again unto the Capitol, and there made a decree, whereby they gave the Consul Opimius extraordinary power and authority, by absolute power to provide for the safety of the commonwealth, to preserve the city, and to suppress the tyrants. This decree being established, the Consul presently commanded the Senators that were present there, to go arm themselves: and appointed the Roman knights, that the next morning betimes every man should bring two of their men armed with them. Fulvius on the other side, he prepared his force against them, and assembled the common people together. Caius also, returning from the market-place, stayed before the image of his father, and looked earnestly upon it without ever a word speaking, only he burst out a-weeping, and fetching a great sigh, went his way. This made the people to pity him that saw him: so that they talked among themselves, that they were but beasts and cowards at such a strait to forsake so worthy a man. Thereupon they went to his house, stayed there all night and watched before his gate: not as they did that watched with Fulvius, that passed away the night in guzzling and drinking drunk, crying out, and making noise, Fulvius himself being drunk first of all, who both spake and did many things far unmeet for his calling. For they that watched Caius,

on the other side, were very sorrowful, and made
no noise, even as in a common calamity of their
country, devising with themselves what would fall
out upon it, waking and sleeping one after another
by turns.

When the day brake, they with Fulvius did awake
him, who slept yet soundly for the wine he drank over
night, and they armed themselves with the spoils of
the Gauls that hung round about his house, whom he
had overcome in battle the same year he was Consul:
and with great cries, and thundering threats, they
went to take the Mount Aventine. But Caius would
not arm himself, but went out of his house in a long
gown, as if he would have gone simply into the
market-place according to his wonted manner, saving
that he carried a short dagger at his girdle under his
gown. So as he was going out of his house, his wife
stayed him at the door, and holding him by the one
hand, and a little child of his in her other hand, she
said thus unto him: "Alas Caius, thou dost not now
go as thou wert wont, a Tribune into the market-
place to speak to the people, neither to prefer any
new laws: neither dost thou go unto an honest war,
that if unfortunately that should happen to thee that
is common to all men, I might yet at the least mourn
for thy death with honour. But thou goest to put
thy self into bloody butchers' hands, who most cruelly
have slain thy brother Tiberius: and yet thou goest,
a naked man unarmed, intending rather to suffer
than to do hurt. Besides, thy death can bring no
benefit to the commonwealth. For the worser part
hath now the upper hand, considering that sentence
passeth by force of sword. Had thy brother been
slain by his enemies, before the city of Numantia:
yet had they given us his body to have buried him.
But such may be my misfortune, that I may presently
go to pray the river or sea to give me thy body, which
as thy brother's they have likewise thrown into
the same: Alas, what hope or trust is left us now,
in laws or gods, sithence they have slain Tiberius?"

As Licinia was making this pitiful moan unto him,
Caius fair and softly pulled his hand from her, and
left her, giving her never a word, but went on with
his friends.   But she reaching after him to take him
by the gown, fell to the ground, and lay flatling there
a great while, speaking never a word : until at length
her servants took her up in a swoon, and carried her
so unto her brother Crassus.

Now Fulvius, by the persuasion of Caius, when all
their faction were met, sent his younger son (which
was a pretty fair boy) with a herald's rod in his hand
for his safety.   This boy humbly presenting his duty,
with the tears in his eyes, before the Consul and
Senate, offered them peace.   The most of them that
were present thought very well of it.   But Opimius
made answer saying, that it became them not to
send messengers, thinking with fair words to win the
Senate : but it was their duty to come themselves in
persons, like subjects and offenders to make their
trial, and so to crave pardon, and to seek to pacify
the wrath of the Senate.   Then he commanded the
boy he should not return again to them but with this
condition he had prescribed.   Caius (as it is reported)
was ready to go and clear himself unto the Senate :
but the residue would not suffer him to go.   Whereupon Fulvius sent his son back again unto them, to
speak for them as he had done before.   But Opimius,
that was desirous to fight, caused the boy to be taken,
and committed him in safe custody, and then went
presently against Fulvius with a great number of footmen well armed, and of Cretan archers besides : who
with their arrows did more trouble and hurt their
enemies than with anything else, that within a while
they all began to fly.   Fulvius on the other side fled
into an old hothouse that nobody made reckoning of,
and there being found shortly after, they slew him,
and his eldest son.   Now for Caius, he fought not at
all, but being mad with himself, and grieved to see
such bloodshed, he got him into the temple of Diana,
where he would have killed himself, had not his very

good friends Pomponius and Licinius saved him.   For
both they, being with him at that time, took his sword
from him, and counselled him to fly.   It is reported
that then he fell down on his knees, and holding up
both his hands unto the goddess, he besought her that
the people might never come out of bondage, to be
revenged of this their ingratitude and treason.   For
the common people (or the most part of them) plainly
turned their coats, when they heard proclamation
made, that all men had pardon granted them, that
would return.

So Caius fled upon it, and his enemies followed him
so near that they overtook him upon the wooden
bridge, where two of his friends that were with him
stayed, to defend him against his followers, and bade
him in the meantime make shift for himself, whilst
they fought with them upon the bridge : and so they
did, and kept them that not a man got the bridge of
them, until they were both slain.   Now there was
none that fled with Caius, but one of his men called
Philocrates : notwithstanding, every man did still
encourage and counsel him, as they do men to win a
game, but no man would help him, nor offer him any
horse, though he often required it, because he saw
his enemies so near unto him.   This notwithstanding,
by their defence that were slain upon the bridge, he
got ground on them so, that he had leisure to creep
into a little grove of wood, which was consecrated to
the Furies.   There his servant Philocrates slew him,
and then slew himself also, and fell dead upon him.
Other write notwithstanding, that both the master and
servant were overtaken, and taken alive : and that his
servant did so straight embrace his master that none
of the enemies could strike him for all the blows they
gave, before he was slain himself.   So one of the
murderers struck off Caius Gracchus' head to carry
to the Consul.   Howbeit one of Opimius' friends
called Septimuleius, took the head from the other by
the way, because proclamation was made before they
fought by trumpet, that whosoever brought the heads

of Fulvius and Caius, they should be paid the weight
of them in gold.   Wherefore this Septimuleius carried
Caius' head upon the top of his spear unto Opimius:
whereupon the scales being brought to weigh it, it was
found that it weighed seventeen pound weight and
two-third parts of a pound, because Septimuleius
besides the horrible murder he had committed, had
also holpen it with this villainy, that he had taken out
his brain, and in lieu thereof had filled his skull with
lead.   Now the other also that brought Fulvius' head,
because they were poor men, they had nothing.   The
bodies of these two men, Caius Gracchus and Fulvius,
and of other their followers (which were to the number
of three thousand that were slain) were all thrown into
the river, their goods confiscate, and their widows
forbidden to mourn for their death.   Furthermore,
they took from Licinia, Caius' wife, her jointure: but
yet they dealt more cruelly and beastly with the
young boy, Fulvius' son: who had neither lift up
his hand against them, nor was in the fight among
them, but only came to them to make peace before
they fought, whom they kept as prisoner, and after
the battle ended, they put him to death.   But yet
that which most of all other grieved the people, was
the temple of Concord, the which Opimius caused
to be built: for it appeared that he boasted, and in
manner triumphed, that he had slain so many
citizens of Rome.   And therefore there were that
in the night wrote under the inscription of the
temple these verses:

> A furious fact and full of beastly shame,
> This temple built, that beareth Concord's name.

This Opimius was the first man at Rome, that
being Consul, usurped the absolute power of the
Dictator: and that without law or justice condemned
three thousand citizens of Rome, besides Fulvius
Flaccus (who had also been Consul, and had
received the honour of triumph) and Caius Gracchus
a young man in like case, who in virtue and reputa-

tion excelled all the men of his years. This notwithstanding, could not keep Opimius from thievery and extortion. For when he was sent ambassador unto Jugurtha king of Numidia, he was bribed with money: and thereupon being accused, he was most shamefully convicted, and condemned. Wherefore he ended his days with this reproach and infamy, hated and mocked of all the people: because at the time of the overthrow he dealt beastly with them that fought for his quarrel. But shortly after, it appeared to the world, how much they lamented the loss of the two brethren of the Gracchi. For they made images and statues of them, and caused them to be set up in an open and honourable place, consecrating the places where they had been slain: and many of them also came and offered to them, of their first fruits and flowers, according to the time of the year, and went thither to make their prayers on their knees, as unto the temple of the gods.

Their mother Cornelia, as writers report, did bear this calamity with a noble heart: and as for the chapels which they built and consecrated unto them in the place where they were slain, she said no more, but that they had such graves as they had deserved. Afterwards she dwelt continually by the Mount of Misenum, and never changed her manner of life. She had many friends, and because she was a noble lady, and loved ever to welcome strangers, she kept a very good house, and therefore had always great repair unto her, of Grecians and learned men: besides, there was no king nor prince, but both received gifts from her, and sent her again. They that frequented her company, delighted marvellously to hear her report the deeds and manner of her father's life, Scipio African: but yet they wondered more, to hear her tell the acts and death of her two sons, Tiberius and Caius Gracchi, without shedding tear, or making any shew of lamentation or grief, no more than if she had told an history unto them that had requested her: insomuch some writers report, that age, or her great misfortunes, had overcome and taken her reason and sense from her, to feel any sorrow.   But indeed they were senseless to say so, not understanding, how that to be nobly born, and virtuously brought up, doth make men temperately to digest sorrow, and that fortune oftentimes overcomes virtue, which regardeth honesty in all respects, but yet with any adversity she cannot take away the temperance from them, whereby they patiently bear it.

THE COMPARISON OF TIBERIUS AND CAIUS GRACCHI WITH AGIS AND CLEOMENES

Now that we be come to the end of this history, we are to compare the lives of these two men the one with the other. First, as touching the two Gracchi: their enemies that most hated them, and spake the worst they could of them, could not deny but that they were the best given to virtue, and as well taught and brought up, as any Romans that were in their time. But yet it appeareth, that nature had the upper hand of them in Agis and Cleomenes. For they having been very ill brought up, both for learning and good manners, for lack whereof the oldest men were almost spoiled: yet did they notwithstanding make themselves the first masters and example of sobriety, temperance, and simplicity of life. Furthermore, the two first having lived in that time, when Rome flourished most in honour and virtuous desires: they were more than ashamed to forsake the virtues inherited from their ancestors. These two last also, being born of fathers that had a clean contrary disposition, and finding their country altogether without any order, and infected with dissolute life: were not therefore any whit the more slack in their desire to do well. Furthermore, the greatest praise they gave unto the two Gracchi was, their abstinence and integrity from taking of money all the time they were in office, and dealt in matters of state, ever keeping their hands clean, and took not a penny wrongfully from any man; where Agis on the other side was offended if any man praised him: for that he took nothing from another man: seeing that he dispossessed himself of his own goods, and gave it to his citizens, which amounted in ready coin to the value of six hundred talents. Whereby men may easily judge, how grievous a sin he thought it to take anything wrongfully from any man: seeing that he thought it a kind of avarice, lawfully to be richer than others.

Furthermore, there was marvellous great difference in their alterations, and renewing of the state, which they did both prefer. For the acts of the two Romans were to mend highways and to re-edify and replenish decayed towns: and the worthiest act Tiberius did was the law Agraria, which he brought in for dividing of the lands of the commonwealth amongst the poor citizens. And the best act his brother Caius also did was the mingling of the judges: adding to the three hundred Senators three hundred Roman knights to be indifferent judges with them: whereas Agis and Cleomenes in contrary manner were of opinion, that to reform small faults, and to redress them by little and little, was (as Plato said) to cut off one of the hydra's heads, of the which came afterwards seven in the place: and therefore they took upon them a change and innovation, even at once to root out all the mischiefs of their country, (or to speak more truly, to take away the disorder which brought in all vice and mischief to the commonwealth) and so to restore the city of Sparta again to her former ancient honourable estate. Now this may be said again for the government of the Gracchi: that the chiefest men of Rome were ever against their purposes: where, in that that Agis attempted, and Cleomenes ended, they had the noblest ground that could be, and that was the ancient laws and ordinances of Sparta, touching temperance and equality: the first, instituted in old time by Lycurgus, the other confirmed by Apollo. Furthermore, by the alterations of the first, Rome became no greater than it was before: where, by that which Cleomenes did, all Greece in short time saw that Sparta com-

manded all the rest of Peloponnesus, and fought at
that time against those that were of greatest power
in all Greece, for the signiory thereof. Whereby
their only mark and purpose was, to rid all Greece
from the wars of the Gauls and Illyrians, and to
restore it again to the honest government of the
race and line of Hercules.

Their deaths, methinks, do shew great difference
of their courages. For the Gracchi fighting with
their own citizens, were slain flying. Of these two
also, Agis, because he would put never a citizen to
death, was slain in manner voluntarily : and Cleomenes
receiving injury stood to his defence, and when he
had no opportunity to do it, he stoutly killed himself.
And so may it be said on the other side, that Agis
did never any noble act of a captain or soldier,
because he was slain before he could come to it.
And for the victories of Cleomenes on the other side,
may be opposed the scaling of the walls of Carthage,
where Tiberius was the first man that at the assault
got up upon the wall, which was no small exploit :
and the peace which he made also at the siege of
Numantia, whereby he saved twenty thousand fighting
men of the Romans, the which had no means otherwise to save their lives. And Caius also in the self
same war, at the siege of Numantia, and afterwards
in Sardinia, did many noble feats of war : so that
there is no doubt, but if they had not been slain so
soon as they were, they might have been compared with
the excellentest captains that ever were in Rome.

Again, touching their doings in civil policy, it
appeareth that Agis dealt more slackly, being abused
by Agesilaus : who likewise deceived the poor citizens
of the division of the lands which he had promised
them. In fine, for lack of courage, because he was
very young, he left the things undone which he had
purposed to have performed. On the other side,
Cleomenes went too roundly to work to renew the
ancient government of the commonwealth again, by
killing the Ephors with too much cruelty, whom he

might easily have won, or otherwise by force have gotten the upper hand. For it is not the part of a wise physician, nor of a good governor of a commonwealth to use the sword, but in great extremity, where there is no other help nor remedy : and there lacked judgment in them both, but worst of all in the one, for injury is ever joined with cruelty. The Gracchi on the other side, neither the one nor the other, began to imbrue their hands in the blood of their citizens. For it is reported, that though they did hurt Caius, yet he would never defend himself: and where it was known that he was very valiant in battle with his sword in his hand against the enemy, he shewed himself as cold again in the uproar against his citizens. For he went out of his house unarmed, and fled when he saw them fight: being more circumspect not to do hurt, than not to suffer any. Therefore they are not to be thought cowards for their flying, but rather men fearful to offend any man. For they were driven, either to yield to them that followed them, or else if they stayed, to stand to their defence, because they might keep themselves from hurt.

And where they accuse Tiberius for the faults he committed, the greatest that ever he did was when he deposed Octavius his colleague from the Tribuneship, and that he himself made suit for the second. And as for Caius, they falsely accused him for the death of Antyllius the sergeant, who indeed was slain unknown to him, and to his great grief: where Cleomenes on the other side, although we should forget the murder he committed upon the Ephors, yet he set slaves at liberty, and ruled the kingdom in manner himself alone : but yet for manners' sake only he joined his own brother with him, which was of the self same house. And when he had persuaded Archidamus (who was next heir to the kingdom of the other royal house) to be bold to return home from Messené unto Sparta: he suffered him to be slain, and because he did not revenge his death, he did confirm their opinion that thought he was con-

14—2

senting to his death. Lycurgus on the other side, whose example he did counterfeit to follow, because he did willingly resign the kingdom unto his brother's son Charilaus, and being afraid also, that if the young child should chance to miscarry, they would suspect him for his death: he exiled himself out of his own country a long time travelling up and down, and returned not to Sparta again, before Charilaus had gotten a son to succeed him in his kingdom. But we cannot set another Grecian by Lycurgus compar-able unto him. We have declared also that amongst Cleomenes' deeds, there were many other greater alterations than these, and also many other breaches of the law. So they that do condemn the manners of the one and the other, say, that the two Grecians from the beginning had an aspiring mind to be tyrants, still practising wars. Whereas the two Romans only, even by their most mortal enemies, could be blamed for nothing else, but for an extreme ambition, and did confess that they were too earnest and vehement above their nature, in any strife or contention they had with their adversaries, and that they yielded unto that choler and passion, as unto ill winds, which brought them to do those things they did in the end. For what more just or honest intent could they have had than the first was: had not the rich men (even through stoutness and authority to overthrow the laws) brought them against their wills into quarrel: the one to save his life, the other to revenge his brother's death, who was slain without order, justice, or the authority of any officer? Thus thou mayest thyself see the difference that was betwixt the Grecians and the Romans: and now to tell you plainly my opinion of both, I think that Tiberius was the stoutest of the four, that the young king Agis offended least, and that, for boldness and courage, Caius came nothing near unto Cleomenes.

NOTES

p. 1. In the early editions this preface is attached to the life of Aemilius Paulus, which, contrary to Plutarch's practice elsewhere, is placed before the Greek parallel life. In modern editions the order has been corrected and the introduction transposed, as here, to precede the life of Timoleon.

p. 1, l. 16. The verse quotation is from a fragment of the *Tympanistae* of Sophocles.

p. 1, l. 19. Democritus of Abdera (about 460 B.C.–370 B.C.), the Laughing Philosopher whose views on physics were adopted later by the Epicureans, as in Lucretius' great poem *De rerum Natura*.

p. 2, l. 21. After the Athenian fleet which had been sent to Sicily had been annihilated by the Syracusans in 413 B.C. Syracuse passed through a period of unrest at home and danger from the Carthaginians abroad, till in 405 the elder Dionysius established himself as despot. Dionysius strengthened his power by making an impregnable fortress of the part of Syracuse which was upon Quail-island (Ortygia) and improving the fortifications of the city. He was thus able to maintain himself against attacks from his subjects (which soon began owing to discontent at his exactions from the hostile party and the taxation needed to pay for his public works), and also to defy the onslaughts of the Carthaginians against whom he carried on war intermittently for many years. He was also able to hold in check the native population—the Sicels—and to carry on war with the peoples of Southern Italy. He also interfered frequently in the affairs of Greece, Syracuse as a colony of Dorian Greeks feeling bound to support the Dorian Greek states which were headed by Sparta. Early in 367 B.C. Dionysius died and was succeeded by his son Dionysius II, a man of much less character and energy than his father. In 357 B.C. Dion, who was brother-in-law to Dionysius II and a disciple of Plato, eager to apply his master's doctrines to practical politics returned from the Peloponnesus with a small force and after some time was able to expel Dionysius from Syracuse. After a struggle which continued till 355 B.C. Dion assumed the reins of government, but soon became as unpopular as his predecessors. As a result he was assassinated in 353 B.C. by Callippus, who reigned as despot for thirteen months. He was then driven from Syracuse and succeeded by Hipparinus, a son of Dionysius I and half-brother of Dionysius II. In 351 Hipparinus died and was succeeded by another brother Nysaeus.

p. 2, l. 40. Nysaeus was expelled and Dionysius II restored in 346 B.C.

p. 3, l. 4. North's statement that Syracuse was the "greatest kingdom that ever was in the world" would have been impossible for Plutarch, remembering countries like Macedon, Persia, or Egypt. What Plutarch says is not "the greatest kingdom" but "the greatest despotism." The mistake is North's, for Amyot translates correctly *la plus puissante tyrannie.*

p. 3, l. 13. Hicetes, or **Hiketas,** as his name is more correctly given, was a Dorian of Syracuse who had made himself master of the Ionic Greek town of Leontini a short distance inland from Syracuse.

p. 3, l. 22. The struggle of the Carthaginians for the possession of Sicily continued for centuries. They had been severely defeated by Gelo, despot of Syracuse, at Himera as long ago as 480 B.C. The struggle however continued till, after the Hannibalic war (218 B.C.–202 B.C.), the Romans broke the power of Carthage, which they ultimately took and destroyed in 146 B.C.

p. 3, l. 26. As Syracuse was a Corinthian colony (founded in 735 B.C.), appeals for help were naturally first made to the mother city. But Plutarch says here not "the Syracusans" but "the Siceliots," *i.e.* the Sicilian Greeks as distinguished from the Sicels, the older inhabitants of the island, who were said to be of the same stock as the Latins. The history of Corinth hardly confirms Plutarch's high praise.

p. 5, ll. 6–7. The English is somewhat clumsy. Amyot says *car c'estoit un homme acervelé, et furieusement espris et perdu de convoitise de regner, que luy avoient mise en la teste une trouppe de gens de basse condition, qui se disoient ses amis.*

p. 5, l. 18. The date of this battle is not exactly known. Cleonae was a small town between Corinth and Argos: in its territory the Nemean games were celebrated.

p. 6, l. 17. Satyrus may have been called Orthagoras, "soothsayer," *i.e.* truth-speaker, as a compliment to his success as a prophet.

Theopompus of Chios (378 B.C.–?300 B.C.) and **Ephorus** (about 400 B.C.–340 B.C.) from Cyme in Asia Minor were the two most important Greek historians of the 4th century B.C. Their works are lost except for some fragments, but much of Ephorus' Universal History from 1090 B.C. to 340 B.C. is preserved in substance by Diodorus Siculus who wrote in the reign of Augustus. Theopompus wrote two large works, one on Greek History continuing the work of Thucydides from 411 B.C. to 393 B.C., the other on the life and times of Philip of Macedon who reigned from 360 B.C. to 336 B.C. This work was very discursive and included even Sicilian History. A large fragment of a Greek historian which was found in Egypt and published in 1907 has been attributed by some scholars to Theopompus, by others with more probability to Ephorus. With Ephorus Plutarch couples Timaeus, but as Amyot omits the latter, North naturally does so also. Timaeus (352 B.C.–256 B.C.) was himself a

Sicilian, the son of the ruler of Tauromenium and may have seen Timoleon, as his father Andromachus was a friend of Timoleon and supported his expedition (p. 13). Timaeus wrote a history of Sicily which came down to 264 B.C. This work seems to have been Plutarch's chief source for the history of Timoleon.

p. 7, l. 28. North's translation is here not very clear; the words translated "and rest confounded in themselves" mean in the original "being driven away from their own calculations," which Amyot translates *est poussé hors des discours, sur lesquels il s'estoit premierement fondé.*

p. 7, l. 33. lickerous-mouthed men: gluttons.

p. 8, l. 10. North here follows Amyot exactly. The original means that Phocion could have wished for the result to be attained but for the policy followed in attaining it to be his.

p. 9, l. 3. The picturesque phrase "Hicetes had carried two faces in one hood" is North's own; the original merely says "letters were brought revealing his change of sides and treachery." Amyot says *des lettres d'Icetes, par lesquelles il apparoissoit clairement qu'il avoit tourné sa robbe, et qu'il estoit traistre.*

p. 9, l. 26. North like his contemporaries uses words appropriate to Christianity for the older pagan religion. Here the "nuns" are only the priestesses of the Virgin as the Greeks generally called Proserpina. Her mother Demeter (Ceres) was also associated in the cult.

p. 9, l. 34. Delphi, the famous oracle of Apollo on the north side of the Corinthian gulf; Delphos to Shakespeare in the *Winter's Tale.*

p. 10, l. 8. North often uses *element* where, as in the Bible, we should expect *firmament*; cp. p. 112, l. 24 and Shakespeare, *2 Henry IV,* IV. iii. 58, " I, in the clear sky of fame, outshine you as much as the full moon doth the cinders of the element " (*i.e.* the stars).

p. 10, l. 22. Like Milton's

> That fair field
> Of Enna, where Proserpine gathering flowers,
> Herself a fairer flower, by gloomy Dis
> Was gathered, which cost Ceres all that pain
> To seek her through the world.
>
> *Paradise Lost,* IV. 268.

p. 11, l. 1. The date of Timoleon's arrival was 344 B.C.

p. 11, l. 5. Rhegium at the Straits of Messina on the Italian side, the natural point at which to watch for the arrival of ships from the East.

p. 12, l. 8. incontinently = forthwith. **It stood him very much upon,** &c. = Amyot's *alleguant que cela faisoit grandement pour la seureté de sa descharge.* Plutarch says merely that it was of importance to him for his safety.

p. 13, l. 2. Tauromenium, the modern Taormina, on the N.E. coast of Sicily.

p. 13, l. 4. For Andromachus and Timaeus see note on p. 6, l. 17.

p. 13, l. 22. The Phoenicians are the Carthaginians, who were a colony from Phoenicia.

p. 14, l. 13. Callippus was the assassin of Dion ; **Pharax** the Lacedaemonian had been an opponent of Dion and commanded Dionysius' army when he retired to Locri.

p. 14, l. 33. The town of Adranum, the modern Aderno, is at the foot of Mt Etna to the S.W. The worship of the god Adranus is said to have come from the East, but this seems doubtful.

p. 15, l. 12. The word *vaward* (cp. Shakespeare's "Their bands i' the vaward are the Antiates," *Coriolanus*, I. vi. 53) is spelt by North (and by his contemporary Sir Philip Sidney) *voward*. It is the same word as *vanward*, the modern *vanguard*, which comes from an old French *avant warde*.

p. 16, l. 7. Catana, N. of Syracuse on the E. coast of Sicily. The name Mamercus is not Greek but Italic, suggesting that M. was either a Sicel by origin or an Italian mercenary like the later Mamertines.

p. 17, l. 9. The relationships of Dionysius recorded in the life of Timoleon will be easily seen from the following table :

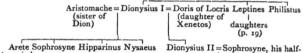

```
                 ┌────────────────┬──────────────┬──────────┐
     Aristomache = Dionysius I = Doris of Locris  Leptines  Philistus
     (sister of   |             (daughter of      |
     Dion)        |             Xenetos)         daughters
                  |                                (p. 19)
 ┌──────┬─────────┴──┬────────┐   ┌──────────────
Arete Sophrosyne Hipparinus Nysaeus   Dionysius II = Sophrosyne, his half-
(married                              |              sister
Dion, her                       sons and daughters put to
uncle)                          death by the Locrians (p. 17).
```

p. 17, l. 21. The verb *go* followed by another verb not preceded by *to* is common in Elizabethan literature, " Go take the city of Catana," p. 22.

p. 17, l. 37. After keeping for some time the participle which is the English construction after *see*, North lapses into the infinitive which is the French construction throughout.

p. 18, l. 33. Plato apparently visited Syracuse three times in the reigns of Dionysius I and II.

p. 18, l. 36. Aristoxenus of Tarentum was a disciple of Aristotle and a distinguished musician. Considerable fragments of one of his works have recently been discovered and published.

p. 19, l. 12. Dionysius I often competed and won second and third prizes for tragedies at the contests in Athens. He is said to have died of excitement on hearing that he had been awarded the first prize for a tragedy at the Lenaean festival at Athens.

p. 19, l. 20. For the construction of the adjective in *Diogenes*

Sinopian cp. Leon Corinthian (p. 22), Timoleon Corinthian (p. 47), Evander Cretan, &c. (p. 77). Diogenes is the famous Cynic philosopher of the 4th century B.C.

p. 19, l. 30. Philistus the historian was in general a supporter of Dionysius, but is not to be confused with the brother of Dionysius I.

p. 20, l. 7. The "castle of Syracuse" was the great fortress made by Dionysius I on the island of Ortygia.

p. 20, l. 12. The town of Thurii, founded by Athens in 443 B.C. but peopled by volunteer colonists from all Greek lands, stood near the site of the ancient Sybaris, which was destroyed in 510 B.C. The Bruttians were wild native tribes who were generally at war with the Greek colonies in S. Italy.

p. 21, l. 24. throughly = thoroughly as in St Matthew iii. 12, "Whose fan is in his hand, and he will *throughly* purge his floor."

p. 21, l. 25. A *mina* was in value about £3. 15s.

p. 22, l. 3. "Une armee effroyable à voir," Amyot. "Mago sailed in, awe-inspiring with his hundred and fifty vessels," Plutarch.

p. 22, l. 10. the barbarous people, "les Barbares," A. The Greek word only means "foreigners."

p. 22, l. 28. crayers were small trading vessels.

p. 23, l. 4. Achradina was the part of Syracuse on the mainland directly opposite to the island of Ortygia. North of Achradina was the district of the quarries in which the Athenians captured in 413 B.C. had been confined, more to the west lay the New Town (Neapolis); west of all three lay the plateau of Epipolae which had been encircled with a wall by Dionysius I.

p. 24, l. 22. In Old English and down to the 17th century the plural of *horse* was the same as the singular, and is so still in dialects. Collectively the form is still used in "a troop of horse."

p. 25, l. 36. hoised: the old verb now obsolete of which the modern *hoist* is a corruption.

p. 26, l. 20. Dinarchus and **Demaretus** are apparently the same persons whom Demosthenes mentions in his speech *On the Crown* as leaders of the Macedonian party in Corinth in the time of Philip and Alexander the Great. In the Greek text followed by Amyot the second name is given as Demaratus and is so copied from him by North.

p. 26, l. 31. In later editions the two sentences are more properly made into one. Fortune, which favoured Timoleon, wished him rather to be admired for his good luck than praised for his own merits.

p. 27, ll. 25-6. The construction of the English is clumsy owing to the use of *so as* followed immediately by *so...as*.

p. 27, l. 39. Syracusans born... = *Voyant...aussi ce peu de Syracusains naturels qui estoient echappez*, Amyot.

p. 28, l. 7. Mago was not crucified, but impaled.

p. 29, l. 11. Athanis was a Syracusan who continued the historical work of Philistus (note, p. 19, l. 30) to the death of Timoleon, and was apparently a contemporary.

p. 29, l. 24. Gelo who became despot of Syracuse in 485 B.C. extended his power over a large part of Sicily and defeated the Carthaginians at Himera on the north side of the island in 480 B.C.

p. 30, l. 1. Apollonia was about the middle of the north coast of Sicily. Leptines also ruled over Engyion which was inland, some distance S.E. of Apollonia.

p. 30, l. 24. Lilybaeum was at the western end of the island.

p. 30, l. 30. an able army=*car aussi estoit-ce une puissance suffisante pour prendre & subiuguer tous les Siciliens*, A. This expedition was in the year 339 B.C. according to some authorities. Others place it between 343 and 341 B.C.

p. 31, l. 1. strangers=foreign mercenaries.

p. 31, l. 18. The Crimesus or Crimisos rises in a mountain ridge south of Himera and flows S.W. till it joins the Hypsas which flows into the sea not far from the ancient Selinus.

p. 31, l. 23. smallage is wild celery.

p. 31, l. 36. The Isthmian games were held every other year in honour of the god Poseidon on the isthmus of Corinth. The Nemean games were held at Nemea in the territory of Cleonae, which borders on Corinth.

p. 32, l. 3. By *pine-apple trees* North means only pines.

p. 32, l. 35. "The Sacred Band" of Carthage was armed with large shields covered with elephant-hide. Diodorus says they were only 2500 in number.

p. 33, l. 20. carts=chariots.

p. 34, l. 3. murrions, the same as morions, helmets without visors.

p. 34, l. 21. fresh-water, though more appropriately used of inexperienced sailors as it often is, is in this sense according to the *Oxford English Dictionary* first found in the present passage, the first passage quoted for sailors belonging to the year 1621.

p. 34, l. 28. plates: plaits or folds, *les plis de leur hocquetons*, A. Plutarch says, "when the bosoms of their under-garments were filled with water."

p. 35, l. 9. This use of *insomuch as* in the meaning of *insomuch that* is first quoted from North. The *Oxford English Dictionary* has no quotation of the use later than 1658. The Greek has merely "and": Amyot connecting with the previous sentence has *dont les uns estans suiuis de pres, furent mis à l'espee emmi la plaine mesme*.

p. 35, l. 28. The "Nomads" are better known as Numidians.

p. 35, l. 38. The double phrase regarding the prisoners represents

Amyot's *Quant aux prisonniers, les soldats en desroberent et destour-
nerent beaucoup.* Plutarch says only "Of the prisoners most were
stolen outright by the soldiers."

p. 37, l. 1. The Bruttians lived in the upland parts of the foot of
Italy. According to Diodorus they were provoked by the mercenaries pillaging the country.

p. 37, l. 11. The expedition of Gisco (better Gesco) was in the
spring of 338 B.C. if the battle of the Crimisos was in 339 B.C.

p. 37, l. 23. The mistaken reading of the manuscripts followed by
Amyot is now emended to Hietae, a town a few miles S.W. of
Panormus (Palermo).

p. 37, l. 29. Philomelus and **Onomarchus** were two brothers who
successively were leaders of the Phocians in the Sacred War 356–
346 B.C. They financed their army by plundering the treasures stored
in the temple of Delphi. Plutarch refers to these men again in an
essay which he wrote on "The tardy vengeance of the Deity"
(*Moralia*, p. 552 F).

p. 38, l. 20. North greatly expands Amyot's expansion of the
original two lines which say merely "These shields of gold and ivory
and painted with purple we took with cheap little shields."

p. 38, l. 25. Neither the site of Calauria nor the river Damyrias
(l. 34) can be certainly identified. **Therewhile** was archaic even in
North's time.

p. 39, l. 15. The plural *ways* so used is very common in the
language of Shakespeare and is so still in dialect. Shakespeare uses
it only with *go*: "Go thy ways to a nunnery," *Hamlet*, III. i. 132.

p. 39, l. 34. The verse is a play upon the words of Medea in
Euripides' play of that name, *v.* 214, where the sense is altogether
different.

p. 39, l. 36. put up in this sense is now replaced by "put up
with." The instances of this usage in the *Oxford English Dictionary*
range from 1573 to 1832.

p. 40, l. 8. passed for in the sense of "cared for," usually with a
negative, is now obsolete.

p. 40, l. 13. Whether Hiketas was really responsible for these
murders is uncertain. The passage in the life of Dion is chap. 58.

p. 40, l. 17. The proper spelling of the name and the position of
the river Abolus are alike uncertain.

p. 41, l. 17. The "degrees" are the ascending rows of seats in
the theatre.

p. 41, l. 22. Thieves and murderers were crucified.

p. 41, l. 30. of the country self is an example of a construction
which became obsolete about North's own time. In it *self* is still an
emphatic adjective like the Latin *ipse.*
In the modern construction "of the country's self" *self* is treated
as a substantive.

p. 41, l. 32. Gela was an important town on the south coast of Sicily, the original inhabitants of which were colonists from Rhodes and Crete. **Agrigentum** (now Girgenti) on a height some distance from the sea was a colony from Gela. The Carthaginians captured and destroyed Agrigentum in 406 B.C., Gela in 405 B.C.

p. 41, l. 33. By "the wars of the Athenians" is meant the great Sicilian expedition of 415 B.C.–413 B.C.

p. 41, l. 37. Elea or Velia was on the coast of Lucania in Italy.

p. 41, l. 38. Ceos, an Ionic island in the Cyclades south of Euboea. As the Syracusans were Dorians, however, we ought possibly to read **Cos**—a large Dorian island not far from Rhodes, on the coast of Asia Minor.

p. 42, l. 17. Timotheus, son of the great Athenian general Conon and himself a distinguished general in many campaigns between 378 B.C. and 356 B.C. **Agesilaus,** the famous lame king of Sparta (399 B.C.–361 B.C.). **Pelopidas** and **Epaminondas,** the two great Boeotian generals during the short-lived Boeotian supremacy (371 B.C.–362 B.C.). Pelopidas was killed when fighting against Alexander of Pherae, a Thessalian chief, in 364 B.C., Epaminondas fell at the battle of Mantinea in 362 B.C. Plutarch's life of Pelopidas is extant, that of Epaminondas, which was apparently the first biography he wrote, is lost.

p. 42, l. 27. It is not known from what play of Sophocles (496 B.C.–406 B.C.) the quotation comes. North does not shine as a versifier. The archaic prefix in *yput* is very common in North's contemporary Spenser, but rare in Shakespeare.

p. 42, l. 31. Antimachus of Claros near Colophon wrote an epic poem on the story of Thebes and an elegiac poem entitled *Lyde*. He flourished about 400 B.C. **Dionysius of Colophon** was a portrait painter and a close imitator of Polygnotus.

p. 42, l. 34. travelled would now be spelt *travailed*.

p. 42, l. 35. tables : pictures. Nicomachus was a painter in the time of Alexander the Great.

p. 42, l. 36. passing, in its old sense of *surpassing*.

p. 43, l. 34. Simonides (556 B.C.–467 B.C.), the famous lyric poet of Ceos. This is a favourite quotation with Plutarch, occurring three times in his extant works.

p. 43, l. 40. North is translating Amyot's *comme Laphystius luy donnast assignation à certain iour, pour venir respondre deuant le peuple à quelque cas, dont il pretendoit le convaincre, ses citoyens se mutinerent, & ne voulurent point que cest adiournement eust lieu.* The Greek says merely "When L. tried to bind him over to answer a certain indictment, he would not allow the citizens to make a noise or prevent him."

p. 44, l. 7. because : to the end that, an obsolete use: *à fin que,* A.

p. 44, l. 36. The English construction is much clumsier than the French : *estant ja bien auant sur son aage, la veuë luy commença premierement à baisser, & vn peu apres il la perdit du tout.*

p. 45, l. 1. a disease inheritable, &c. : *vn accident de maladie hereditaire à sa race,* A.

p. 46, l. 21. The quaint phrase " took him by the back " is North's own.

p. 46, l. 23. The plural *funerals* (cp. obsequies) was common in earlier English : " His funerals shall not be in our camp," Shakespeare, *Julius Caesar*, v. iii. 105.

p. 48, l. 4. In early Rome the population consisted of the patricians and their clients on the one hand and of the plebeians or common people on the other. The plebeians had no political rights.

p. 48, l. 6. The early history of Rome is contaminated with many Greek stories, some, like this one, being very foolish. According to the generally received chronology, Pythagoras is later than Numa. The story was obviously invented in order to connect the name Aemilius with a Greek word of almost the same spelling (*haimylios*) meaning " plausible " or " clever." Mamercus has better authority than Marcus.

p. 48, l. 14. At the battle of Cannae, in S.E. Italy, Hannibal the Carthaginian disastrously defeated the Romans in 216 B.C. The fellow-consul of Paulus in this battle was Gaius Terentius Varro.

p. 48, l. 22. to let : to hinder. So St Paul says (*Romans* i. 13) " Oftentimes I purposed to come unto you, but was let hitherto." For the substantive see p. 114, l. 31.

p. 48, l. 25. By " Scipio the Great " is meant Scipio Africanus the elder, the conqueror of the Carthaginians at Zama in 202 B.C. The younger Scipio Africanus who captured and destroyed Carthage in 146 B.C. was a son of Aemilius Paulus who was adopted by his own cousin, the son of the elder Scipio Africanus.

p. 49, l. 3. To plead causes as a barrister was in ancient Rome as in modern England a common avenue to political promotion.

p. 49, l. 17. The Aediles might be roughly defined as Police Commissioners. One of their duties was to celebrate the public games, and if this was done successfully the aedile was likely to be elected to higher office. In later times there was a regular sequence of offices, with intervals between them, culminating in the consulship.

p. 49, l. 22. The Augurs at Rome formed a " college " or guild, to membership of which rising politicians aspired. Aemilius differed from most of his colleagues in regarding the position as a duty and not merely as an honour (l. 29).

p. 50, l. 15. neither corrupting them for a second charge is in the original " not suing for a second period of command by currying favour in the first."

p. 50, 1. 30. The war with Antiochus the Great of Syria was in 191 B.C. "In the south parts" is a far from correct translation of A.'s *en Levant*.

p. 50, 1. 31. The false concord "that ways" is common in earlier English and is still in dialects. Cp. Dame Quickly's "come a little nearer this ways," *Merry Wives of Windsor*, II. ii. 50. It has always been commonest with numerals used collectively as in "a thirty thousand" below (l. 39).

p. 50, 1. 32. in the neck, like "took him by the back," p. 46, l. 21, is a picturesque phrase of North's own. Aemilius was in Spain from 191 B.C. to 189 B.C. At first he suffered a severe defeat but later was very successful and was voted a triumph on his return to Rome.

p. 50, 1. 34. In modern English "they sent Aemilius *as* Praetor." On military service the lictors carried twelve axes in front of a consul; the praetor, who was a step lower in the official career, had six carried before him. Aemilius is a proconsul, *i.e.* an acting consul, with a consul's rights and privileges.

p. 52, 1. 5. This was Quintus Fabius Maximus nicknamed Cunctator, "Wait and see," the famous dictator in the Hannibalic war. He died at a great age in 203 B.C. His son who had also been consul pre-deceased him. For the relations of the Scipios see note on p. 48, l. 25.

p. 52, 1. 10. Cato is the famous Censor, M. Porcius Cato (234 B.C.–149 B.C.). Plutarch wrote lives of both Fabius Maximus and Cato.

p. 52, 1. 33. The Ligurians were in the mountains above the Gulf of Genoa and at one time extended farther west and south.

p. 53, 1. 4. the strait of Hercules' Pillars: the straits of Gibraltar.

p. 53, 1. 22. These boats had presumably three oars a side; in the only other place where the Greek word occurs it means having three banks of oars.

p. 53, 1. 34. curiously: with greater care or zeal : *un peu trop curieusement*, A.

p. 53, 1. 38. hunts: old word for *hunters*. The Common Hunt of the City of London was abolished in 1807 (*O.E.D.*): "instructors in hunting," Plutarch : *des piqueurs & dompteurs de cheuaux & des veneurs Grecs*, A.

p. 53, 1. 39. matters of commonwealth : affairs of state.

p. 54, 1. 5. Perseus was the son of Philip V of Macedon whom the Romans under Flamininus had defeated at the battle of Cynoscephalae in 197 B.C. (l. 17 and p. 55). Perseus succeeded his father in 179 B.C.

p. 54, 1. 11. King Antiochus in the third year of the war (189 B.C.) was defeated by the Romans at Magnesia in Asia Minor.

p. 54, 1. 32. The dynasty was founded by Antigonus, one of the generals of Alexander the Great, who after the death of Alexander made for himself a great kingdom mainly on the Hellespont (the Dardanelles) and in Asia, but was defeated and slain at the battle of

Ipsus in 301 B.C. His son Demetrius Poliorketes (the City-sacker) escaped and established himself first at Athens and afterwards in Macedonia, from which he was expelled by Pyrrhus in 287 B.C. Demetrius himself fled to Asia, but his son Antigonus Gonatas was able to establish himself in Greece and became king of Macedon in 277 B.C. He was succeeded by Demetrius II in 239 B.C., who died in 229 B.C. and was succeeded by Antigonus Doson (p. 55, l. 1), at first nominally as guardian of the child Philip, but actually king till 220 B.C. Philip then came to the throne at the age of 17.

p. 55, l. 38. For this collective use of the word *weapon* cp. p. 62, l. 36.

p. 56, l. 7. The story of Demetrius the victim of his father's jealousy fanned by Perseus is told by Livy the Roman historian in great detail (Book 40).

p. 56, l. 16. For *miserable* in this sense literary English now uses *miserly*, though this usage survives in dialect.

p. 56, l. 31. Publius Licinius was defeated near Larissa in Thessaly in 171 B.C.

p. 56, l. 36. Oreus : at the north end of the island of Euboea.

p. 56, l. 40. foists or fusts were light vessels with both sails and oars. Amyot seems either to have had a bad reading in the MS. from which he was translating or to have confused the Greek word for fifty with that for ships with five banks of oars. The correct translation is " he made himself master of four galleys with five banks of oars."

p. 57, l. 2. Hostilius was defeated in 170 B.C.

p. 57, l. 9. The Dardanians were a Thracian tribe.

p. 57, l. 14. Most scholars regard the Bastarnae as being not Gauls but Germans. But the ancients had much difficulty in distinguishing between the peoples of the north.

p. 57, l. 15. The Illyrians held the Adriatic coast north of Greece.

p. 57, l. 18. The Gauls probably required no bribes from Perseus to invade the southern lands. They had passed into Italy about 400 B.C., sacked Rome about 390 B.C., invaded Greece in 281 B.C., and established themselves in the heart of Asia Minor. Another great wave of invasion fell upon Italy in 106 B.C., the onslaught of the Cimbri and Teutoni.

p. 57, l. 28. well stepped on in years : *fort auant en son aage*, A. The phrase more commonly used in Elizabethan English is " well stept in (or into) years."

p. 58, l. 14. Ordinarily the two consuls for the year cast lots for the provinces in which they were to conduct warlike operations, but, as three generals had already been unsuccessful, no doubt it was felt that the war in Macedonia was too serious to be left to the chance of the lot.

p. 58, l. 19. Owing to the Roman custom of exposing female children, it is rare to find so many as three daughters in a family. Unlike boys, Roman girls in the second century B.C. and later had no *praenomen, e.g.* Gaia, Lucia, &c., but if there were two were simply called by the family name, *e.g.* Antonia, with the addition of *major* or *minor*. Thus Tertia is not a girl's proper name but merely No. 3. Cicero (*de Divinatione*, II. 83) calls her simply Aemilia, though in I. 103, where the story is given at length, the name is Tertia as here.

p. 58, l. 24. she meant it by : *ce qu'elle entendoit d'vn petit chien*, A. This use of *by* with verbs of saying and thinking is now obsolete. Cp. Shakespeare, *Merchant of Venice*, II. ix. 25, "What many men desire ! that 'many' may be meant *By* the fool multitude, that choose by show."

p. 60, l. 14. Maedica, the territory of the Maedi, a Thracian tribe.

p. 61, l. 14. It was a saying of Philip of Macedon, the father of Alexander the Great, that he could take any city through the gate of which a beast of burden laden with gold could pass.

p. 61, l. 16. Alexander destroyed the spoils when he made his expedition to India, as Plutarch tells us in the life of Alexander, chap. 57.

p. 61, l. 35. a fond and foul part : *commit vn cas meschant &° mal-heureux*, A.

p. 62, l. 24. by tract of time to eat him out with charge : Plutarch says "thinking to wear him out by delay and expense."

p. 64, l. 37. Perrhaebia is a district S. of Macedonia and S.W. of Mt Olympus. Python and Petra are on opposite sides of the Olympus range.

p. 65, l. 3. Publius Cornelius Scipio Nasica. In this family there were members of this name in six successive generations. This one had a great reputation for shrewdness and was nicknamed Corculum, "Brainy," in consequence. His father was a cousin of the elder Africanus, whose elder daughter Corculum married. North's "son adopted" is an inaccurate translation of A.'s correct rendering *gendre*. From Corculum's rather vainglorious memoirs Plutarch drew some of the historical facts recorded in the Lives (cp. p. 66, l. 26).

p. 65, l. 13. Polybius (about 204 B.C.–122 B.C.), one of the most accurate of Greek historians. He lived many years at Rome, was an intimate friend of Aemilius, and the tutor and lifelong friend of his son the younger Africanus.

p. 66, l. 1. North, knowing no Greek, scans Eumelus wrongly with the middle syllable short.

p. 66, l. 15. The Cretan was no doubt one of the light-armed force attached to the Roman army.

p. 66, l. 16. An inaccurate rendering of A.'s *luy alla descouurir le tour &° circuit que faisoient les Romains.*

p. 66, l. 21. strangers, *i.e.* mercenaries.

p. 66, l. 40. Pydna was a town in Macedonia on the coast road to the north.

p. 67, l. 20. champion : champaign, level ground. North hardly brings out the meaning of the rest of the sentence. Plutarch says that it was suitable "for a phalanx, which requires level ground to stand on and an even area in which to move." The phalanx was a section of the Macedonian army made up of units arranged with 16 men in front and 16 deep. It was armed with very long spears which made movement except in a straight line difficult and on rough ground it could not maintain its cohesion. Livy (XLIV. 37) says this was so here.

p. 67, l. 23. The archers are called naked men, as having no body armour.

p. 68, l. 21. According to Livy the Roman soldiers were not frightened by the eclipse because one of their officers, C. Sulpicius Gallus, had calculated when it would take place and had explained it to them beforehand.

p. 69, l. 10. The twenty-first victim, says Plutarch, indicated victory to those on the defence. Hence Aemilius does not directly attack the Macedonians.

p. 69, l. 36. Aemilius did not "pass by" but "went up to" the troops.

p. 70, l. 6. and their thighs with tasses : *les iambes·armees de greues et de cuissots*, A. Plutarch mentions only greaves.

p. 70, l. 16. The "brave purple cassocks" are in the original "red coats."

p. 71, l. 22. Of this Posidonius hardly anything is known. He must not be confused with the philosopher (*c.* 130 B.C.–46 B.C.), from whom Cicero borrowed many of his ideas.

p. 71, l. 29. a stripe of a horse : he had been kicked on the leg by a horse, says Plutarch.

p. 72, l. 7. The Paelignians lived in the Apennines in central Italy. Near neighbours of theirs on the E. were the Marrucinians for whom Amyot mistakenly read Terracinians in l. 23. Tarracina (earlier Anxur) was a Volscian town on the west coast of Italy.

p. 72, l. 29. Mt Olocrus was to the S.W. of Pydna.

p. 73, l. 14. private : individual, Amyot *particuliers* : Plutarch says " Aem. explained these things to the leaders and the leaders to the soldiers."

p. 73, l. 40. beaten : *au squadron des vieux routiers Macedoniens*, A.

p. 74, l. 2. great Cato : Cato the Censor.

p. 75, l. 10. far forth night : *bien auant en la nuict*, A. This construction of *forth* is now obsolete. The latest example given by the *Oxford English Dictionary* is a hundred years earlier than North.

p. 76, l. 6. Scipio: Africanus the younger destroyed Carthage in 146 B.C., and Numantia in Spain in 133 B.C.

p. 76, l. 15. Pella was the capital of Macedonia; N.W. of Thessalonica (Salonika).

p. 76, l. 37. Eudaeus: in modern texts **Eulaeus.**

p. 77, l. 14. Amphipolis: an important town on the river Strymon (Struma), founded by the Athenians in 437 B.C., seized by the Spartans with its inhabitants' consent 424 B.C., later occupied by Philip of Macedon. **Galepsus,** S.E. of Amphipolis, on the coast.

p. 78, l. 32. Sagra: the Sagras was a river in S. Italy where in the 6th century B.C. (the exact date is uncertain) 10,000 men of Western Locri defeated 130,000 men of Croton.

p. 78, l. 35. Mycale on the W. coast of Asia Minor. The battle took place in 479 B.C.

p. 79, l. 1. After the battle of Lake Regillus (499 B.C.). The story of the "great twin brethren" is told in Macaulay's *Lays of Ancient Rome.*

p. 79, l. 13. Amyot translates Ahenobarbus more correctly *ayant barbe blonde comme cuivre.* Both North and Amyot are wrong as to the colour. Plutarch says red.

p. 79, l. 16. Domitian's reign (81 B.C.–96 A.D.) was disturbed by a rising headed by L. Antonius Saturninus, the governor of Upper Germany, in 89 A.D. He was soon defeated by Appius Norbanus, the governor of Lower Germany, who remained loyal.

p. 80, l. 11. As in Epimenides' verse quoted by St Paul (*Titus* i. 12) the Cretans were "always liars, evil beasts."

p. 82, l. 32. brag as an adjective has been long obsolete.

p. 83, l. 7. Plutarch merely says "from the royal store."

p. 83, l. 20. Phidias (*c.* 490 B.C.–432 B.C.), the sculptor of the Parthenon, afterwards made the famous chryselephantine statue of Jupiter at Olympia in Elis.

p. 84, l. 18. The sons that were learned are obviously Fabius Maximus and Scipio Africanus.

p. 84, l. 25. This simplicity of life was characteristic of the Tubero branch of the Aelian family. Aemilius' grandson who played a considerable part as statesman and Stoic philosopher in the second half of the second century B.C. followed the earlier practice of the family.

p. 84, l. 37. Epirus is the mountainous country thinly peopled by poor highlanders, N.W. of Greece.

p. 85, l. 28. Oricum was near the Acroceraunian promontory and about the nearest point to Italy.

p. 86, l. 9. Servius Sulpicius Galba had been a tribune of the soldiers in the campaign. The story is told almost exactly in the same form by Livy XLV. 35 ff.

p. 86, l. 34. The vote of the first tribe against Aemilius was important, because, being chosen by lot, its vote was supposed to indicate the will of heaven, and the other tribes were almost certain to follow its example.

p. 87, l. 13. Marcus Servilius Geminus must have been a very old man at this time, since he was holding important offices as early as 203 B.C. He was no doubt chosen to address the soldiers as himself a very distinguished soldier. He had been more than once a commissioner for establishing colonies in conquered territory in Italy, which were occupied by the same class as the common soldier, and Servilius would be regarded as sympathetic with them.

p. 87, l. 25. Amyot had here a bad reading *Libyes* "Africans" for *Ligyes* "Ligurians" (see p. 52, l. 33). North betrays his ignorance of geography and makes nonsense by inserting "other."

p. 88, ll. 5 ff. This long sentence, though the general meaning is preserved, is rather paraphrased than translated by Amyot, and North carries the paraphrase still farther. In Dryden's translation revised by Clough it is thus given: "Yet to such a height of power is malice arrived amongst you, that a man without one scar to show on his skin, that is smooth and sleek with ease and home-keeping habits, will undertake to define the office and duties of a general before *us*, who with our own wounds have been taught how to judge of the valour or the cowardice of commanders." Servilius' action shows that the proper pronoun is *us* and not *you* as in North and Amyot.

p. 89, l. 24. North converts the weapons of Aemilius' time into those of his own. Plutarch is less elaborate: the weapons were in a carefully ordered disorder, helmets on shields, breastplates on greaves, Cretan round shields, Thracian wicker shields and quivers mingled with horses' bridles, &c.

p. 92, l. 13. On such occasions the soldiers' songs were mostly jests at the expense of their general. The more abuse they could heap upon him, the more likely in their view he was to escape the envy of Nemesis.

p. 92, l. 23. The passage of Homer to which Plutarch apparently refers is *Iliad* XXIV. 527 ff.:

> Two coffers lie beside the door of Jove,
> With gifts for man: one good, the other ill;
> To whom from each the Lord of lightning gives,
> Him sometimes evil, sometimes good befalls.
> LORD DERBY's translation.

p. 92, l. 37. fear: in the sense of frighten now only archaic or in dialects. For the two uses of frighten and dread side by side see p. 93, ll. 22, 23.

p. 93, l. 28. Aemilius must have had a fair wind. The steamer from Brindisi to Corfu in good weather takes 10 to 12 hours. The journey from Corfu to Delphi would now be much more expeditious.

p. 94, 1. 31. The construction is irregular: to see that his children are alive, &c.

p. 95, 1. 17. chancellor: *il seruit de scribe & de greffier aux magistrats de Rome,* A. Plutarch says " was under-secretary to the magistrates."

p. 95, 1. 26. contribution: it was, as Plutarch says, henceforth unnecessary to levy the property tax (*tributum*). The Romans, however, had a great windfall in 133 B.C. when the last king of Pergamum bequeathed his kingdom to them.

p. 95, 1. 27. Hirtius and **Pansa** were consuls in 43 B.C. Both fell besieging Antonius at Mutina (Modena) during their year of office.

p. 96, 1. 1. Scipio's competitor for the censorship in 142 B.C. was Appius Claudius Pulcher, the father-in-law of Tiberius Gracchus. There was no " family of the Appians," Appius being a *praenomen.* The family name was Claudius. The mistake is Plutarch's.

p. 96, 1. 15. a common sergeant: a herald. The word translated "a prattling fellow" is merely a proper name, Philonicus. Plutarch tells us elsewhere that he was a taxgatherer.

p. 96, 11. 30 ff. The Censors amongst other duties revised the roll of the Senate, striking out those they considered unworthy and restoring others. They could also deprive a knight of the horse with which the State supplied him.

p. 96, 1. 38. sessors: an obsolete form of *assessors.*

p. 97, 1. 4. Aemilius named Lepidus as President of the Senate and struck three senators off the roll. The sentence is clumsily expressed.

p. 97, 1. 8. Quintus Marcius Philippus, the other Censor in 164 B.C., had like Aemilius fought against the Ligurians, had been an envoy in Macedonia and as consul had carried on an ineffective campaign there in 169 B.C.

p. 97, 1. 16. Velia on the S.W. coast of Italy. The phrase " took sea " in this sense is now obsolete and has been replaced by " took ship," which is also old.

p. 97, 1. 34. perseverance: persistence. This example is nearly three hundred years earlier than that given in the *Oxford English Dictionary.* Amyot translates more accurately *sans qu'on eust apperceu auparauant, ny qu'on se fust douté d'aucune alteration.*

p. 98, 1. 9. Spain, Genoa (Liguria), **Macedon,** the three provinces where Aemilius had commanded. The action showed the goodwill of those who had been under his rule.

p. 98, 1. 12. North introduces the church as he did nuns in the life of Timoleon (p. 9). A. more accurately *pour aider à le porter.* Aemilius died in 160 B.C.

p. 100, 1. 18. Gylippus, the Spartan general who defeated the Sicilian expedition of the Athenians in 413 B.C. Thucydides says nothing of his disgrace in Sicily. But he was banished from Sparta many years afterwards for embezzling part of the money which Lysander had commissioned him to take to Sparta. For Callippus and Pharax see p. 14 and notes.

p. 102, 1. 10. The quotation is supposed to come from a play "The Shepherds" of which only some twenty lines are preserved.

p. 102, 1. 29. Theophrastus (378 B.C.–c. 285 B.C.) was Aristotle's successor in the Peripatetic school. The work which Plutarch quotes is lost.

p. 103, 1. 7. Phocion, the Athenian statesman (402 B.C.–317 B.C.), whose life also was written by Plutarch.

p. 103, 1. 8. Antipater (about 397 B.C.–319 B.C.), the Macedonian general who was left to control Macedonia and Greece when Alexander the Great went to the East. Phocion and Antipater were brought into contact in various political negotiations, especially after the battle of Krannon in 322 B.C. when Antipater deprived Athens of all possessions beyond her own frontiers.

p. 103, 1. 33. The plural "Gracchi," following the classical concord, is logically more correct after two names than the modern English fashion of putting it in the singular.

p. 104, 1. 32. Sparta had the unique distinction of having two kings of different families reigning at the same time. The families were the Eurypontidae and Agiadae (see p. 105, l. 7).

p. 104, 1. 35. Agesilaus, the lame king, in whose long reign (398 B.C.–361 B.C.) the power of Sparta greatly declined.

p. 104, 1. 39. Archidamus shared in many of his father's exploits and later served abroad in Crete and elsewhere as a soldier of fortune. While helping the men of Tarentum he was defeated and slain by the Messapians (who lived in the heel of Italy) in 338 B.C.

p. 105, 1. 2. Agis III who had attempted to raise rebellion against the Macedonian power in Alexander's absence was defeated by Antipater and slain when besieging Megalopolis in Arcadia (331 B.C.).

p. 105, 1. 8. Pausanias defeated the Persians at Plataea in 479 B.C. He was not king of Sparta but guardian of the child king Pleistarchus.

p. 105, 1. 12. The younger Pausanias was charged with treason because he had been unduly friendly to the Athenians after their downfall in 404 B.C. and because, through his late arrival, the great Spartan general Lysander had been defeated and slain at Haliartus in Boeotia in 395 B.C.

p. 105, 1. 23. Areus fell defending the liberty of Greece against Antigonus Gonatas (see p. 54) in 265 B.C. after a reign of forty-four years. **Acrotatus** died soon afterwards while fighting against Aristo-demus, despot of Megalopolis.

p. 105, l. 38. Seleucus: the founder of the Seleucid line of kings in Syria; he died in 281 B.C.

p. 106, l. 12. a plain Spanish cape: *vne poure meschante cappe*, A. North forgets that a Spartan of Agis' day would not have much connexion with Spain. This short mantle was in fact the ordinary garb of the Spartan.

p. 106, l. 17. The governing Spartans (or Spartiates) were a very small minority, the body of the population consisting of Helots, who were serfs bound to the soil, and of Perioeci, who were free men but had no political rights. Consequently the minority lived perpetually under a kind of military *régime*, with all the hardships of camp life, in order to be able to defend themselves at any time from their own hostile countrymen. This *régime* they attributed to an ancient reformer, Lycurgus (see his life by Plutarch).

p. 106, l. 20. The Spartans overthrew the Athenian Empire in 404 B.C. Under Lycurgus' *régime* only iron money was allowed in Sparta; after the Spartan victory, gold and silver and other luxuries began to be smuggled into Sparta.

p. 106, l. 24. Lycurgus had divided the Spartan territory into a number of equal portions which could be neither subdivided nor sold, but remained in the same families from generation to generation. **Epitadeus**, whose date is uncertain, was one of the committee of five Ephors, or overseers, who in fact, if not in name, controlled the Spartan government. The effect of his law, whereby the ancestral allotments could be sold, was that landed property gradually became concentrated in a very few hands.

p. 107, ll. 2–4. which made all honest sciences, &c.: *qui fut cause d'y faire cesser tous exercices honestes & liberaux, & d'y introduire les mechaniques, auec enuie & haine à l'encontre de ceux qui possedoient les biens*, Amyot.

p. 107, l. 27. Lysander was a descendant of the famous general Lysander who fell at Haliartus in 395 B.C.

p. 108, l. 8. friends: *amis*, A.: a very loose translation of the Greek word which means "poor retainers," free men working for a daily wage.

p. 108, l. 19. depart: in Tudor and earlier English = part, in its various senses. "Till death us do part" in the marriage service was in its original form "till death us depart."

p. 108, l. 22. Seleucus and **Ptolemy**, the wealthy kings of Syria and Egypt.

p. 108, l. 37. In Sparta women had more freedom and more esteem than at Athens.

p. 109, l. 11. to let: to prevent this enterprise succeeding (cp.

note on p. 48, l. 22). Observe that with the negative meaning contained in *let*, the following *not* is superfluous, but is often found in earlier English, where two negatives did not make an affirmative.

p. 109, l. 29. Pellene was in the valley of the Eurotas some six miles N.W. of Sparta ; **Sellasia**, about four miles due east of Pellene ; **Taygetus**, the great mountain range running from north to south between Sparta and Messenia ; **Malea**, the most southerly point of the long eastern peninsula.

p. 110, l. 16. Thalamae, now Kutiphari, on the south-western side of Taygetus, not far from the Gulf of Messenia. The local form of the goddess' name was Pasipha. Enquirers of the oracle slept in the temple and got their answer in a dream.

p. 110, l. 19. Ammon, whose most famous shrine was on an oasis in the Libyan desert, is generally identified with Zeus himself.

p. 110, l. 20. Cassandra carried off by Agamemnon at the sack of Troy had shrines under the name of Alexandra at Amyclae (near Sparta) and at Leuctra in Laconia.

p. 110, l. 23. Phylarchus, a native either of Athens or of Naucratis in Egypt, wrote a history of this period.

p. 110, l. 24. Amyclas, the hero after whom Amyclae was named. The story of Daphne is elsewhere connected with Arcadia, not with Sparta.

p. 111, l. 18. Strangers were not encouraged at Sparta and frequently orders were issued by the authorities that they should be expelled.

p. 111, l. 32. Terpander, the inventor of the seven-stringed lyre and the Dorian musical mode, came from Antissa in the island of Lesbos ; **Thales** or **Thaletas** is mentioned in Plutarch's life of Lycurgus as coming from Crete ; **Pherecydes**, an early prose writer, came from the island of Syros. Spartan severity increased in the fifth century B.C.

p. 111, l. 39. Phrynis, in the early part of the fifth century B.C.

p. 112, l. 2. Timotheus flourished about 400 B.C. A poem of his was discovered in Egypt and published in 1903. It is more remarkable for high-sounding phrases than for sense, and would not have commended itself to the simple taste of the Spartans.

p. 112, l. 4. did not far off prevent: *n'eussent pas voulu de loing obuier*, A. There is nothing in the Greek corresponding to " far off " or *de loing*.

p. 112, l. 15. The people at Sparta had very little power and could only say Yes or No to the proposal laid before them.

p. 112, l. 24. in the element: *du ciel*, A.

p. 112, l. 32. The oracle was not at Olympus (a mountain in Thessaly) but at Olympia in Elis, where was the great temple of Olympian Zeus.

p. 113, l. 6. The goddess of the Brazen House (Chalcioecos) was not Juno but Athena. The mistake is Amyot's. The temple was so named because covered with bronze tiles.

p. 113, 1. 16. incensed : "urged on, incited," an obsolete use. Cp. Shakespeare, *King Lear*, II. iv. 309, "And what they may incense him to, being apt To have his ear abused, wisdom bids fear."

p. 113, 1. 40. Tegea was in Arcadia on the main road leading from Sparta to the north.

p. 114, 1. 22. The documents were called *clāria* because the security for payment was the allotments of land (*clāros*).

p. 114, 1. 31. let: hindrance. The word has been revived in connexion with lawn tennis.

p. 114, 1. 33. The Achaeans occupied a number of small towns on the S. side of the Corinthian Gulf. These towns formed a league among themselves, which, in the decadence of Athens and Sparta, became an important power in Greece, especially in the period when the league was under the leadership of Aratus.

p. 114, 1. 36. The Aetolians in N.W. Greece, on the N. side of the Corinthian Gulf, had formed a similar league. They were jealous of the Achaeans and were abetted by Antigonus Gonatas in attempting to check the extension of their league. The Aetolians were threatening the Achaeans by an invasion through Megara on the isthmus of Corinth.

p. 114, 1. 37. Aratus of Sicyon (about 270 B.C.–213 B.C.) began his career by freeing Sicyon from the Macedonians when he was twenty years old. He was elected on seventeen occasions general of the Achaeans. His life was written by Plutarch.

p. 115, 1. 36. Baton of Sinope (on the Black Sea) was a Greek historian who lived apparently in the second half of the third century B.C. Only a few fragments of his works are preserved.

p. 116, 1. 14. The combination "tallages and taxes" (*les tailles et tributs*, A.) represents but one word in Plutarch. It is frequently employed in older English for all kinds of arbitrary taxation.

p. 116, 1. 16. North hardly brings out the meaning of Plutarch even as expressed by Amyot. The Spartan year was a lunar year of 354 days. In order to make this year agree with the solar year of 365 days, an additional month was added three times in eight years —in the third, fifth and eighth year. Agesilaus arbitrarily added this month in a year when it ought not to have been added.

p. 116, 1. 38. By the temple of Neptune is meant apparently the famous temple of Poseidon on Mt Taenaros, at the extreme end of the central of the three peninsulas in which the Peloponnesus ends to the south.

p. 119, 1. 14. For "provoked" the Greek has "embittered," Amyot *incita & irrita*.

p. 120, l. 19. The "sergeants," A. *sergens,* are in the original "servants," a word to which "sergeant" was originally equivalent. The Dechad or "Receiver" was probably a lower dungeon, like the Tullianum at Rome, but it is known only from this passage.

p. 121, l. 39. The earlier English "fact" is used both of a noble deed or exploit and of an evil deed or crime. The former sense is obsolete and the latter survives only in such legal phrases as "accessory after the fact." See *O. E. D.*

p. 121, l. 40. The Dorians had come into the Peloponnesus or Morea from northern and north-western Greece in the 12th or 11th century B.C.

p. 122, l. 8. Cleombrotus fell in the battle of Leuctra in Boeotia when the Spartans were defeated by Epaminondas in 371 B.C. **Philip** is Philip of Macedon, the father of Alexander the Great.

p. 122, l. 10. The history of the conquest of Messenia by the Spartans is very uncertain. The Spartan legend made Theopompus conquer Messenia in the first Messenian war (about 743 B.C.–724 B.C.) and assigned the exploits of Aristomenes, the Messenian national hero, to the second Messenian war (685 B.C.–668 B.C.).

p. 122, l. 28. Down to the 17th century "heir" is both masculine and feminine.

p. 122, l. 29. For Gylippus see note on p. 100, l. 18.

p. 123, l. 1. The phrase "insomuch as" in this sense has now been replaced by "insomuch that."

p. 123, l. 29. Sphaerus is said to have written a work on the constitution of Sparta. His native town of Olbia was situated near the mouth of the river Borysthenes, the modern Dnieper.

p. 123, l. 32. Zeno (about 340–263 B.C.) **of Citium,** in Cyprus, was the chief representative of the Stoic school of philosophers.

p. 123, l. 35. By the "ancient Leonidas" is meant the hero who fell at Thermopylae in 480 B.C. with his three hundred defending the pass against the Persians.

p. 123, l. 36. Tyrtaeus, according to the legend, was a lame Athenian schoolmaster, who, in reponse to an oracle which told the Spartans to get a leader from Athens, was sent in contempt by the Athenians. His military songs, however, were so inspiring that the Spartans defeated the Messenians in the second Messenian war (about 640 B.C.).

p. 124, l. 19. North seems to have taken Empnistae as a proper name, whereas it is an infinitive meaning "to be inspired." He was misled by A. who prints it with a capital but translates it correctly *comme qui diroit, estre inspiré.* In Sparta and other states there was a custom, which still prevails among the Albanians, that a youth was taken in charge by an older man who taught him his military duties and was generally extremely devoted to him. The name given to the elder man was *eispnēlas*, "inspirer," while the younger was called *aïtas*, "listener."

p. 124, l. 40. For Aratus see note, p. 114, l. 37.

p. 125, l. 15. Belbina was on the upper waters of the Eurotas in the N.W. of Laconia. The temple of Athene (more correctly Athenaeum) was a little to the east of Belbina.

p. 125, l. 18. Megalopolis was a town in Arcadia built by Epaminondas to block communication between Sparta and Elis.

p. 125, l. 22. Tegea and **Orchomenus** were towns in Arcadia, N. of Sparta.

p. 125, l. 32. let, hindered; see note, p. 48, l. 22.

p. 125, l. 38. Democritus A. is in some editions of North Democrites, but should be Damocrates.

p. 126, l. 8. Caphyae, N.W. of Orchomenus in Arcadia. **Methydrium** was in the mountains about 15 miles S.W. of Caphyae; for some time its population was amalgamated with that of Megalopolis.

p. 126, l. 13. Aristomachus, who had earlier been the second tyrant or unconstitutional ruler of that name in Argos, had been prevailed upon by Aratus to resign and bring Argos into the Achaean League. Soon after (227 B.C.) he became the general of the League.

p. 126, l. 14. Pallantium was in Arcadia between Tegea and Megalopolis.

p. 126, l. 20. In older English, verbs which ended in *t* or *d* dropped or assimilated the ending *-ed* of the past tense and past participle. Thus here *lift* for *lifted* (participle). The past tense is thus found in Shakespeare, *Henry VI*, I. i. 16, "He ne'er lift up his hand but conquered."

p. 126, l. 21. The use of *remember* in the sense of *remind* is now rare.

p. 126, l. 27. Elis is separated from Arcadia by Mt Lycaeon.

p. 126, l. 33. Mantinea was an important town in Arcadia, N. of Tegea.

p. 126, l. 38. Messene was on Mt Ithome in Messenia. It had been built when Messenia was taken from the Spartans by Epaminondas in 370 B.C.

p. 126, l. 39. There had been no king of the other royal family at Sparta since the death of Eurydamidas, the infant child of Agis by Agiatis, afterwards wife of Cleomenes.

p. 127, l. 8. For Phylarchus see note on p. 110, l. 23 and p. 150, l. 24.

p. 127, ll. 19-20. North is less clear than A.'s *laquelle luy fournissoit argent tant comme il vouloit & luy aidoit à se pousser en auant.*

p. 127, l. 25. To avoid confusion with the battle of 371 B.C. at Leuctra in Boeotia, this engagement is sometimes called the battle of Ladokia from another place in the neighbourhood of Megalopolis.

p. 127, l. 27. For the construction "city self" see note on p. 41, l. 30.

p. 127, l. 30. The "bogs and quagmires" represent a "deep ravine" of the original.

p. 127, l. 31. Lydiadas was a native of Megalopolis who, like Aristomachus at Argos, had made himself despot, but ultimately renounced his rule and brought the city into the Achaean League (235 B.C.). He was three times general of the League. Aratus was jealous of him and was charged with having caused his death in this battle (227 B.C.), by leaving him in the lurch.

p. 127, l. 36. The Tarentines, named from Tarentum in Italy which had first organised such a force, were light cavalry armed with javelins. The Cretans were archers and not necessarily natives of Crete.

p. 128, l. 8. self: very, same.

p. 128, l. 34. For this meaning of "feel" we now use "sound." It was common till the 17th century.

p. 128, l. 40. Heraea was an Arcadian town near the border of Elis.

p. 129, l. 1. Alsaea is probably corrupt, the name being otherwise unknown. The best modern authority suggests *Aliphera* which is to the south of Heraea, rather than *Alea*, far away to the east, north of Mantinea, or *Asea*, east of Megalopolis.

p. 129, l. 17. Samothracians is a curious corruption of a Spartan word *mothakes*. They were the sons of serfs who, being foster-brothers of noble Spartans, had been given liberty without political rights, and were often, as the history of Gylippus and Lysander shows, persons of great ability.

p. 129, l. 21. Agesilaus is a misreading for Agylaeus in the old texts of Plutarch.

p. 129, l. 28. above ten: probably "not more than ten," a negative having dropped from the Greek text. The context shows that the number of the dead was small.

p. 129, l. 34. The meaning of "Fear" in this passage is not *terror*, but *awe*, or *reverence*.

p. 130, l. 1. Aristotle's statement probably occurred in his Constitutional Histories, of which that of Athens (rediscovered and published in 1891) is the only extensive portion preserved.

p. 130, l. 4. chins, *mentons*, A., ought to be "moustaches."

p. 130, l. 14. of one = by one, viz. the poet Stasinos of Cyprus.

p. 130, ll. 16 ff. Homer, *Iliad* III. 172 and IV. 431.

p. 131, l. 12. Nothing is known of Asteropus.

p. 131, l. 36. The story of King Charilaus (better read Charillus) is told in the life of Lycurgus, chapter 5.

p. 132, l. 16. For the Aetolians see note on p. 114, l. 36. The Illyrians, who occupied a district corresponding roughly to the modern Albania, made raids into Greece at periods when the Greek states were unable to defend themselves. Amyot's word *Esclauons* is really an anachronism, there being no Slavonic people in that area in ancient times.

p. 132, l. 19. Megistonous was not his father-in-law but his step-father. This misuse of the term is found occasionally even in good authors down to the present day. Amyot has *beau-pere.* The word which Plutarch uses is also almost peculiar to himself in this sense.

p. 132, l. 26. their neighbours: the unenfranchised middle class of the towns in Sparta.

p. 132, l. 28. pikes : Cleomenes really armed his men with the Macedonian *sarisa,* which was 21 ft. long or more, instead of the much shorter Spartan spear *doru.*

p. 132, l. 34. Sphaerus : see note on p. 123, l. 29.

p. 132, l. 35. insomuch " as " where we now use *that :* see note on p. 35, l. 9.

p. 132, l. 37. diet : Cleomenes restored Lycurgus' system of common meals.

p. 133, l. 21. kings in all Greece : Macedonian, Egyptian, and Syrian kings who were of Greek origin at this time and spoke Greek.

p. 134, l. 15. three boards : the Greeks reclined on couches at meals. There were apparently only two persons on each couch and thus the whole party consisted of six persons.

p. 134, l. 28. North's pottle was a liberal Elizabethan measure of two quarts, Cleomenes' measure was somewhat less than a pint.

p. 134, l. 30. every followed by the plural " they " is common in older English.

p. 135, l. 15. Pherae, better spelt Pharae, was on the river Pirus, about ten miles south of Patras.

p. 135, l. 19. Hyperbatas seems to have been general in 224 B.C.

p. 135, l. 23. Dyme was the most westerly town of Achaea. **Hecatombaion,** which was probably a temple, is mentioned only here and in the life of Aratus.

p. 135, l. 25. against, here in the sense of hostile.

p. 135, l. 32. Langon should be Lasion, in Elis, on the borders of Arcadia.

p. 135, l. 34. in hard state : *estans les Achæiens fort au bas,* A.

p. 135, l. 35. The parenthesis though true in fact is not in the Greek text, but was introduced by A.

p. 136, l. 10. Lerna was on the Gulf of Argolis opposite to Nauplia.

p. 136, l. 17. parliament : the assembly of the Achaean League at Aegion in Achaia.

p. 136, l. 32. thirty years, in the Greek thirty-three, seems intended for the whole period of Aratus' political activity (245 B.C.–212 B.C.). Otherwise Plutarch should have said twenty-three.

p. 137, l. 4. Antigonus Doson, king of Macedonia, was called in by Aratus in 223 B.C. Aratus had expelled Antigonus Gonatas in 243 B.C. from Acrocorinthus, the very lofty citadel of Corinth which commands the entrance to the Peloponnese. The three most important strategic points in Greece were Acrocorinthus, Chalcis in Euboea, and Demetrias in Thessaly, which were known as the three fetters of Greece. Plutarch seems not to distinguish clearly here between the two kings called Antigonus. It was apparently Gonatas not Doson of whom Aratus had spoken ill.

p. 137, l. 13. Aratus we are told in the life of Aratus, chap. 34, rescued Athens in 229 B.C. by bribing the commander of the Macedonian garrison Diogenes. An extant inscription of the period, now in the museum at the Piraeus, gives the credit to Diogenes and says nothing of Aratus.

p. 137, l. 16. the ladies' chambers : Philip (afterwards Philip V of Macedon) who was the ward of Antigonus seduced the wife of Aratus' son.

p. 137, l. 23. Sicyon was an important town west of Corinth. **Tritaea,** an insignificant place not far from Patras.

p. 137, l. 25. The coarse bread and rough cloak were characteristic of the Spartans, as the crown and purple robe were of the kings of Macedon.

p. 138, l. 18. This wrestling school also called Cyllarabis, p. 148, was 300 paces outside Argos.

p. 138, l. 22. to send him back, &c. " To distrust and drive him away" in the Greek: *monstrer qu'ils se desfiassent de luy, & le renuoyer sans rien faire,* A.

p. 138, l. 30. Cleomenes was technically correct, as Aegion was the regular meeting place (see note on p. 136, l. 17).

p. 138, l. 35. The division of land among the citizens generally and the abolition of debts was a regular party cry in Greek cities. Even in Athens the famous Solon had passed a measure for the abolition of debts. The nobles naturally were very hostile to such proposals.

p. 139, ll. 1 ff. Pellene, an Achaean town west of Sicyon; **Pheneus,** on the W. side of a small plain in Arcadia, S.W. of Pellene; **Pentelium,** mentioned only here and in the life of Aratus, was presumably a fort on the mountain S.W. of Pheneus.

p. 139, l. 8. The games which, as the name suggests, were originally held at Nemea, in a valley between Phlius and Cleonae, had at some period before this time been moved to Argos, which is in a much larger plain S. of Nemea.

p. 139, l. 15. Aspis, a flat-topped hill north of the theatre at Argos, so named perhaps because its shape suggested the round shield of the Argives.

p. 139, l. 25. Pyrrhus, the king of Epirus, who after fighting against the Romans 280 B.C.–275 B.C. was killed at Argos in 272 B.C.

p. 139, l. 38. When this expedition of the Aetolians against Sparta took place is unknown. It has been vaguely referred to already (p. 132, l. 16). Many of the Helots no doubt took service voluntarily with the Aetolians.

p. 140, l. 11. Phlius and **Cleonae** lay to the north of Argolis over the mountains, Phlius on the road to Sicyon, Cleonae on that to Corinth.

p. 140, l. 20. A fuller account of these incidents is given in the life of Aratus, chap. 40.

p. 140, l. 36. Troezen, Epidaurus and **Hermione** were all in the long peninsula of Argolis.

p. 141, l. 1. Tritymallus is apparently the person who is called Tripylus in the life of Aratus (c. 41), where he is said to have been the first envoy and Megistonous the second.

p. 141, l. 14. Geranea is the highest point in the range of mountains in Megaris, N.W. of the isthmus of Corinth.

p. 141, l. 16. Cleomenes could not fortify the isthmus of Corinth when Acrocorinthus was in the hands of the Macedonians; he therefore garrisoned the mountain passes to the S.E. in order to prevent the Macedonians invading the Peloponnese. All Greek armies had a wholesome dread of the Macedonian phalanx.

p. 141, l. 26. Lechaeum, the port of Corinth on the west, as Cenchreae was on the east.

p. 141, l. 32. This temple of Juno was on the Heraeum promontory, which projects into the Corinthian Gulf, W. of the Geranea range. Sicyon was on the opposite coast to the S.W.

p. 141, l. 38. This Aristoteles is known only by this important incident which is referred to in the life of Aratus (c. 44) and in Polybius' History II. 53.

p. 142, l. 8. Timoxenus was the general who succeeded Aratus in supreme command of the Achaean League, p. 135, ll. 34 ff.

p. 142, l. 35. The vaults and arches may be those of a subterranean passage or of a watercourse. Remains of both have been discovered in the neighbourhood.

p. 143, l. 1. The Cretans were so famous as archers that archers are so named even when they do not come from Crete.

p. 143, l. 13. Polybius (II. 54) tells us that Antigonus at this time was elected Commander in Chief of the Achaeans and their allies in a meeting held at Aegion in the beginning of the winter of 223 B.C.

p. 143, l. 34. Cleomenes' first negotiations must have been with Ptolemy Euergetes, who died before the end of 220 B.C. and was succeeded by Ptolemy Philopator soon after Cleomenes arrived in Egypt (p. 154, l. 34).

p. 144, l. 13. There was a famous temple of Neptune (Poseidon) on the promontory of Taenaros, which ends the central peninsula of the southern Peloponnese.

p. 144, l. 21. the gods: *au demeurant les affaires iront comme il plaira à Dieu*, A. more correctly, Plutarch using here the vague word (*daimon*, Providence) in the singular.

p. 144, l. 23. Cleomenes had at least two children ; possibly the youngest as requiring special care was sent with Cratesiclea.

p. 144, l. 25. hoise: see note on p. 25, l. 36.

p. 144, l. 39. A fuller account of Antigonus' proceedings is given in the life of Aratus (c. 45). The name of Orchomenus was changed to Antigonea after its old population had been removed, the leading man being murdered and the rest either carried off to Macedonia or sold as slaves.

p. 145, l. 2. The Helots, who were serfs bound to the soil, were thus valued at about £19 each. As there were 60 minas in a talent, the number of the Helots must have been 6000.

p. 145, l. 4. armed: the Greek says "armed in addition." Cleomenes had already 4000 (p. 132, l. 27).

p. 145, l. 6. The Leucaspides or "white shields" of Antigonus were picked Macedonian troops named from their large white shields, which were an imitation of the "silver shields" of Alexander the Great.

p. 145, l. 9. Megalopolis, "Great City," was a new town founded by Epaminondas of Thebes after the battle of Leuctra in 371 B.C. The inhabitants of 38 rural hamlets of Arcadia were combined to form the new town, which was intended to block Sparta's access to Elis and N.W. Greece (p. 125, l. 18).

p. 145, l. 18. Sellasia was directly N. of Sparta on the road to Tegea. The sites of Rhoeteum and Helicus are unknown, and the names are possibly corrupt.

p. 146, l. 10. Thearidas is possibly the grandfather of Polybius the historian.

p. 146, l. 36. Philopoemen (252 B.C.–183 B.C.) **of Megalopolis** makes his first public appearance at this time. He was afterwards on many occasions Commander in Chief of the Achaean League.

p. 146, l. 38. nor also is an unusual combination. North's contemporaries would instead of *also* have put *neither* at the end of the clause.

p. 147, l. 11. The tables and pictures are the same thing and there is but one word to represent them in the Greek, though A. has *les tableaux, images, & peintures.*

p. 147, l. 12. defaced is too mild for A.'s *ruina ou gasta* which is closer to Plutarch.

p. 147, l. 17. pulpit, in the Latin sense, the speaker's platform. Common in the 16th century, now obsolete.

p. 147, l. 21. amazed: rather " utterly dismayed."

p. 148, l. 23. scythes : *avec de longues perches faittes en forme de rançons,* A. Plutarch says "shaped like a Thracian sword," which had a broad and very long blade.

p. 148, l. 26. Cyllarabis: called Cyllarabium p. 138, l. 18.

p. 148, l. 35. The temple of Juno is the famous Argive Heraeum about five miles from Argos.

p. 148, l. 39. From the Heraeum Cleomenes would pass to Mycenae and thence by a mountain road N.W. to Phlius.

p. 148, l. 40. Oligyrtus was a fort in the mountains of Arcadia about 15 miles directly west of Phlius. A road from Sicyon to the central Peloponnese passed it and went on by Orchomenus to Mantinea.

p. 149, l. 9. unfiled: still surviving in dialect. The positive form appears in Shakespeare's " For Banquo's issue have I filed my mind " (*Macbeth,* III. i. 65).

p. 149, l. 12. the sinew of affairs would be a more accurate translation. The metaphor had been common since Demosthenes' time.

p. 149, l. 14. Demades was a contemporary of Demosthenes and at first a supporter of his policy. But being taken prisoner at the battle of Chaeronea in 338 by the Macedonians and having attracted the attention of King Philip by his wit, he was set free and came back to Athens as a strong supporter of the Macedonian side. Plutarch often refers to him as a very clever but unscrupulous orator.

p. 149, l. 18. The text is uncertain. "The baker was wanted first, the pilot after," Clough. Another suggestion is " First wet your dough, before kneading it."

p. 149, l. 21. There were five kings of Sparta named Archidamus. The one meant was Archidamus II, 469 B.C.–427 B.C.

p. 149, l. 39. Macedonia was often raided by the mountaineers to the west and north-west.

p. 150, l. 9. North of Sparta near the road to Tegea.

p. 150, l. 24. Phylarchus : a historian contemporary with Cleomenes and said to have been very partial to him and hostile to Aratus and the Achaean League. He is said to have written in a striking and dramatic style. Plutarch is supposed to have drawn much from him in the lives of Agis and Cleomenes.

p. 150, 1. 26. The Acarnanians lived in N.W. Greece, west of the river Achelous.

p. 150, 1. 35. Damoteles was really in command of a body of young men, who acted as a kind of secret police, wandering about Laconia at night and spying upon the Helots, of whom the governing class, the Spartiates, who were very few in numbers, stood in continual dread.

p. 151, 1. 20. The battle of Sellasia which utterly ruined Sparta was fought probably in 222 B.C., but according to many authorities in 221 B.C.

p. 151, 1. 35. extreme as an adverb; common in the 16th and 17th centuries but now obsolete.

p. 151, 1. 40. Gythium: S. of Sparta on the N.W. coast of the Gulf of Gythium.

p. 152, 1. 13. tisick: consumption, in the Greek *phthisis*. The word is so spelt also in Shakespeare's *Troilus and Cressida*, V. iii. 101.

p. 152, 1. 20. lungs and lights is an Elizabethan tautology, both substantives meaning the same thing and being etymologically connected. Cp. "As if his lungs and lights were nigh asunder brast," Spenser, *Faerie Queene*, VI. iii. 269.

p. 152, 1. 28. Cythera: off the southern coast of Laconia, is the modern Cerigo.

p. 152, 1. 29. Aegialia, the modern Cerigotto between Crete and the Peloponnese. The original of p. 154, l. 9 has another form, Aegiala.

p. 152, 1. 30. Cyrene on the north coast of Africa belonged at this time to Egypt.

p. 153, 1. 2. The Spartans regarded themselves as descended from Hercules, the Dorian invasion of the Peloponnese being known as the "Return of the Heraclids."

p. 154, 1. 34. Ptolemy Philopator at this time succeeded his father Euergetes. He was the worst kind of Oriental despot.

p. 155, 1. 8. Ptolemy murdered his brother Magas, his mother Berenice and his father's brother, Lysimachus.

p. 155, 1. 20. Sosibius was the chief minister throughout the reign of Philopator, whom he encouraged in his vicious courses. Agathocles his colleague in the guardianship of the boy successor Ptolemy Epiphanes murdered him. The account here given closely resembles that in the historian Polybius v. 36.

p. 155, 1. 34. every wagging of a straw is North's own graphic addition instead of "to be frightened of everything."

p. 156, 1. 3. all what: as in Shakespeare's *Timon of Athens*, IV. ii. 35, "To have his pomp and all what state compounds."

p. 156, 1. 6. After the death of Antigonus the Aetolians (from N.W. Greece) invaded the Peloponnese. This caused a war with the Achaean League which lasted till 217 B.C.

p. 156, 1. 13. North's language here is an adaptation to the proceedings of his own time of "in religious orgies and festal processions."

p. 156, 1. 22. Apis: the sacred bull of Memphis which was regarded as a god.

p. 156, 1. 28. The quotation is from Homer, *Iliad* I. 491 f.

p. 156, 1. 32. maliced: the verb seems confined to the 16th and 17th centuries. The reason for Nicagoras' ill-will is said, quite differently, by Polybius to have been his friendship for Archidamus, the brother of King Agis, whom Polybius says (probably falsely) that Cleomenes murdered (cp. p. 211, ll. 38 ff.).

p. 156, 1. 38. sands: *sur la greue du port*, A. Cl. was walking on the quay.

p. 157, 1. 4. horse of service: war-chargers.

p. 157, 1. 32. Nothing else is known of Ptolemy the son of Chrysermus.

p. 158, 1. 22. Canobus or **Canopus**, at the western mouth of the Nile, fifteen miles from Alexandria.

p. 158, 1. 37. by means of: here in the sense of " by reason of," now obsolete. So Bacon (*New Atlantis*) writes " by means of our solitary situation."

p. 159, 1. 1. taken in: the *Oxford Dictionary* gives no precise parallel to this use = imbibed.

p. 159, 1. 2. coat: the chiton or under-garment. The stitching was undone in order that the arm might have free play.

p. 160, 1. 27. Cleomenes died about the end of 220 B.C., or the beginning of 219 B.C.

p. 160, 1. 38. splitted: cp. Shakespeare, *Antony and Cleopatra*, v. i. 24, " that self hand...hath...splitted the heart."

p. 161, 1. 2. flay: a mistranslation. Cleomenes' body, whether for insult or some other reason, was sewn up inside a skin.

p. 161, 1. 14. Taenarum: see note on p. 116, 1. 38.

p. 162, 1. 26. The ancient notion that bees were bred from the bodies of cattle is well known from the passage on the subject in Virgil's *Georgics*, IV. 281 ff.

p. 163, 1. 6. Tiberius Gracchus the elder was consul in 177 B.C. and again in 163 B.C. He triumphed over the Spaniards in 178 B.C. after his praetorship, and over the Sardinians in 175 B.C.

p. 163, 1. 12. North should have said "after the death of *her* father," but was misled by A.'s *apres la mort du pere*. Scipio Africanus the elder died in 183 B.C.

p. 164, 1. 2. Which Ptolemy is referred to is not certain, and his suit is not referred to elsewhere. It has been suggested that this was Ptolemy Euergetes of Cyrene whose dispute with his brother Philometor, king of Egypt, was decided by the Senate, and who visited Rome in connexion with it twice, the second time in 154 B.C.

p. 164, 1. 6. The younger Scipio African was the son of Aemilius Paulus who was adopted by the son of the first Scipio Africanus (p. 48, l. 25).

p. 164, 1. 14. "Castor the tamer of horses and Pollux good with his fists" says Homer.

p. 164, 1. 28. jetted : darted about. The earliest instance of this sense in the *Oxford Dictionary* is from 1635.

p. 164, 1. 29. pulpit : platform (p. 147, l. 17).

p. 164, 1. 30. Cleon : the famous demagogue at Athens, killed in battle at Amphipolis 422 B.C.

p. 164, 1. 36. excellently applied : rather "carefully finished."

p. 164, 1. 37. full of fineness and curiosity : *figuree, embellie & fardee*, A. ; in the Greek "persuasive and brilliant."

p. 164, 1. 39. a convenient ordinary : *simple & sobre*, A. ; "inexpensive and plain," Plutarch.

p. 165, 1. 3. Drusus was put up as a rival demagogue by the senatorial party opposed to Gaius Gracchus.

p. 165, 1. 5. The drachma was about the value of a French franc.

p. 165, 1. 12. with great uncomeliness, &c.: *iusques à dire des iniures, & à confondre son parler*, A. more correctly.

p. 165, ll. 20 ff. Cicero, from whom the story comes, says the note on the pipe was to urge him to greater effort or to warn him against too great energy, which has been misunderstood by Plutarch. Quintilian, Plutarch's contemporary, thought it was merely a pitchpipe to give Gracchus the appropriate key-note.

p. 165, l. 26. tenants : rather "subjects" (of the state).

p. 165, 1. 34. one self time : cp. Shakespeare, *Twelfth Night*, I. i. 39, "when...fill'd Her sweet perfections with one self king."

p. 166, 1. 1. fellow : "deemed worthy of the priesthood," Plutarch. North adopts a modern phraseology, as he does elsewhere, when he calls the vestal virgins nuns (p. 180) or the Pontifex Maximus the High Bishop (p. 171).

p. 166, 1. 5. Appius Claudius Pulcher was consul in 143 B.C. and Censor in 137 B.C. He was a member of the commission of three appointed under Tiberius Gracchus' legislation and some of the boundary stones then set up with the names of the commissioners engraved on them still exist. He was not President of the Senate but held the honorary position of Leading Senator (*Princeps Senatus*).

p. 166, l. 16. Antistia : Claudius names his wife by her family name,

16—2

Roman ladies at this period having no individual name (see note on p. 58, l. 19). She probably belonged to the family of the Antistii Veteres, the most distinguished branch of the Antistian clan who, unlike the Claudii, were not patricians but plebeians.

p. 166, l. 24. Polybius, the Greek statesman, soldier and historian, the friend of Scipio Africanus the younger.

p. 166, l. 37. Fannius: a Roman historian, son-in-law of C. Laelius, the bosom friend of the younger Scipio. His work which seems to have been a History of his own times is lost. He took a prominent part in affairs, was tribune of the plebs in 142 B.C., proconsul in Spain in 141 B.C., and consul in 122 B.C., when, as head of the government, he was forced to take action against Gaius Gracchus, although personally sympathising with his policy.

p. 167, ll. 3–5. Treasurer : *i.e.* Quaestor, the financial official who accompanied a Roman Governor to a province. The Governor in this case was C. Hostilius Mancinus who was sent to Hispania Tarraconensis (the district of Tarragona) in 137 B.C. At the time Numantia was in revolt against Rome, Mancinus was beaten and disgraced, and Numantia held out till taken and destroyed by Scipio Africanus the younger in 133 B.C.

p. 167, l. 29. Tiberius Gracchus the elder had fought successfully in Spain as a praetor in 180 B.C.

p. 168, l. 2. The books of account were, as Plutarch's word shows, tablets of wood, which were covered with wax and written upon with a sharp metal point, the *stilus,* called by North a bodkin, p. 200, l. 16. Tiberius' accounts would be audited at the end of his year of office and the accounts deposited at the Treasury (*Aerarium*).

p. 168, l. 29. The Romans like other ancient nations thought an offering "of a sweet-smelling savour" was pleasing to the gods. In earlier and more simple times they had used sweet-smelling garden herbs, but by Gracchus' time the Romans had much traffic with the East, and incense, though still very expensive, had come to be used by them in offerings.

p. 169, l. 5. Cicero tells us (*de Officiis,* III. 109) that Titus Veturius and Spurius Postumius the consuls who were defeated by the Samnites at the Caudine Forks in 321 B.C. made a peace with the Samnites which was regarded by the Senate as disgraceful and was rejected. The Romans, somewhat hypocritically, assumed that the peace could be unmade by surrendering to the Samnites the two consuls and the two tribunes of the people Tiberius Numicius and Quintus Maelius who had negotiated the peace and by so doing had, it was contended, exceeded their powers. The Samnites refused to accept them and they returned into the Roman camp unharmed. Mancinus was handed over to the Numantines in the same way. They too refused to accept him and he stood between the two armies for a whole day in his shirt. He afterwards returned to Rome and an important question arose as to his legal status—whether or not he was a citizen after having been handed over to the enemy. His citizenship was ultimately restored to him by a special statute.

p. 169, l. 24. The "learned men" were such as Diophanes and Blossius (p. 170).

p. 169, l. 40. Plutarch seems not to have understood very clearly the Roman difficulties with regard to land. In the second Punic War (218 B.C.–202 B.C.) Hannibal ravaged for many years consecutively the rural districts of Italy, so that the population had to abandon their homesteads and take refuge in the towns. When the war was over, no effort was made to reinstate the farmers who had no capital of their own, and gradually the wealthy nobles annexed without title the derelict lands, thus creating a large and dangerous landless class in the towns. From this class was drawn material for the continuous wars on every shore of the Mediterranean which were carried on throughout the second century B.C. The farms annexed by the nobles were converted into great domains worked by slave labour. Gracchus is said (p. 171) to have been so much impressed by the disappearance of the free small farmer when he was passing through northern Italy on his way to Spain that he revived the idea of the Licinio-Sextian laws of 367 B.C. by which the area of public land an individual could hold was severely restricted.

p. 170, l. 3. The Roman measure translated "acre" was only about two-thirds of an acre.

p. 170, l. 23. Laelius was consul in 140 B.C. His surname *Sapiens* may have been thus given to him in irony or, as others think, because he was interested in philosophy.

p. 170, l. 24. Tiberius became tribune in 133 B.C.

p. 170, l. 26. Diophanes was a Greek rhetorician from Mitylene in the island of Lesbos. Regarded as an accomplice of Gracchus he too was put to death in 132 B.C.

p. 170, l. 27. Blossius, a Stoic philosopher from Cumae who also was arrested and examined as to the proceedings of Gracchus. When asked if he would have set fire to the Capitol had Gracchus bidden him, he first replied that Gracchus would never have given such an order. Under pressure, however, he said if Gracchus had given him such an order, he would have carried it out, as he would have been sure that Gracchus thought such an action in the interest of the people. He ultimately escaped to Asia where he committed suicide.

p. 170, l. 30. Antipater, also a Stoic philosopher from Tarsus in Asia Minor, the teacher of Blossius and of Panaetius from whom Cicero drew much.

p. 170, l. 36. Spurius Postumius was possibly the consul of 110 B.C.

p. 171, l. 3. Nothing is known of this work of Gaius Gracchus. Speeches of the two brothers were known to Cicero and some fragments are still extant.

p. 171, l. 13. The writing was not by "bills" but by scribbling on the walls. Such announcements may still be seen at Pompeii.

p. 171, l. 21. the High-bishop, *i.e.* the *Pontifex Maximus*, a title which, curiously enough, has been assumed by the Pope. Publius Licinius Crassus was consul in 131 B.C. He also was a Scaevola by descent, his father having been adopted by Publius Crassus. **Publius Mucius Scaevola** was consul in 133 B.C.

p. 171, l. 31. These proposals for compensation were not embodied in the later form of the law.

p. 172, l. 33. troth : here in the sense of truth, which is the literal translation of the Greek. Cp. Shakespeare, *Midsummer Night's Dream*, II. ii. 36, "And to speak troth, I have forgot our way."

p. 173, l. 9. pass with it : a rare usage. Here clearly in the sense "are satisfied." The only example in the *Oxford Dictionary* is more than sixty years later and in a different sense.

p. 173, l. 36. The law Tiberius proposed was a *iustitium* or cessation of all public business.

p. 173, l. 39. The temple of Saturn contained the Treasury (*Aerarium*) and the public accounts.

p. 173, l. 40. The Treasurers are the Quaestors (p. 167, ll. 3–5).

p. 174, l. 3. The praetors who remained in Rome during their year of office dealt with legal matters.

p. 174, l. 12. The **dolon** was a kind of sword-stick, the dagger being concealed in a whip shaft.

p. 174, l. 16. The pots are the urns into which the voters put the *tabellae* (little tablets, not papers) by which they recorded their votes.

p. 174, l. 21. Manlius, the consul of 149 B.C., was a great lawyer. As there were three consuls of the name of Fulvius between 153 B.C. and 134 B.C., it is not certain which is meant.

p. 175, l. 17. would be doing with him: would deal with his case, take a vote regarding him.

p. 176, l. 21. The three commissioners Plutarch says (more exactly) were elected ; Roman writers say, no doubt wrongly, they were appointed by Tiberius.

p. 176, l. 40. Publius Scipio Nasica Serapio had been consul in 138 B.C., was now *Pontifex Maximus* and leader of the aristocratic party. Plutarch says "he had acquired very much public land, and took it ill to be forced to give it up."

p. 177, l. 4. nine oboli : about 1s. 3d. The ordinary practice was for the state to provide full equipment and maintenance for persons on such a commission.

p. 177, l. 27. Plutarch says Attalus *Philometor*, *i.e.* Attalus III, king of Pergamum in Asia Minor. The mistake as usual is Amyot's. Of Eudemus nothing is known. Attalus died in 133 B.C.

p. 177, l. 31. This law of Tiberius is not mentioned elsewhere: the application of the revenues from Asia was regulated later by Gaius Gracchus.

p. 177, l. 36. to furnish them towards house: *pour eux meubler*, A. "For equipment" is the literal translation.

p. 178, l. 3. This Pompey was the consul of 141 B.C., now one of the Censors.

p. 178, l. 9. Quintus Metellus Macedonicus, a famous statesman and orator, consul in 143 B.C.

p. 178, l. 10. The censorship of C. Claudius Pulcher and Ti. Sempronius Gracchus in 169 B.C. was regarded as particularly severe.

p. 178, l. 18. T. Annius Luscus had been consul in 153 B.C.

p. 178, l. 21. Annius really challenged Tiberius to a legal wager (*sponsio*) of a sum of money, which would fall to the winner of a lawsuit on the subject.

p. 178, l. 22. fact: in the sense of evil deed, crime, the only use of the word in Shakespeare. Cp. p. 121, l. 39 note.

p. 178, l. 24. holy and untouched: the tribunes of the people were *sacrosanct*, any person who injured them being dedicated to the infernal deities. The action of Tiberius in ejecting Octavius from his office was therefore regarded by all parties as a shocking breach of all law.

p. 180, l. 4. Tarquinius Superbus, the seventh king of Rome, was expelled, the immediate cause, according to the legend, being the cruel maltreatment by his son Sextus of Lucretia the wife of L. Tarquinius Collatinus.

p. 180, l. 11. The vestal virgins, six in number, had for one of the main duties of their priesthood to keep perpetually alight the sacred fire in the temple of Vesta. If through the carelessness of a vestal the fire was allowed to go out, she was scourged by the Pontifex Maximus, who had to relight it by rubbing together two pieces of wood (the primitive fire-drill).

p. 180, l. 38. It was forbidden, by a resolution of the people (*plebiscitum*) in 342 B.C., to stand for any public office a second time within ten years.

p. 181, l. 2. Every citizen had to serve in the army, if required, from his 18th to his 46th year.

p. 181, l. 4. billed: enrolled. North, here following Amyot, expands greatly Plutarch's statement which is merely "reducing the period of military service."

p. 181, l. 6. The persons qualified to serve on juries had heretofore been all of senatorial rank; to these Gracchus added an equal number from the wealthy middle class. His aim was to secure impartial justice in the lawcourts, senatorial juries being biased in favour of litigants of their own class.

p. 181, l. 27. brought their tents: this follows Amyot closely, but Plutarch probably only meant "bivouacked in the open air."

p. 181, l. 29. The Romans often took auspices by the behaviour of chickens when food was offered them. They were kept in a coop, and if, when the coop was opened, they rushed upon the food and dropped some of it on the ground, this was a good sign. If they did not leave the coop or would not eat, it was a bad sign. The Roman admiral who in the latter circumstances had the hardihood to kick the coop into the sea with the remark that if the chickens did not eat they should drink, was naturally believed to have met with disaster as a consequence.

p. 182, l. 35. Mucius was the presiding magistrate at the election.

p. 182, l. 40. M. Fulvius Flaccus was later a commissioner with Gaius Gracchus and Appius Claudius for the dividing of public land, and consul in 125 B.C.

p. 183, l. 13. long gowns: the Roman toga, which had to be girt up for easy walking.

p. 183, l. 14. sergeants: Roman lictors.

p. 183, l. 28. The consul is the presiding magistrate, Quintus Mucius Scaevola.

p. 184, l. 4. states: magnates, an obsolete use of the word.

p. 184, l. 9. trestles and chairs: an expansion after Amyot. Plutarch says "some benches being smashed, they picked up the pieces and the feet."

p. 184, l. 17. Tiberius left behind his toga, and fled in his undergarment (*tunica*).

p. 184, l. 22. Of Satureius and Rufus nothing further is known.

p. 184, l. 29. Individuals charged with treason had been executed on many occasions in the 377 years between the expulsion of the kings and the murder of Tiberius Gracchus, but there had not been before an extensive massacre of sympathisers as in this case.

p. 185, l. 11. A commission was appointed to try the supporters of Gracchus and from it there was no appeal, as in ordinary legal proceedings, to the people.

p. 185, l. 14. Nothing is known of Villius (or Billius as his name is given by Plutarch), but his punishment is that of a parricide, who was sewed up in a leathern bag with a snake, a cock, an ape and a dog, and cast into the sea or running water.

p. 185, l. 29. Aristonicus, said to have been the illegitimate son of Eumenes II, king of Pergamum, was a pretender to the crown of Pergamum and maintained himself for several years very successfully against the Romans. In 130 B.C. he was defeated and captured by Perpenna, taken to Rome and executed.

p. 185, l. 36. Crassus served on the commission only a short time. In 131 B.C. he was consul and being sent next year against Aristonicus was entirely defeated by him, captured as a refugee by Thracians and murdered by order of Aristonicus.

p. 185, l. 38. Cornelius Nepos (still alive in 27 B.C.) wrote a number of brief lives of eminent men which are still extant.

p. 185, l. 40. Decimus Junius Brutus, consul 138 B.C., triumphed over the Gallaeci and Lusitanians in 132 B.C.

p. 185, l. 9. Nasica was sent as a member of a commission to investigate the proceedings of Aristonicus at Pergamum, and died there. As *Pontifex Maximus* (North's "chief Bishop") he ought not to have left Rome.

p. 186, l. 28. The verse of Homer is *Odyssey* I. 47.

p. 186, l. 37. In the Greek there is a further sentence "An account in detail of these events is given in the biography of Scipio," which has been dropped by Amyot, presumably because Scipio's biography is lost.

p. 187, l. 5. insomuch as : p. 35, l. 10 note.

p. 187, l. 18. Vettius' lawsuit is not mentioned elsewhere.

p. 187, l. 26. Treasurer : *Quaestor* (p. 167, l. 3 n.). Lucius Aurelius Orestes was consul in 126 B.C.

p. 187, l. 28. Gracchus' enemies were glad that he went to Sardinia because they hoped the bad climate would kill him.

p. 187, l. 30. else : otherwise, in other circumstances ; cp. Shakespeare, *Comedy of Errors*, v. 50, "Hath not else his eye Stray'd his affection in unlawful love ?"

p. 188, l. 34. in the neck of that : close upon, now only in dialect but very common in the 16th and 17th centuries (*O.E.D.*).

p. 188, l. 36. Micipsa, king of Numidia, son of Masinissa who had been friendly with Africanus, whose grandson Gracchus was.

p. 189, l. 3. Rather "to continue Caius his Treasurer." They thought that Gracchus, out of respect for his chief, would not return till he did.

p. 189, l. 26. Fregellae, in the S.E. of Latium on the north side of the river Liris. The town, which seems to have been of considerable importance since the Hannibalic war, when it took the side of Rome, supported the demands of the Italic peoples for citizen rights or right of appeal to the people when formulated by Fulvius Flaccus in 125 B.C., and ultimately took up arms against Rome. The enemies of Gaius Gracchus attributed this movement to his influence.

p. 189, l. 34. The field of Mars (*Campus Martius*) was the great level space on the E. side of the Tiber, opposite the Vatican Hill.

p. 190, l. 6. remembering : "putting in" mind. Cp. Shakespeare, *Richard II*, III. iv. 14, "It [telling tales of joy] doth remember me the more of sorrow."

p. 190, l. 9. Faliscans, the inhabitants of Falerii, on the other side of the Tiber, N. of Rome. This incident and the persons mentioned are otherwise unknown, but as it is not mentioned in the early books of Livy, it has been suggested that it took place in the last war with Falerii in 241 B.C. The Genucii were an influential plebeian family.

p. 191, l. 1. Gaius Popillius Laenas was consul in 132 B.C. Cicero says that after Gracchus' death, Popillius was recalled from exile at Nuceria in Campania. The other consul of 132 B.C., Publius Rupilius, was dead.

p. 191, l. 29. The restoring of the colonies was the reviving of the law enacted by Tiberius and of the commission appointed under it, which had been suspended in 129 B.C. at the instigation of Scipio Africanus the younger.

p. 191, l. 32. In a citizen army, like that of the Romans, these advantages given to the army would win much support for Gracchus. The law appears to have been carried but not acted upon after his death.

p. 191, l. 37. The proposal to enfranchise the allied states of Italy would naturally find less support, as it would weaken the influence of native Romans upon the elections.

p. 192, l. 1. The result of the corn law was that the corn which came from the tributary provinces was distributed at less than cost price to the poor people in Rome. This proceeding spoilt the market for the newly established farming colonies and brought about their failure, while at the same time it impoverished the treasury.

p. 192, l. 15. The palace where the senators sat was on the site of the Church of St Adriano on the N.W. of the Forum. The Comitium, "meeting place," was the open space between the Senate House and the Forum. An orator speaking from the Rostra—the platform at the western end of the Forum—would have to turn to his left to address a crowd in the Comitium. To address a crowd in the Forum he had only to look straight before him. This subtle insult to the Senate is attributed by Cicero to C. Licinius Crassus, tribune in 145 B.C.

p. 192, l. 36. This was Quintus Fabius Maximus, the son of that son of Aemilius Paulus (see p. 52, l. 5) who was adopted by the son of Fabius Maximus the dictator. He was thus the nephew of Scipio Africanus the younger (p. 76, l. 6 n.). Fabius was praetor in 124 B.C. and commanded an army in Spain as pro-praetor in the following year. In 121 B.C. he was consul, along with Opimius, and won a great battle over the Gaulish tribe of the Allobroges at the junction of the Isère and the Rhone.

p. 193, l. 7. The "garners" were to hold the large supplies from which the cheap corn for the populace should be drawn.

p. 193, l. 30. North seems here to have misunderstood Amyot's *car il les faisoit tirer à droite ligne à trauers les champs solides,* which is itself inaccurate for "the roads went straight through the estates without deviation."

p. 193, l. 33. Amyot seems to have had here a bad reading in his Greek text (*ammou khōmasin aktois* of the first edition, where the words are wrongly divided instead of *khōmasi naktēs, oi* and *ē* in medieval and modern Greek being pronounced alike). The gravel was not "brought hither" but "rammed hard."

p. 193, l. 38. In the original there is nothing about "line or plummet."

p. 194, l. 26. Fannius, who appears to be the son-in-law of Laelius (p. 166, l. 37), though some think him a different person, was so "slack a friend" to Gracchus that one of his chief claims to fame in later times was a speech he made against Gracchus' proposals.

p. 194, l. 31. The state land at Tarentum and at Capua had been let on lease, and Gracchus, by proposing to establish colonies there, was carrying further the proposals that Tiberius had made with regard to dividing state domains amongst farmers (pp. 169, 170).

p. 194, l. 32. By Latins Plutarch means the communities in various parts of Italy which had rights of trade and marriage like Roman citizens, but not the full franchise. This is the same proposal as that referred to before (p. 191, l. 37).

p. 194, l. 39. This Drusus who was put up by the aristocracy thus unscrupulously to outbid Gracchus was the father of the Drusus who perished in 91 B.C. in an honest attempt, like Gracchus' own, to enfranchise the Italic peoples.

p. 195, l. 11. and were, &c. The sentence is loosely constructed. Rather " eager and striving for no other end but to outdo Gracchus in pleasing and gratifying the mob, like the characters in a comedy." Plutarch may be referring, as some think, to an amusing scene in Aristophanes' play *The Knights,* where the sausage seller and the Paphlagonian make extravagant bids of all kinds in rivalry for the favour of the populace.

p. 195, l. 23. These twelve colonies were never established, but were merely the bait to draw the populace away from Gracchus.

p. 195, l. 35. " When Drusus proposed that not even in the field should any Latin be degraded by flogging, they supported the bill."

p. 196, l. 16. Both Tiberius and Gaius Gracchus made the mistake of appointing their own relatives commissioners under their laws. It was a legitimate point for Drusus to make against Gaius.

p. 196, l. 18. Nothing is known of Rubrius. Carthage had been destroyed by the younger Scipio in 146 B.C. and its rebuilding prohibited by a curse. Gracchus, as a tribune, had no right to leave Rome.

p. 196, l. 27. Fulvius is said to have been also a tribune in this year. He was a firebrand, and had been concerned in the insurrection at Fregellae (p. 189, l. 26).

p. 197, l. 1. Scipio Africanus the younger was found dead in bed in 129 B.C. As he had been active against the continuance of Tiberius Gracchus' commission for the division of the public lands, it was supposed that he had been assassinated by the popular party. But there is no certain evidence to this effect.

p. 197, l. 7. Plutarch's life of Scipio is lost.

p. 197, l. 22. **the voice goeth**: it is said. Cp. Shakespeare, *King Henry VIII*, IV. ii. 11, "Prithee, good Griffith, tell me how he died"......" Well, the voice goes, madam."

p. 197, l. 23. **had...appeared**: this usage common at all times is specially common in Elizabethan English. Cp. Dame Quickly's "I had myself twenty angels given me this morning," *Merry Wives of Windsor*, II. ii. 73.

p. 197, l. 24. **the staff of his ensign** should read "of his first ensign." The colonists were in military order and carried flags.

p. 197, l. 37. The name should be read Lucius Opimius. He was consul in 121 B.C.

p. 198, l. 4. **set beside the saddle**: a common Elizabethan phrase for to defeat or overthrow (see *Oxford Dictionary* under *saddle* 2 *b*).

p. 198, l. 12. **where**: would now be " whereas." Cp. Shakespeare, *Love's Labour's Lost*, II. i. 103, "Were my lord so, his ignorance were wise, Where now his knowledge must prove ignorance." The Palatine was in Gracchus' time the aristocratic quarter.

p. 198, l. 26. **confederates**: we should now say " allies."

p. 198, l. 33. **sergeants**: the consul's lictors.

p. 199, l. 2. **fencers at the sharp**. Similarly in the *Life of Romulus*, Chapter X, " a combat of fencers (called *Gladiatores*) fighting at the sharp," *i.e.* not with foils. The ordinary place for these shows to take place in the republican period of Rome was the market-place (*forum*).

p. 199, l. 14. **fact**: see p. 121, l. 39 note.

p. 199, l. 27. What North supposed a Sardonian was is not clear, but probably a Sardinian, in which form the word sometimes appears. The use of the word to qualify " laughter " appears as early as Homer.

p. 200, l. 16. **bodkin**: used to translate the Greek *grapheion*, the sharp instrument with which the ancients wrote on wooden tablets covered with wax (cp. p. 168, l. 2).

p. 201, l. 10. The tautology " all the whole " is common in Elizabethan English ; cp. Shakespeare, *Romeo and Juliet*, IV. ii. 32, " All our whole city is much bound to him," and the phrase in the English Prayerbook " we and all thy whole Church."

p. 201, l. 37. **drinking drunk**. Examples of this usage in the *Oxford Dictionary* range from 1474 to 1660.

p. 202, l. 6. Fulvius had defeated in 125 B.C. the " Transalpine

Ligurians" when he was sent to conduct a campaign against the Salluvii, a tribe of Gauls who were ravaging the territory of Marseilles.

p 202, l. 12. The district of Mount Aventine was occupied mainly by plebeians and lay S.W. of the Palatine.

p. 202, l. 29. naked is often used in the sense of "unarmed" as in 2 *Henry VI*, III. ii. 234, "Thrice is he armed that hath his quarrel just, And he but naked, though locked up in steel, Whose conscience with injustice is corrupted." Here there is but one word in the Greek.

p. 203, l. 35. hothouse: in the sense of hot baths, common till the 18th century.

p. 203, l. 39. The temple of Diana was upon the Aventine.

p. 204, l. 1. Pomponius, a Roman knight who is said elsewhere to have defended Gracchus as Horatius did the bridge in the days of old—the wooden bridge of l. 14.

p. 204, l. 21. Philocrates: a Greek slave or freedman.

p. 204, l. 29. "The temple of the Furies" should read "the temple of Furrina," an old Italian goddess. The mistake is Plutarch's. The correct name is given by Cicero but with the same explanation as Plutarch gives. Some remains of the shrine have been found in recent years on the Janiculum.

p. 205, l. 15. confiscate: an old form of the participle when the stem of the verb has a *t* or *d* in the final syllable: cf. "lift" l. 19 below. "Situate" may still be seen sometimes in advertisements of land or house property.

p. 205, l. 17. jointure: now used only of the provision made for a wife in case of the death of her husband. In the 16th century often as here in the sense of dowry.

p. 205, l. 25. A temple of Concord had existed for centuries. Opimius restored it by order of the Senate.

p. 205, l. 32. North's verses miss the point of the original which turns on a play upon the word meaning "concord."

p. 205, l. 37. Opimius had many imitators, like Marius and Cinna.

p. 206, l. 4. Opimius was sent as ambassador to Jugurtha, king of Numidia in N. Africa, in 117 B.C., was bribed by Jugurtha, discovered, convicted 110 B.C. and died miserably in exile at Dyrrhachium (now Durazzo, on the coast of Albania).

p. 206, l. 26. The promontory of Misenum on the coast of Campania was the site of many country houses of the wealthy Romans.

p. 207, l. 6. which regardeth honesty in all respects follows Amyot faithfully. But A. seems to have had a bad text here, which, as in the first edition, read *kalá* "good things" instead of *kaká* "evil things." The latter suits the sense and is now universally adopted. The clause ought to read "while attempting to avert evils."

p. 209, 1. 18. indifferent : impartial. Cp. Shakespeare, *King Henry VIII*, II. iv. 17, " having here No judge indifferent, nor no more assurance Of equal friendship and proceeding."

p. 209, 1. 36. the first instituted : rather " for which Lycurgus was voucher to them, and Apollo to him."

p. 211, 1. 6. North seems to have misunderstood Amyot here ; " lacked " ought to be present tense, for the unwise physician and the bad governor (statesman) behave so at all times.

p. 211, 1. 7. one : rather the latter, the bad statesman.

p. 212, 1. 2. counterfeit : pretend. Cp. Shakespeare, *As you like it*, IV. iii. 174, " counterfeit to be a man," a passage in which there are several plays on the different meanings of the word.

p. 212, 1. 3. Lycurgus, on the death of his brother Polydektes, acted only as trustee till the child Charilaus was born whom he at once saluted as king.

p. 212, 1. 32. thou mayest thyself. This is not addressed to any reader as might be supposed but probably to Gaius Sosius Senecio to whom several of the lives were certainly dedicated.

For EU product safety concerns, contact us at Calle de José Abascal, 56–1°,
28003 Madrid, Spain or eugpsr@cambridge.org.

www.ingramcontent.com/pod-product-compliance
Ingram Content Group UK Ltd.
Pitfield, Milton Keynes, MK11 3LW, UK
UKHW012328130625
459647UK00009B/149